DO NOT REMOVE
CARDS FROM POCKET

ALLEN COUNTY PUBLIC LIBRARY

FORT WAYNE, INDIANA 46802

You may return this book to any agency, branch,
or bookmobile of the Allen County Public Library.

DEMCO

D1058736

ECCENTRIC LIVES
AND PECULIAR NOTIONS

John Michell

ECCENTRIC LIVES
AND PECULIAR NOTIONS

Harcourt Brace Jovanovich, Publishers
San Diego   New York   London

Library of Congress Cataloging in Publication Data

Michell, John F.
Eccentric lives and peculiar notions.

Bibliography: p.
Includes index.
1. Eccentrics and eccentricities—Biography.
2. Curiosities and wonders.
I. Title.
CT9990.M5   1984   920'.02 [B]   84-4543
ISBN 0-15-127358-8

Printed in Great Britain

First American Edition

A   B   C   D

CONTENTS

A DREADFULLY
PERSISTENT LOVER

The woodcock is hard to shoot because of its zig-zag flight, and Mr John Rutter Carden of Barnane Castle, Tipperary, was generally known as Woodcock Carden because he also seemed impervious to gunshot. On many occasions he had been fired at by his Irish tenants, but he always escaped. Once he caught and overpowered two snipers, marched them off to the local gaol and had them hanged.

This was during the first half of the nineteenth century, when landlord-shooting was a common event in Ireland. Woodcock Carden, born in 1811 and educated in England, had come into his Irish estates on attaining his majority. They were in poor shape. The tenants had long lost the habit of paying rent, and they made it plain to their new landlord that they were not inclined to do so in future. Carden issued an ultimatum: pay or quit; but the tenants were obstinate and many said they would do neither. War broke out between the two parties. Barnane Castle was made ready for a siege. Its entrances were strengthened with metal sheets and stout timbers, and it is said that Carden even had the stairs cut away, substituting ladders which could be removed if the castle was attacked, allowing the defenders to fight it out floor by floor.

On one of their raids the tenants brought with them several teams of horses with the idea that, if they could not catch Woodcock Carden, they could at least spoil the view from his windows by ploughing up his lawns. But they quickly withdrew when Carden appeared on the battlements and threatened them with a swivel-mounted cannon which he had installed on the castle roof.

Nothing in the early history of Woodcock Carden indicated that it was his destiny to become an Irish popular hero. He was generally liked and respected by his landed neighbours; even the tenants came to concede that, apart from his strict insistence on receiving rent, he was a reasonable enough landlord. As a magistrate and deputy-lieutenant for the county, he was a representative of English authority, more likely to be feared than loved. By the end of his career, however, mobs of the same people who had once tried to kill him were cheering him in the street.

In his middle age Woodcock Carden created a public scandal, which ruined him while making him famous. Scandals in Ireland are much prized for the entertainment they provide, and the participants in them who attract the greatest popular support are not always those who appear morally or legally to be in the right, but those who conduct the affair in the most spirited fashion. For the scandal which overwhelmed him Mr Carden confessed himself entirely and alone to blame, but that did nothing to discourage the Cardenites of the 1850s who celebrated their hero in many romantic ballads inspired by his disgrace.

Woodcock Carden made his name as a most spectacular victim of love. He had always liked and been liked by women in general, and he was rumoured to have had several love affairs which for some reason had left him with a prejudice against heiresses. He was over forty, however, and had still not married; nor did it seem likely that he ever would, for when, in July 1852, he was invited to stay and dine with his friends, the Bagwells of Eastwood, County Cork, the reason he later gave for accepting was that it amused him to laugh at people making love.

A common opinion in the years which followed was that for this impiety Woodcock Carden was condemned through the rest of his life to suffer continual anguish and never again to know happiness or peace of mind. At the Bagwells' dinner he was introduced to neighbours, the Honourable Mrs George Gough of Rathronan House and her young sisters, Laura and Eleanor Arbuthnot, who had recently come to live with her, their parents being dead. Eleanor was a considerable heiress, but Carden instantly fell in love with her. She was eighteen years old, sweet, pretty and innocent. She showed no particular interest in him, nor did her family seem altogether friendly, and in a moment of foreboding Mr Carden decided to leave the house at once before his emotions became too violently aroused. The hostess however persuaded him to stay on a while, and from that moment he was a doomed man.

That fact was not immediately apparent. Carden and the Goughs became friends, riding together, staying at each other's houses and attending the same parties. Eleanor was polite to Mr Carden in the normal way, but he never found the opportunity to declare his love. He used to say afterwards that had he proposed to her direct, and had she refused him, that would have been the end of the matter. But direct proposals were not in fashion at the time, so John Carden did the correct thing by applying to Mrs Gough for her sister's hand in marriage. This, he was told, was impossible. Eleanor had not the slightest partiality for him and was not yet ready to think about marrying anyone. Mr Carden was advised to give up all thoughts of Eleanor as his bride and to forget the whole affair once and for all.

That was the one thing he was completely unable to do. The conviction grew on him that Eleanor was not really indifferent to his love but merely shy of admitting it, that she was influenced by her family against him and that, if he could talk to her on her own for a sufficient period of time, she would come to recognize her true feelings. It grew to the point where he believed that the family were holding her prisoner and that she was pining away for love of him. Finally it became an obsession. Eleanor had to be rescued. He wrote her a passionate note asking her to elope with him. She naturally showed it to her relations, and Carden was in disgrace. He wrote again with grovelling apologies, but the Goughs were deeply offended and refused all further communications. Eleanor sent a brief note to say she could not forgive the insult offered her.

For a time John Carden appeared crushed. He pondered all kinds of wild schemes to put an end to his agony, including emigration to the West Indies. Finally it was the maddest of all which took root in his mind. He would have to abduct Eleanor by force. Only thus could she be removed from the influence of her repressive family and brought to acknowledge her secret love for him.

In the course of 1853, the year after their first meeting, relations between Carden and the Goughs gradually mended. As neighbours of the same class and interests they could hardly avoid meeting at local events and parties, and on several occasions Carden saw Eleanor and even talked to her, though never alone. That autumn, while travelling to Scotland to stay with his friend, Lord Hill, on the isle of Skye, he found himself on the same boat as the Goughs and the Arbuthnot girls, who were on the way to a ball. On learning from his host that the ball was to be at Inverness, he immediately left Skye, made a rapid journey across Scotland and appeared at the party unexpectedly. There he annoyed

Eleanor by persistently staring at her and following her about the room. The next day he walked over twenty miles to Forres merely to catch a glimpse of her from the roadside as she went by in a carriage.

At Inverness he began making active preparations for the abduction. His plan was to snatch her away from her family and carry her by relays of horses to the Galway coast, where a yacht would be ready to receive her and sail them both to Skye. There, he imagined, Lord Hill would be prepared to receive them. For her comfort on the voyage he made expensive purchases of ladies' clothes and luxurious items for her dressing table. A fine yacht was his next acquisition, and he spent a great sum on fitting it out with the utmost elegance. To put her at ease he staffed the yacht with old servants from Barnane with whom she would be familiar.

Meanwhile he kept up his campaign of pestering Eleanor. When she and her family went to enjoy a season in Paris, Woodcock Carden flitted after them and considerably spoilt their pleasure by dogging their footsteps. He would pace up and down outside their lodgings, run behind their carriage and, when they dined out, make himself a distant nuisance by spying on Eleanor from a table across the dining room. When they returned to Ireland he followed.

The abduction plan was now complete, but its execution was delayed by an accident. Eleanor fell from her horse and badly damaged her ankle. Carden was barred from visiting Rathronan House, so his only contact with her was through mutual friends, whom he constantly badgered for news of her condition. He imagined she was being neglected. His one ally at Rathronan was Eleanor's brother, William Arbuthnot, a mild young man who responded kindly to the friendship Carden pressed upon him. William was due to go to India, and it was planned that Eleanor should travel part of the way with him. That was Carden's last hope. He believed that William would occasionally let him see her, which, he claimed, would have made him happy enough to abandon the abduction scheme. But when the time came for William to leave, early in 1854, Eleanor's injured ankle kept her at home. Carden went several times to Rathronan to plead with Mr Gough for permission to see her, and when this was refused he wrote a passionate letter offering to make over all his money to Mr Gough's family if they would allow him to marry her. This, of course, only made matters worse. Finally the ankle was better, and Mrs Gough took Eleanor off to Paris for a convalescence. Naturally Mr Carden went there too, travelling in his new yacht. This time, however, he refrained from approaching them, knowing by now how much his presence annoyed them.

Back in Ireland, the yacht was anchored off Galway, horses were made ready at intervals along the road to the coast, and Woodcock Carden instructed the toughest, most reliable men on his estate in the parts they had to play in the abduction of Miss Arbuthnot. In the last week in June these characters were to be seen loitering in the neighbourhood of Rathronan House, Mr Carden with them. As a last-minute precaution, having heard that abducted girls were sometimes prone to hysteria, he had provided himself with two phials of chloroform which, the doctor had told him, was the best treatment for such cases.

On Sunday, 2 July, his opportunity arose. That morning the three sisters, Mrs Gough, Laura and Eleanor, went to church at Rathronan, about a mile from their house. With them was the family governess, Miss Lyndon. Mr Carden was hanging about the churchyard and he followed them in for the service. While it was going on a few drops of rain fell, and the Goughs' coachman, Dwyer, who had driven the ladies in an open carriage, thought it best to return home and exchange it for a closed vehicle.

When the church service was over Mr Carden was nowhere to be seen, but on the drive home, near the gates of Rathronan House, the ladies spotted him riding towards them. As he passed their carriage he turned his horse and followed them. By now they were used to this sort of behaviour, so were not particularly alarmed. But Woodcock Carden was no longer a mere abject pest. Suddenly their carriage jolted to a halt. Three men sprang from a ditch, seized the horses' heads, cut the reins and threatened Dwyer with knives. At the same time Carden leapt off his horse and ran to the opening at the back of the carriage with the intention of dragging Eleanor Arbuthnot out of it.

Had the ladies been in the open car in which they went to church the abduction would probably have succeeded, but the substitution of the closed vehicle proved fatal to Carden's plans. They were sitting in pairs opposite each other, with Miss Lyndon between Eleanor and the carriage's rear entrance. As Carden reached in to grab Eleanor, Miss Lyndon struck at him with her fists until his face was covered in blood. Seeing that she must first be disposed of, he dragged her from the

11

carriage and hurled her to the side of the road. At that stage the drama took a turn towards farce. Carden's men, seeing a lady flying headlong out of the back of the carriage, supposed that she was the object of the abduction and began ushering her into a brougham which was stationed in concealment nearby. Thus Carden found himself on the point of running off with the governess – which, he said later, would have been a just punishment for him.

A separate struggle was now going on all around the carriage. Two men from the Rathronan estate had run up and joined forces with Dwyer against the attackers. Mrs Gough, fearing the imminent destruction of the whole party, climbed from the carriage and ran towards the house, screaming for help. Carden was heard to say, 'I know I shall be hanged for this.' In fact the punishment at that time for abduction was transportation for life.

Two of the ladies being now out of the carriage, Carden renewed his attempt at Eleanor. Her sister, Laura, was still with her, and both girls resisted him as fiercely as the governess had done. He managed finally to pull Laura out, and had almost succeeded in extracting Eleanor when one of the opposing party struck him a hard blow on the head. He replaced Eleanor gently in the carriage and then reeled back, calling on his men to complete the operation. As they tried to comply, a number of Mr Gough's men appeared on the scene to reinforce the Rathronan party. In desperation Carden called upon his supporters to shoot them with firearms he had provided. But it was plain by now that the day was lost. The Carden gang made for the brougham and took flight, their leader preceding them on horseback. He had not gone far before he felt faint and had to sit in the brougham. The horses were whipped up and the foiled abductors set off at full gallop.

The chase that followed has passed into history as the most exciting ever heard of in Tipperary. Carden and his men had a racing start and excellent horses, but the police were quickly alerted and mounted men were soon hot in pursuit. Even though hindered by the bad state of the roads, the brougham had covered twenty miles at a fabulous rate before it was overtaken. The capture chanced to take place just outside a police station, and although Carden's men showed fight they were soon overpowered by the mass of policemen who ran out against them. Carden was arrested by officers with drawn sabres and driven off to the prison at Cashel.

Disgraced and humiliated, Woodcock Carden found himself the people's hero. A large crowd, mostly of women, gathered round the prison gates to cheer him as he entered. The Irish gentry were also on his side. Many of them visited his cell to commiserate on the failure of his sporting attempt and to wish him better luck in future. His trial at Clonmel was a great social event. The noble families of Ireland, particularly the wives and daughters, clamoured for seats. There were not enough to go round, and the High Sheriff, in charge of allocating them, became an abiding enemy to those he could not accommodate.

Three charges were brought against Mr Carden: actual abduction, attempted abduction and felonious assault, the last referring to a serious injury suffered by one of the Rathronan men during the fight. To the delight of the accused man Eleanor Arbuthnot appeared in court as a witness. He instructed his counsel on no account to bother her with questions, but she readily admitted the vital point, that Mr Carden had not quite succeeded in dragging her from the carriage, and therefore, it was held, no actual abduction had taken place. On the charge of attempted abduction John Carden was inevitably found guilty, and the judge sentenced him to two years' hard labour. The third charge, of felonious assault, aroused great indignation among the spectators in court. It was generally considered to be excessively vindictive, and there were prolonged cheers and much waving of handkerchiefs by the ladies when the jury quickly dismissed it. When news of this verdict spread, so did the jubilation. Vast crowds celebrated outside the court-house. In the London *Times* (2 August 1854) it was recorded with disapproval that 'three vociferous cheers were given for Carden of Barnane'.

By all classes of Irish society Woodcock Carden was adopted as the man of the hour. A few sour comments appeared in the newspapers, one editor remarking that Mr Carden 'stands more in need of a straight-waistcoat than of a wife', but for the most part Cardenite sentiments prevailed. They grew even stronger when it was learnt that Carden had nobly refused to sign a paper offering him immediate release from prison if he would undertake never again to 'annoy or molest' Miss Arbuthnot. It was inconceivable to him to undertake such a thing, his whole life being dedicated to the pursuit of Eleanor. Instead he offered to enlist as a common soldier in the Crimea. This was rejected by the authorities, and Carden served out his two years, awaiting only the day of release for the recommencement of his campaign.

Freed in 1856 he left prison quietly so as to avoid a demonstration in his honour. He had no interest in his own cult, nor did he share the popular view of himself as a romantic hero. At his trial and for the rest of his life he was apologetic about the trouble he had caused Eleanor and her family. Yet he never faltered in his determination to win her. He proceeded at once to India, hoping to persuade William Arbuthnot to intervene on his behalf, but the young man was unhelpful. He next applied to the Lord Lieutenant of Ireland and to the head of the Gough family, Viscount Gough of Loughcooter. Both these dignitaries received him kindly and with good advice, but Mr Gough of Rathronan was adamant and refused to have anything more to do with him.

His delusion that Eleanor was secretly in love with him survived and flourished. A maid at Rathronan was dismissed, and Carden persuaded himself that the reason was that she had been caught smuggling out a loving note to him from Eleanor. In the course of trying to find the maid and question her, he met one of her relations who took advantage of his mania by pretending to be in contact with Eleanor who, she said, was desperately in love and dying to see him. Somehow the affair ended in court, where Carden was ordered to cease from persecuting the Gough family and Eleanor swore before the magistrate that she detested Mr Carden, was in fear of him and never wanted to see him again. This produced absolutely no effect on Carden who took the episode as another example of the coercion which Eleanor suffered.

For years to come, wherever Eleanor went, in Ireland or abroad, John Carden went there too, a pitiful shadow, sometimes trying irresolutely to approach her but usually just loitering in the vicinity of her presence. Once, it is said, he found her alone in a room in Paris. She told him to leave at once, otherwise she would do so. He went out of the room and back to Ireland, retiring to Barnane Castle.

It was no longer the grim fortress from which Woodcock Carden had once repulsed the assaults of his tenants. With the idea of attracting Eleanor he had had it done up and furnished in style. There was even a turkish bath in one of the towers. This may have given him the notion of opening the place as an hotel. Arrangements were made, but instead of admitting the public Carden went in for private hospitality, entertaining neighbours and travellers with notable generosity until his death in 1866.

Apart from the maniac Carden, who was responsible for the whole affair and destroyed himself on his own account, the person who suffered most was poor innocent Eleanor Arbuthnot. By the Cardenites she was cast as the villain of the piece, accused of haughtiness, heartlessness, English arrogance and encompassing the ruin of a high-spirited Irish gentleman. After the trial her family thought it best for her not to appear in public in case people hissed her in the street. Her reputation was utterly spoilt. According to every account of people who knew her she was kind, charming and good-natured, as perfect a creature almost as Woodcock Carden held her to be. She never married. In later life she left Ireland and lived in Edinburgh, concerning herself with the education of her nephews, Laura's children.

Opinions expressed in England about the Arbuthnot Abduction affair were different from those which prevailed in Ireland. In its reports and leading article about it (3 August 1854) *The Times* kept up a tone of sarcasm. Mr Carden was compared to a knight at the farcical Eglintoun tournament, and the writer supposed that in County Tipperary even the Rape of the Sabines might easily be tolerated. The demonstrations in court by the Cardenites, particularly the females, gave *The Times* an opportunity of sharpening its wits on the barbarous Irish. Abduction, said *The Times*, might be cheaper than a wedding, but it was to be hoped that the primitive style of courtship apparently popular in Ireland would not spread to England where young heiresses and their protectors might not so appreciate it.

In Ireland Woodcock Carden was not quickly forgotten. For many years 'Carden's Wild Domain' was a favourite country song, and his exploits as a crazy lover were recounted in numerous verses. The example below has been attributed to Percy French, the once well-known composer of 'Abdulla Bulbul Amir' and 'The Mountains of Mourne':

On the Terrace, Barnane

I sit beside the fountain's brim
And in my fancy picture him
Wayward, wilful, strong of whim
    An elemental man

And she a maid of many charms;
He longs to hold her in his arms,
And so – excursions and alarms
    And all that costly plan

To carry off that maiden sweet
Relays of horses! steamship fleet!
But one thing wanted to complete
  This happiness for life.

And that one thing the man has missed!
For maid and myrmidons resist.
She strikes him with her little fist
  She will not be his wife.

Oh, lovers in the long ago
Our ancestors were wild to know
And you were but a backward throw
  To prehistoric time

When prehistoric man would say
To maiden neither yea or nay
But bear her to his cave away;
  A custom, not a crime.

Had I been judge, no County Jail
Had been the climax of the tale.
Of course I'm an unusual male,
  And, tho' she'd none of him,

I'm with "The Woodcock" hand and
glove.
For I have known the pangs of love
And so this web of verse I've wove
  Around the fountain's brim;

And sitting near the stately fane
He built for her, but built in vain,
I fancy they might meet again
  In some serener sphere

And find no flicker of the fire
That filled that too tempestuous squire.
He'll know no passionate desire
  And she no maiden fear.

THE STRANGE ADVENTURE
OF A
SOMERSET GENEALOGIST

About fifteen years ago a conspicuous couple were regularly to be seen at the bus stop in front of the Abbey at Glastonbury. The man, clad in the kilt and bonnet of a Highlander, looked very old with his thin white face and whiskers. His name was Sir Ian Stuart-Knill, and his wife, about twenty years younger, was known as Lady Eve. They lived some miles away in an old people's bungalow on the council estate at Edington, a little village near Burnham-on-Sea. It was easy to get to know them because Eve would tell anyone who had caught her eye about the adventures they were having together. They made wonderful partners, for Sir Ian was a scholar, a lover of ancient history, documents and pedigrees, while Lady Eve was a natural mystic and knew how to move back in vision into times past. They would take local buses to some ancient spot, preferably associated with King Arthur, where Eve would go into a trance and see its history pass before her eyes, while Sir Ian took notes of what she described, and later checked her information against the evidences of scholarship. They were thus at a considerable advantage over the archaeologists, whose excavations they liked to visit. The mystically received knowledge they passed on to the diggers was not always accepted gratefully, but the Knills did not mind. They pitied those whose vision of the past was limited to the scrutiny of old bones and potsherds.

In a way the Knills were very ordinary people, just poorer, simpler and more kind-hearted than most. One could visit them for tea and look at photograph albums in a normal way, and yet their experience of life had evidently been quite different from anyone else's. Showing a photograph of an old family cat, for example, Lady Eve would tell the story of how it never climbed the trees in the usual way with its claws, but hugged the trunk and swarmed up it like a sailor. Another photograph showed the former Knill estate in Herefordshire, and Sir Ian would explain that they had had to leave it because the land was unworkable. A battle had once been fought there, leaving the fields so encumbered with buried pikes and suits of armour that it was impossible to plough it.

In the course of ordinary conversation the Knills would gossip about some of the people they had met recently at ancient sites. Eve's particular favourites were the Beaker Folk whom she sometimes came across at holy wells. One of them had a most beautiful beaker and would offer her a drink of water out of it. She also knew Merlin and had several encounters with Queen Guinevere. These contacts were of great value to Sir Ian because his life-long study was the genealogy of King Arthur.

A dramatic incident had determined his career and caused him to become the leading expert on his subject. On his sixth birthday his grandfather had treated him to a minstrel show followed by tea at his London club. A strange old man came in, greeted the grandfather and enquired who the little boy was. When told, he put his hands on Ian's shoulders and said, 'Never forget, my boy, that the royal blood of Arthur flows in your veins.' The old man was the Poet Laureate, Lord Tennyson.

Ian Stuart-Knill never forgot that he was a descendant of King Arthur. The following year, 1898, his grandfather died, repeating with his last breath the words of Tennyson and leaving the boy with a large box of papers relating to Arthur's pedigree.

Originally Ian was called John Knill until a growing conviction that he was of pure Scottish descent, not shared by the rest of his family, caused him to make appropriate changes to his name and adopt full Highland dress. His eventful career included service at different times in all three of the Armed Forces and a variety of civilian jobs. In military circles he made his name for his expertise in gunnery. The rapid development of the machine gun during the First World War was largely due to his inventiveness. His main interest, however, was always genealogy, and his ambition was to fill the gaps in the chain of descent from King Arthur to himself. After many years of research he finally succeeded, at the age of eighty. His *Pedigree of Arthur*, published in 1971, traced the line from King Arthur to the Knills and, by another branch, to Queen Elizabeth II, and took it back through St Joseph of Arimathaea and the Holy Family to King David of Israel. The genealogical charts were displayed at Glastonbury Town Hall, and the Knills acted as guides to visitors.

Many of their stories about King Arthur and his knights were quite new and surprising, and some people were inclined to laugh at them. But, as Sir Ian would gently point out, few of his critics knew anything about the subject, having never studied it for themselves, whereas he had spent sixty-three years on it.

In his *Pedigree* Sir Ian acknowledged the clairvoyant assistance of his wife, through which he had solved many of the problems of King Arthur's lineage. Yet for many years his researches had been frustrated. Somewhere in the Middle Ages there was a gap in the family tree which neither he nor Eve had been able to bridge. Finally the missing information turned up. It happened in a remarkable way, providing Sir Ian with one of his best stories. This is how he told it.

Much of his research was done at the library at Burnham-on-Sea, but he could only go there once a week when the local bus passed through Edington, making the return journey early in the evening. One summer's day, after lunch, Sir Ian caught the bus, arrived in Burnham and set out on foot to the nearby library. As usual, he made straight for the shelf of books on old English history. He knew them all quite well, but on this occasion there was a stranger among them, an elderly volume in a battered leather binding. Sir Ian took it down and opened it. It was on the subject that most concerned him, and his first glance revealed, clearly set out, the very piece of information about the family of King Arthur which he had sought in vain for most of his life. It was something to do with the marriage of the daughter of some semi-mythical person to another such person who was one of the crucial characters in Sir Ian's work of genealogy, and there was reference to a document, no longer in existence, in which this event was recorded. At one stroke Sir Ian had his proof and the authority for it. He drew out his notebook intending to copy out the passage, but before he could begin the librarian announced that she was about to close, and he had to leave.

That evening he compared the new information with the facts already established by previous researches, and the two fitted perfectly. His next opportunity for going to Burnham for another reading of the old book was in a week's time, when the bus ran again, and he awaited the moment eagerly. The day arrived, he entered the library and went up to the shelf. The book was no longer there. He asked the librarian about it, and she said there was no such book and that Sir Ian was wrong in thinking that he had visited the library the previous week. She had been on duty then and would have recognized him because of his kilt. The baffled genealogist took the bus back to Edington. Yet, even though its source was no longer in evidence, he had the information he needed to complete his life's work, and *The Pedigree of Arthur* displayed no gap in the line of descent from King Solomon through King Arthur to the Stuart-Knill grandchildren.

After telling this story Sir Ian would say, 'Whether I actually laid hands on the book or whether I fell asleep at the bus shelter in Burnham and dreamt it all, I shall never know for certain. But however it happened, I was able to solve the problem of Arthur's pedigree.' He would laugh with pleasure at the thought of his successful career. Soon after the book was published he died, and Lady Eve began a career of her own, writing and editing books of poetry for a publisher.

LOYALISTS OF THE
FLAT EARTH

M ost people nowadays believe the scientific doctrine that the earth is a revolving globe, though there are still some in remote parts of the world who have not heard that news and retain the common-sense view that it is flat. And there are others of that same opinion, who have heard all that science has to say on the matter, but reject it, usually because it conflicts with the Bible but also for other possibly good reasons.

The long association between Christianity and the flat-earth theory begins in the sixth century when a Greek monk of Alexandria, Cosmas, who had travelled widely in the East, retired to a cloister in Sinai and wrote his *Christian Topography*. In it he refuted the 'false and heathen' notion that the earth is a sphere, and showed that it is really a rectangular plane arched over by the firmament which separates us from heaven. The inhabited earth, with Jerusalem at its hub, is at the centre of the plane, and it is surrounded by oceans beyond which lies Adam's paradise. The sun revolves round a north polar mountain, circling its peak in summer and its base in winter.

Christian Topography was well received by the Church, whose policy at the time was to eradicate all previous knowledge and establish itself as the sole authority in religion, philosophy and science. The flat-earth theory, hitched on to the geocentric cosmology of Ptolemy, prevailed among clergymen (if not among navigators) until the sixteenth century, when Copernicus called it in question by venturing the idea that the earth is a planet orbiting the sun. He was not very assertive. The preface to his book emphasized that the heliocentric system was merely a hypothesis, and Copernicus avoided controversy with the reviewers by dying on the day it was published.

Copernicus first derived his theory from esoteric studies of the Pythagorean and other ancient traditions. His successor, Galileo, challenged the flat-earth believers to scientific experiments. One of theirs was to shoot a cannonball vertically into the air. When it fell to earth near the cannon they claimed to have proved that the earth was not moving. Galileo explained that the reason why the ball was not left behind by the spinning earth was that it partook of the same motion. The argument went on for years, but heliocentricism was in the air. It won its way against the Inquisition and finally triumphed with the cosmological system of Sir Isaac Newton. The Church found that it could after all live with the round-earth idea, and that references in the Old Testament to the four corners of the earth and the pillars on which it rests might have been intended, not literally, but as figures of speech.

Not everyone caved in so easily. Upholders of scripture, such as Mr Hine the British Israelite hero of a later chapter, have constantly preserved the image of the earth's corners and pillars, and a rearguard of the old flat-earth experimenters have constantly supported them. Sir Richard Phillips, who tried to convert scientists to the flat or 'planist' doctrine at the end of the eighteenth century, could hardly have been motivated by religion, for he was imprisoned for dealing in atheist literature. Nor did the great nineteenth-century planist 'Parallax' (in ordinary life Mr Samuel B. Rowbotham) base his arguments entirely on the Bible. His proofs of the flatness of the earth were drawn from experiment and reason.

The scene of the classic battles between the planists and the 'globularists', as they are called in the jargon of cosmological controversy, is a long, straight stretch of canal, the Old Bedford Level in Cambridgeshire, in particular an uninterrupted length of about six miles between Welney and Old Bedford bridges. Over such a distance, according to the globularists, an object placed near the water-line at one bridge should be rendered invisible from the other bridge by the curvature of the earth. Rowbotham denied that that was the case. He claimed that the surface of the water in the Old Bedford Level was perfectly flat throughout, thus discrediting globular theory, and he undertook to prove it so.

For nine months of 1838 Rowbotham lodged in a wooden hut on the bank of the canal's six-mile stretch. During that time he conducted a long series of experiments, always with the same result. Standing in the canal near one bridge, with a telescope a few inches above the water, he obtained clear views of barges beyond the other bridge and other distant objects near the canal's surface which orthodoxy said should not be visible. For many years, up to 1870, he repeated and varied on these experiments, demonstrating to parties of believers and sceptics alike the heretical sights offered by the Old Bedford Level. These were carefully detailed in his major work, *Zetetic Astronomy* (from the Greek verb *zēteo*, meaning 'I find out for myself'), which ran to 430 pages and has ever since been the standard authority for anti-globularists.

Other experiments described in *Zetetic Astronomy* included sightings of distant ships and landmarks far across oceans which conventional globularist theory, according to Rowbotham, said should be hidden by the earth's curve. He repeated the old tests with vertically projected cannonballs, reporting that after about half a minute aloft they sometimes fell right back into the cannon's mouth, and he performed new ones which involved firing balls upwards, forwards and backwards from moving trains. So elaborate is his case, and so gently and reasonably argued, that the lay reader, after finishing his book, feels the need for a new Galileo to reaffirm the globularist faith.

Many would-be Galileos did in fact arise. The Victorians took their science seriously, and earnest people took it upon themselves to issue detailed refutations of the works of Parallax. Sometimes they would confront him at the public lectures he gave during zetetic tours of Britain. However, as the astronomer Richard Proctor admitted, Rowbotham was not easily argued down. Unlike most of his opponents, he was a professional controversialist, and he was well schooled in the tricks of the lecture hall. Proctor attended one of his lectures at Plymouth, where a party of naval officers had come determined to rout him. When pressed too closely on any point, Rowbotham would thank the questioner, tell him he had now enjoyed his fair share of the discussion and invite some other gentleman to speak. For those who came to laugh he had another good tactic: he would infuriate them by the reasonableness of his manner, provoking them to unreasonable conduct and thus winning sympathy. One man, said Proctor, had to be restrained from attacking Mr Rowbotham with his cane.

Matters came to a head at the Old Bedford Level in 1870 when Mr John Hampden of Swindon, a graduate of Oxford University and a devotee of Parallax, was so carried away by the zetetic doctrine that he issued a challenge to the globularists, staking the large sum of £500 on the result of a new experiment to be carried out on the famous six-mile stretch of canal. The wager was accepted on behalf of science by Mr Alfred Russel Wallace, the co-discoverer with Charles Darwin of the theory of evolution. Unwise speculations had left him short of money, and he was advised by his senior colleague, Sir Charles Lyell, that he could profit from the foolishness of the flat-earthers and teach them a lesson at the same time. It was agreed that each party should nominate a referee, and Mr J.H. Walsh, editor of *The Field,* was made stake holder.

On the evening of Monday, 28 September, Mr Wallace took the train up to Downham Market in Norfolk, accompanied by Mr William Carpenter, a journeyman printer and author of a book upholding the flat-earth theory, whom Hampden had appointed as his referee. They found a mutual interest in spiritualism and dined happily together at the Crown Hotel, riding out next day to the Old Bedford Level. They paced along its tow-path between the two bridges, and at mile intervals they erected marker discs on poles at the same height above water-level. That evening they were joined by Mr Walsh, acting as Wallace's referee, and John Hampden arrived next morning.

The idea was for a telescope to be levelled from bridge to bridge along the tops of the markers. Wallace predicted that the discs would be seen 'rising higher and higher to the middle point, and thence sinking lower and lower to the furthest one.' Hampden's party said that all the markers would be observed to stand at the same height, thus proving that the water-level was indeed flat. This experiment was unsatisfactory; the markers were not quite in a straight line and the viewers could not be certain which one was which. Mr Walsh had to leave that evening and his place as Wallace's referee was taken by a local surgeon, Mr M. Coulcher. The following day was spent at Kings Lynn where Wallace borrowed a better telescope, a surveyor's Troughton model with built-in spirit-level.

The vicinity of the Old Bedford Level was sparsely populated, but on the morning of the fifth of March a crowd of locals gathered at Welney bridge for the scientific entertainment. Wallace had spent the previous day, when fog had prevented any fieldwork, in devising a new, simpler experiment. The top of Welney bridge was found to be 13 feet 4 inches above the water, a signal was placed at the same height on the face of Old Bedford bridge and a disc on a pole was erected midway between the two bridges, also at a height of 13 feet 4 inches. Through the new telescope, levelled on the parapet of Welney bridge and directed towards the signal six miles away, Wallace and Coulcher supposed that the centrally placed disc would appear raised above the line of sight. Hampden and Carpenter supposed otherwise and so did most of the rustic onlookers. Neither side was disappointed. The globularists saw exactly what they wanted to see, the disc standing about five feet above the signal, and the flat-earth representatives saw the same thing; but the conclusions they each drew from the sight were quite different. Mr Carpenter actually jumped for joy when he noticed that the apparent gap between the cross-hair on the telescope and the central disc was the same as between the disc and the far signal. The cross-hair, he said, represented the position of the observer, and the fact that the disc and the signal appeared to recede from it, due to perspective, by equal intervals, meant that a dead straight line could be drawn through all three marks. He claimed the victory on behalf of Mr Hampden.

Wallace was furious. In vain he explained that the telescope had been properly levelled and the position of the cross-hair had nothing to do with the matter. When Carpenter held his ground, he demanded that the local clergyman be sent for to make a final judgment on the spot. The idea was vetoed by his opponents, and the parties drove back to Downham Market in gloomy silence.

Up to then they had spent amicable evenings together, sharing carriages to the canalside each day, but the dispute put an end to all fraternizing with the enemy. The upholders of the Bible dined separately from the unbelievers, and on the train next morning they travelled in different compartments. Before leaving, Mr Carpenter had called on Mr Coulcher to persuade his fellow referee that the wager should be settled in favour of the flat earth. He was so insistent and the argument became so unpleasant that the surgeon summoned a policeman to throw him out of the house.

Since there was no chance of the referees agreeing, or even communicating further with each other, an umpire was appointed, Mr Walsh – which seems a bit unfair since he was Wallace's referee in the first place. He took care, however, to listen to Carpenter's side of the case, and referred his objections to a firm of instrument makers, who dismissed them. He then published the reports of both umpires in *The Field*, pronounced judgment in favour of the globularists and paid the £1,000 stake over to Mr Wallace.

All this was extremely galling to old Parallax, who had given Hampden and Carpenter their ideas in the first place, but had not been consulted about the Old Bedford Level challenge. He dissociated himself from the whole business, and scolded his disciples as bungling innocents for allowing themselves to be fooled by crafty men of science. In a pamphlet, *Experimental Proofs*, he explained the trick which Wallace had played at the Old Bedford Level. Instead of the three level markers required for the experiment, there had been only two, the telescope taking the place of the third. The result, although it appeared to indicate that the earth was round, was merely an effect of perspective. John Hampden hired Parallax to go up again to Welney bridge and repeat his former experiments, and this he did, confirming once more the flat-earth doctrine. Armed with his results, and with two pamphlets which they had each written to show how they had been cheated, Hampden and Carpenter disputed the award in favour of Wallace. The matter ended up in court, where in 1876 three judges of the Queen's Bench carefully avoided having to rule on whether the earth is round or flat, but decided that wagers on the subject were not legally binding and that since Mr Hampden disagreed with the umpire's decision he was entitled to his money back.

Sad to say, this was not the end of the matter. Ever since the umpire's decision had gone against him, John Hampden had nurtured a sense of grievance, which grew into a monstrous obsession. For the next sixteen years he persisted in a ruthless campaign of vilification against Alfred Wallace, writing poison-pen letters to his wife, family and friends and abusing him to his professional colleagues. The tormented scientist had to sue him for libel and on several occasions had him arrested; but all in vain. Hampden now saw himself as a religious martyr, and even sentences of up to a year in prison failed to divert him from his course. In order to avoid payment of damages awarded against him by the courts for his libels against Wallace and Walsh, he passed over all his assets to his son-in-law and declared himself bankrupt. Alfred Wallace came to regret bitterly his involvement in the shape-of-the-earth controversy. In his autobiography, *My Life*, he wrote that Hampden's persecutions had blighted a large part of his life, and the cost of the ensuing law-suits had almost ruined him financially.

William Carpenter migrated to America and flourished there as a most prolific writer on the flat-earth theory. He became a well-known figure on the streets of Baltimore, loitering outside schools and colleges and pressing his pamphlets and arguments on pupils going in and out.

Lady Blount

For many years after Wallace's experiment, the Old Bedford Level was regularly visited by flat-earth researchers and their rivals. James Naylor reported in the *Earth Not a Globe Review* (March 1897) that he had discovered the cause of Wallace's apparent success: that the hairline on the telescope he used had distorted the view along the canal. Proper use of the instrument showed him that the water-surface was level. He was answered in 1901 by Mr H. Yule Oldham, who conducted another experiment with poles and addressed a paper to the British Association for the Advancement of Science, stating that all was well with globular theory. The effect of his paper was not, however, what he intended. Far from stilling controversy, it stirred up the formidable Lady Blount. On her shoulders had fallen the mantle of Parallax, and she proved herself worthy of it.

Born Elizabeth Anne Mould Williams, she married in 1874 a staid baronet, much older than herself, Sir Walter de Sodington Blount (pronounced 'Blunt'). The present baronet remembers her simply as an old lady whom he visited in about 1923, shortly before her death, when he was six years old, and the only tradition that remains of her in the family is that she was an out-and-out crank. The most direct indication of the state of her mind and of her marriage is in a fantastic novel she wrote, *Adrian Galilio*. She herself is the heroine, disguised only in name as Lady Alma, alias Madame Bianka the zetetic lecturer. Her fictional husband is the oddly named Sir Rosemary Alma, a Roman Catholic like Blount. He is old, cold-hearted and mean, and he forbids his young wife the company of her fellow Protestants. She responds by taking a priest for a lover. To him she delivers passionate speeches about the Bible and the flat earth, and has almost converted him when they are both shot down by the priest's jealous housekeeper. Recovering separately, the lovers undergo amazing transformations, as do all the other characters in the novel, the priest becoming a licentious baronet in Paris while Lady Alma, now Madame Bianka, takes to the lecture hall circuit, winning many to the true zetetic faith. Much of her propaganda is put out as doggerel verses set to music, for Lady Blount was an ecstatic, and a feature of her actual lectures was her singing of hymns in praise of the flat-earth doctrine.

After bearing two sons to her first husband, Lady Blount embarked on a second marriage in which she had two daughters. But most of her energy went into her work. She inherited the Universal Zetetic Society, which Rowbotham had founded in New York in 1873, with a branch ten years later in London. Under her full-time management the Society flourished. She was a tireless pamphleteer, and streams of magazines and other papers issued from her house at Kingston, Surrey. One of them was the Society's official journal, *The Earth*, which she edited, published and mostly wrote. It circulated, she claimed, in almost all countries, apart from Russia where it was banned. She enjoyed polemics, particularly with a clear-cut opponent such as her rival editor, Mr Blatchford of *The Clarion*, a crusading atheist. On one point only, she agreed with him: that, in the words of Thomas Paine, 'modern astronomy and the Bible can not be held together in the same mind, and he who thinks he believes both knows very little of either'. Her deepest scorn was for the compromising Christians who pretended that the Bible and modern science could be made compatible.

Among her following were a number of clergymen, or ex-clergymen, one of the latter being Mr E. V. Mulgrave, a leading contributor to *The Earth*, whose religious convictions, she said, 'rendered it imperative that he should dissever himself from the Established Church'. At Speakers' Corner in Hyde Park he caught Mr Blatchford in the act of uttering blasphemies and told him off in the name of God. Challenged by Blatchford to produce proof of the existence of God, Mulgrave replied, 'Sir, I doubt your existence. Prove it to me.' The atheist was so confused by this demand that 'he came off his stand and went out of the park in haste'.

With her firm faith and thorough knowledge of the works of Parallax, Lady Blount was proof against all the arguments which globularists could bring against her. The classical demonstration of the earth's rotation by means of a pendulum she dismissed on the grounds that all it demonstrated was the motion of the pendulum, not that of the earth, and she could quote cases, unknown to her lecture audiences, where a pendulum had not behaved as science said it should. Nor did she fear that most popular proof of a spherical earth, the 'hull down' effect exhibited by ships crossing the horizon, which leaves their masts visible after the hull has vanished from sight. Rowbotham had shown her how to answer that one, by calling it a trick of perspective, particularly noticeable in stormy weather when the hulls are hidden by waves. She also claimed that in calm seas a telescope could often restore a ship to sight after it had supposedly disappeared beyond the earth's curve. In his book Rowbotham had gone in great detail into the hull down effect, ending by turning the tables on the globularists and claiming it as one of the best proofs of planist theory.

Ever since 1870, Alfred Wallace's experiments with poles at the Old Bedford Level, supported later by Oldham's tests, had been a stumbling-block in the path of flat-earth faithists. In 1905 Lady Blount led an expedition to the Old Bedford Level in order to prove once and for all that the earth is flat. Rejecting the 'three pole trick', as she called it, she returned to the original methods of Rowbotham. She hired a photographer, Mr Clifton of Dallmeyer's, who in May 1904 went up to the Bedford Level, equipped with the firm's latest Photo-Telescopic Camera. The apparatus was set up at one end of the clear six-mile length, while at the other end Lady Blount and some scientific gentlemen hung a large, white, calico sheet over the Bedford bridge so that the bottom of it was near the water. It was about 15 feet square, and had been made for her by some ladies who lived nearby. Mr Clifton, lying down near Welney bridge with his camera lens two feet above the water level, observed by telescope the hanging of the sheet, and found that he could see the whole of it down to the bottom. This surprised him, for he was an orthodox globularist and round-earth theory said that over a distance of six miles the bottom of the sheet should be more than 20 feet below his line of sight. His photograph showed not only the entire sheet but its reflection in the water below. That was certified in his report to Lady Blount, which concluded:

'I should not like to abandon the globular theory off-hand, but, as far as this particular test is concerned, I am prepared to maintain that (unless rays of light will travel in a curved path) these six miles of water present a level surface.'

The photograph was published in *The Earth* and other journals, and Lady Blount enjoyed her triumph. A long correspondence took place in the popular science magazine, *English Mechanic*, in which the orthodox tried to explain away the photograph as something to do with 'refraction' or 'mirages', while Lady Blount responded voluminously in prose, verse, songs and quotations from the Bible. She reminded readers of Richard Proctor's statement in one of his authoritative works on astronomy: 'If with the eye a few inches above the surface of the Bedford Canal, an object close to the water, six miles distant from the observer can be seen, then manifestly there would be something wrong with the accepted theory.' That test had now been made, and the accepted theory had come out of it badly. On the strength of it Lady Blount proclaimed that the earth's flatness had been scientifically proved.

There is obviously a need for further experiments at the Old Bedford Level.

The flat earth today

The flat-earth movement became dormant in Britain in the early 1970s with the deaths of its last active promoters, Samuel and Lillian Shenton of Dover. They blamed its decline on the 'anti-God, globe-earth indoctrination' of modern education. Yet there are always a few Zetetics who take their own view of things and will dispute orthodoxy down to its very roots. One of the most obstinate was William Edgell of Radstock, Somerset, head of the well-known building firm still active in that town. In his book, *Does the Earth Rotate?*, he complained that whenever he asked his teachers at school for proof of the round-earth theory, all he received from them was smiles. The object of his book was to persuade authority to reform the education system in accordance with reason, by which he meant the flat-earth doctrine. He described simple experiments by which anyone could disprove the theory of the earth's rotation. These included the usual throwing of balls aloft from moving trains, cars and liners, and he also showed how to convince oneself with a telescope that the Pole Star is a mere 5,000 miles distant, not the fantastic 3,680,000,000,000,000 miles given in textbooks.

Like many independent thinkers, Mr Edgell was an inventor. He discovered such useful devices as the automatic weighing machine and the free-wheel for bicycles, and he also invented the airless tyre at a time when everyone else was concentrating on the pneumatic version. His much repeated motto was 'Truth will always win.'

America, the haven of heretics, still boasts a Flat Earth Society, energetically managed by Mr Charles K. Johnson and his wife Marjory of Lancaster, California. It incorporates the remnants of other organizations, such as the Zetetics, the Shentons' group and the followers of Wilbur Glen Voliva of Zion, Illinois. That city was long the headquarters of American flat-earth loyalists, several thousands of them, who largely populated it. They were members of the Christian Apostolic Church, founded in 1895 by John Alexander Dowie, a Scottish prophet and faith-healer. His rejection of the spherical earth followed, as is usually the case, from his literalizing of the Bible. Ten years later, he himself was rejected by the sect in a revolt led by Voliva, who ruled Zion until he died in 1942. His was a strict government, based on the code of the Scriptures, as he interpreted them. Much of the city's income was from fines on unwary visitors for crimes such as smoking in the street, driving at more than five miles an hour and whistling on Sunday. There were also profits from Zion Industries, a highly successful manufacturing business run by Voliva on behalf of the community.

Voliva also ran a powerful radio station, daily proclaiming the flatness of the earth and prophesying its imminent destruction. In this respect he was like Rowbotham, who believed that the earth would shortly be consumed by fire. Voliva set several successive dates for the cataclysm, and their uneventful passing did nothing to weaken his authority over the people of Zion. He used to offer $5,000 to anyone who could prove that the earth was not a flat plane, and since he was impervious to anyone else's arguments he never found it necessary to pay out.

Charles Johnson, heir to all the flat-earth kingdoms of the west, is very religious and patriotic. He and Marjory live in a lonely house with many dogs, cats and chickens, but without piped water or electricity. They regard themselves as the last bastion of true Christian orthodoxy in a world corrupted by socialism, atheism and the heresy of a revolving earth. They blame this largely on Britain where these evils were nurtured and where, so they say, the Church of England first established the round-earth dogma. But they are hardly less scornful of the Bible-belt fundamentalists of their own country, who, while holding the line against Darwinism and the anti-scriptural theory of evolution, have given way on the basic issue about the shape of the earth.

Modern photographs of the earth from space, showing it as a globe, present a challenge to the Johnsons which Parallax, Blount and Voliva never had to face – though no doubt they would have been equal to it. The Johnsons simply deny that the space programme ever took place. The whole thing was a hoax. In their outspoken journal, *Flat Earth News*, they say that the NASA scientists and the world's rulers are all well aware that the earth is flat, but the British Government prevents them from revealing that fact. Arthur C. Clarke was hired to write the script for the first moon landing, and the valuable rights to the production were allotted to America at a Kennedy-Khrushchev meeting in return for Cuba. Hollywood was well able to simulate Armstrong's historic walk on the moon's surface. As proof of this, the Johnsons have dug up a 1950 film, *Destination Moon,* which closely prefigures the NASA effort nineteen years later. They are well aware of the conspiracies going on around them; nor are they alone in their scepticism. Quite a number of books have been published in America which question the authenticity of the 1969 moon landing. Charles Johnson claims that the majority of people do not really believe in it. 'There's a certain lurking sanity in everyone's mind,' he says.

There are very few instances where a person with decided views on whether the earth is flat or spherical has ever been converted to the opposite belief. A notable case was President Paul Kruger of the Transvaal Republic. In 1900, while on his way into exile on board a Dutch man-of-war, he was invited by the captain to step onto the bridge and watch the process of navigation. As a member of the fundamentalist Dutch Reformed Church, Kruger believed literally in the pillars and corners of the flat earth. He learnt from the captain that the ship was navigated on the basis of the earth being spherical, inspected the sextant and other instruments, and then went below for his Bible and threw it into the sea. If the earth was really a globe, he said, then the Book was untrue and of no further interest to him.

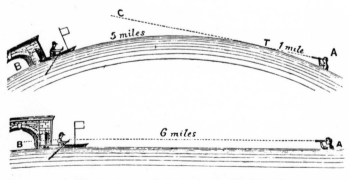

The question at issue in the Bedford Level
experiment, illustrated by Parallax (see p.22).

John 'Woodcock' Carden, the unpopular Irish landlord, became a folk hero for his attempted abduction of a young heiress, Eleanor Arbuthnot. It led to 'the most exciting chase ever heard of in Tipperary'. (1, 2)

Lady Blount, the vigorous campaigner on behalf of the flat-earth doctrine and literal interpretation of the Bible. She both lectured and sang ecstatically at her meetings, and publicized her cause by street processions, as illustrated by this picture from her fantastic novel, *Adrian Galilio*. (3, 4)

Charles and Marjory Johnson of Lancaster, California, the last stubborn defenders of flat-earth doctrine. (5)

Views and comments published by William Carpenter, the flat-earth representative at the Old Bedford Level experiment of 1870 which failed to convince him that the earth is really a globe. Below: Mr Edgell of Radstock's twentieth-century riposte to Galileo, showing that his house, if moving with the earth, would be safe from overhead bombs. (6,7)

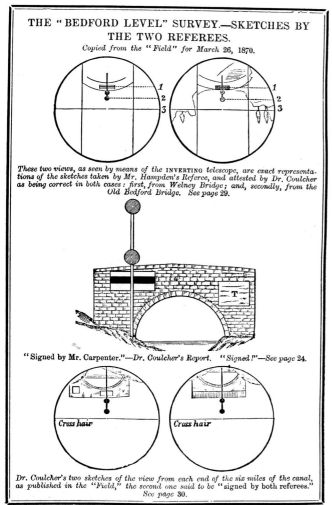

THE "BEDFORD LEVEL" SURVEY.—SKETCHES BY THE TWO REFEREES.

Copied from the "Field" for March 26, 1870.

1
2
3

1
2
3

These two views, as seen by means of the INVERTING telescope, are exact representations of the sketches taken by Mr. Hampden's Referee, and attested by Dr. Coulcher as being correct in both cases: first, from Welney Bridge; and, secondly, from the Old Bedford Bridge. See page 29.

T

"Signed by Mr. Carpenter."—Dr. Coulcher's Report.   "Signed!"—See page 24.

Cross hair

Cross hair

Dr. Coulcher's two sketches of the view from each end of the six miles of the canal, as published in the "Field," the second one said to be "signed by both referees." See page 30.

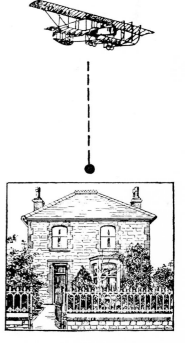

In the name of humanity,
Koresh,

Cyrus Teed, known as Koresh, the American visionary who believed that the earth is hollow and established an ideal community in Florida for his disciples. Below is his plan of New Jerusalem, which he intended to be the nucleus of a new world-order based on his teachings. (8, 9)

The crucial experiment to test Cyrus Teed's belief that the earth's surface is concave was performed in 1897. The geodetic staff of his community used their 'Rectilineator',essentially a giant spirit-level, to project an 'air line' over several miles along the coast of Florida. The results appeared to confirm Teed's theory. Inset is the view along the Rectilineator as the air line approaches nearer to the ground. (10, 11)

Colonel Charles de Laet Waldo Sibthorp, M.P. for Lincoln 1826-55, made his name in Parliament for his xenophobia and his opposition to every reform and innovation. He was hated by Queen Victoria for the part he played in cutting down the allowance paid to her foreign-born Consort. Sibthorp denounced the Great Exhibition of 1851 as an alien plot, and called upon God to smite the Crystal Palace with hailstones and lightning. A *Punch* cartoon shows him hurling a brickbat through its glass wall. (12, 13)

Below: Miss Bevan at the age of twenty-two. As Mrs Nesta Webster, she wrote spine-chilling accounts of hidden forces beneath the surface of history. Her belief that civilization was threatened by a conspiracy of occultists and Freemasons had considerable influence in the period between the two World Wars. Left is her arch-enemy, Adam Weishaupt, founder of the Bavarian Illuminati in 1776, whom she identified as the source of the French and all subsequent revolutions. (14, 15)

Below are four of the numerous notes and letters which Baron de Güldenstubbé, the nineteenth-century spiritualist, found written on the notepads which he left beside tombs and statues in Paris. 'Messages from beyond the grave' were received from Plato, Cicero, Mary Queen of Scots and other notables, as well as from more ordinary correspondents. The most interesting of the examples shown here is, top left, the scrawl of Heloïse, the tragic twelfth-century heroine. It was obtained in the Père-Lachaise cemetery from the tomb she shares with her lover, Abelard.

In London, de Güldenstubbé patronized the fashionable medium, Mrs Guppy who, though she weighed seventeen stone, was credited with the feat of levitation, illustrated left, passing by air from her house in Hampstead to another at Clerkenwell. (16, 17)

N: 55.

N: 56.

Allez mon cher Louis, allez tous trois à St Denis demain à onze heures.

M

N: 57.

N: 58.

Mon très cher Ami, quelle jouissance pour moi de pouvoir vous assurer de ma main d'outre-tombe que vous avez eu raison en ce qu'il y a de plus consolateur pour l'homme!— Oui, nous existons, nous pensons, nous agissons, nous prenons part aux maux ainsi qu'aux moments etc.

THE COMMUNITY
THAT DWELT WITHIN
THE EARTH

At about the same time as Lady Blount and the Zetetics were proving through experiments at the Bedford Level canal that the earth was flat, another group of experimenters were using similar methods to show that it was in fact a hollow shell, inhabited on its inner surface. The motto of this group was 'We live inside.'

Their leader and prophet was Dr Cyrus Teed, known to them as Koresh, a Hebrew version of his first name. He was, to say the least, a most unusual person. Born in 1839 in New York State, he became a practitioner of 'eclectic medicine', a system combining orthodox science with a religious outlook and the use of herbs and other natural remedies. From there he progressed to alchemy. Energy and matter, he believed, were two different forms of the same thing. It should therefore be possible to convert one into the other, and thus to transmute matter from its original nature into something quite different.

At Deerfield, New York, he set up an 'electro-chemical' laboratory, and one autumn evening in 1869 he discovered the philosopher's stone. Once matter had been reduced to energy, the secret of reconstituting it as matter of another kind lay in the use of polar magnetism. This implied that the earth and solar system constituted a perpetual, self-regulating battery, divinely created and comprehensible by human intelligence. He reasoned thus: 'Form is a fundamental property of existence; therefore, that which has not form has no existence. Limitation is a property of form. The universe has existence; therefore it has form, hence it has limitation.'

The unsettling notion of infinite space, inherent in modern cosmology, could be banished. Dr Teed had explained the universe in rational terms, and to him therefore was given the responsibility of leading mankind into a new age of perfect knowledge and serenity.

As he pondered his discovery he fell into a state of visionary trance. The gentle voice of the Mother of the Universe spoke to him, and then she herself appeared, bathed in a light of purple and gold. She confirmed that he was the chosen instrument for redeeming the world, and promised that as both his mother and bride she would come to earth and assist in his appointed mission. The promise was fulfilled some years later when Dr Teed had another encounter with the Universal Mother in the person of Mrs Annie Ordway of Chicago who became thereafter his constant guide and companion.

It was not until he was nearly fifty that Dr Teed, as a reincarnation of the royal prophet Cyrus or Koresh, began to attract a serious following. Ever since the time of his vision, he had combined medical practice with preaching, lecturing and experimenting with the formation of ideal communities, intended as the nuclei of a future world-order based on his teachings. Such experiments were common at the time. Settlements throughout the United States were pioneered by the disciples of charismatic leaders, such as Joseph Smith's Mormons, the Perfectionists of Oneida and the Californian Brotherhood of the New Life. Many of them, like the Shakers, were communistic and celibate, and Teed, who had similar ideas, planned to unite them all into one body under his leadership. But the doctrines of Koresh were so outstandingly peculiar that none of the other groups found it possible to accept them. He acquired, however, a fair number of individual adherents, particularly among educated and professional people in Chicago, and there in 1888 was founded the Koreshan Unity. Its members pooled their resources and lived together as a community, pledging themselves to celibacy and abstention from alcohol, tobacco and opium, under the joint rule of Koresh and the Universal Mother, Mrs Ordway.

The Koreshans acknowledged Dr Teed as the Messiah, destined to replace Christianity with the new scientific religion, Koreshanity. Its cosmology was summarized as follows: 'The universe is a cell, a hollow globe, the physical body of which is the earth; the sun is at the center. We live on the inside of the cell; and the sun, moon, planets and stars are all within the globe. The universe is eternal, a great battery, and perpetually renews itself through inherent functions, by virtue of which it involves and evolves itself.'

By imitating the self-sustaining processes of life through the science of alchemy, it would be possible to achieve immortality and bodily resurrection. When the whole world accepted Koreshanity, it would come under divine rule and the primeval Golden Age would be restored.

From the account so far, it could easily be assumed that Teed was a mere fanatic or charlatan preying on the gullible. He had, of course, to suffer the accusations which have always been brought against such cult-leaders: that he seduced and swindled his followers, alienated their family affections and so on. It is true that most of his following was female, and his vivacious, dark eyes were said to have had a fascinating effect. But no charges of misconduct were ever substantiated against him, and those who best knew him always spoke of Koresh as a sincere, honest, kind individual and a selfless leader. As long as he lived, his followers enjoyed happy, prosperous lives in the paradise he was perfecting for them and the whole world.

Koreshanity was not designed as a minority movement, but for universal acceptance. To achieve that, its promoters had to produce scientific proof that its basic tenets were true, and they also had to publicize it. From their very beginning they were excellent propagandists. They operated their own printing press and issued well-produced editions of Koresh's writings, regular magazines, broadsheets and pamphlets. But when it came to proving that the surface of the earth was concave, rather than convex as orthodoxy had it, Dr Teed was in some doubt as to the best procedure. Like the flat-earthers, he experimented with sightings along a straight line of canal, the Old Illinois Drainage Canal in his case, and from these and similar tests elsewhere he was able to theorize that the earth's apparent convexity was due to optical illusion. As evidence for this he pointed out that a ship which, to the naked eye, is almost invisible over the horizon can be restored fully into sight by the use of a telescope. This was the same observation which old Parallax in England had earlier used as evidence for the flat-earth thesis. It certainly did not amount to the scientific proof of concavity which the Koreshan movement needed. Not until 1897 was that proof finally obtained, by an historic experiment on the coast of south-west Florida.

Meanwhile, the community had moved house. In 1894 Dr Teed and Mrs Ordway had been prospecting in Florida, seeking a location for New Jerusalem, the projected capital city of the Koreshan new world-order. They discovered the ideal spot at Estero, a few miles south of Fort Myers. It was, said Koresh, a natural magnetic centre, most suitable for the future hub of universal commerce, education and government. The land he wanted was occupied by a German settler, but the promise of eternal life and an honoured position at the centre of New Jerusalem persuaded the owner to part with his holding, and the Koreshans were soon established in their new colony.

One of the attractions of Estero, from Teed's point of view, was that it was near the flat coastline which provided a perfect testing-ground for his theory of the earth's concavity. For years he had been looking for a scientist who could design the appropriate experimental equipment. Finally he met the right man, Ulysses Grant Morrow. Teed and Morrow wrote a book together, *The Cellular Cosmogony*, describing their procedure in proving scientifically that the earth's surface slopes upwards.

The instrument they used was called a Rectilineator. Morrow designed it and had it built to accurate specifications. It consisted of several sections, the main feature of each being a double T-square twelve feet long. They were made of seasoned mahogany with brass fittings and braced with steel tension bars. Two uprights supported each section at heights which were adjustable. The idea was for the first section to be levelled so that the horizontal surface of the T-square was parallel with the surface of a body of water, and 128 inches above it. The second section was then to be placed against the first and attached to it with screws, extending the 'air line' another twelve feet. In the same way a third was to be added to the second, and the first section was then to be brought round to the other end to prolong the line still further. As the sections leap-frogged each other the air line would be increased by successive twelve-foot lengths. According to the 'globularists' or followers of Copernicus, the water line should gradually fall away from the air line because of the curvature of the earth. Believers in a flat earth would expect the two lines to remain absolutely parallel. Morrow and Teed, believing that the earth's surface was concave, were confident that the air line produced by the Rectilineator would approach nearer and nearer to the water line and eventually hit it. Thus, on the morning of 18 March 1897, when the first section of the Rectilineator was erected and levelled on the beach at Naples, Florida, by the surveyors of the Koreshan Geodetic Staff, three rival theories were placed in competition with each other. The question as to whether the earth's surface was concave, convex or flat was about to be determined scientifically.

Calculations based on the theory of the convex globular earth show that a line drawn tangent to its surface and projected in one direction should, at one mile from the point of contact, be eight inches above the earth. For every additional mile thereafter, according to the accepted formula, the distance between the tangential line and the earth's surface should increase by the square of the number of miles multiplied by eight inches. Thus after two miles the distance should be $2 \times 2 \times 8 = 32$ inches, after three miles $3 \times 3 \times 8 = 72$ inches and so on. These figures are based on the official doctrine that the earth's diameter is about 8,000 miles, and Teed and Morrow agreed with the calculation. But they turned the whole thing inside out. They declared that 8,000 miles was the distance across the earth's hollow interior, and that its surface curved upwards, according to the established formula, rather than falling away.

After a month's work on the beach at Naples, the Koreshan Geodetic Staff had extended the air line made by the Rectilineator a distance of one mile. Results at this stage were promising: the air line, which at the start had been 128 inches above the surface water line, was now 8.02 inches nearer to it, almost exactly as Teed had predicted, and at the end of the second mile the distance between the two lines had diminished by 30.62 inches, close enough to the 32 inches his theory required. The Rectilineator was extended another half-mile, and the survey was then carried further by means of sighting poles and telescopes levelled on the Rectilineator's air line. This line, it was found, hit the water line at a distance of four and an eighth miles from the starting point. In that distance, therefore, the earth's surface had curved upwards by 128 inches, which Teed and Morrow judged near enough to the calculated figure to justify the Koreshan cosmology.

No one has ever seriously attempted either to debunk or to repeat the Rectilineator experiment, but it is natural for those who can not bring themselves to accept its results to wonder how they were obtained. The Rectilineator apparatus, though cumbersome, was scientifically sound, and so was the principle behind its use, and one can hardly suppose that the Koreshan surveyors, who lived by the doctrines of their leader, were engaged in an elaborate conspiracy of deception. Perhaps the answer lies in the malleable, obliging nature of the universe, which reflects every image projected upon it and gives every experiment a tendency to gratify the experimenter.

Koresh, his celibate community and his eccentric world-view were obvious targets for press ridicule, which they attracted in full measure.

Yet among his followers the Cellular Cosmogony worked well. It may be that, the more outrageous and exclusive are the beliefs which a group holds in common, the more effective they are in holding that group together in defiance of the outside world. At any rate, the Koreshan community flourished. In the early years of this century there were about two hundred settlers at the site of New Jerusalem at Estero and in smaller colonies elsewhere. The appearance of these energetic Yankees in sparsely populated south Florida had a profound effect on the district's economy. The Koreshans, many of whom were skilled in various crafts and trades, husbanded their lands, planted orchards, introduced new crops and livestock and founded useful industries. These included a saw-mill, a boat-building yard, a concrete factory and, for domestic purposes, a bakery, a cane-mill, a steam-laundry and a well-equipped printing shop. Members chose the work for which they were best adapted, and the products of farms, gardens and workshops were distributed according to need at the village store, where the surplus was sold to neighbours. A pleasure park, laid out along the Estero creek, was stocked with many different kinds of fruit trees and vegetables as well as ornamental plants and was furnished with picturesque urns made by the sculpture department. Cultural life centred on the school for general and Koreshan studies and the Art Hall. There were held regular exhibitions, concerts, lectures, feasts, festivals and religious services. The Koreshans dined communally, men and women at separate tables, a routine which was often varied by picnics in the park or further afield on one of the islands off the coast. On pleasant evenings they would place their orchestra in a boat and follow it round their bay in a flotilla, watch the sunset to the strains of music and sail home by moonlight.

To his faithful, hard-working flock Cyrus Teed was a good shepherd. He ruled in conjunction with Annie Ordway and a council of seven women, representing the seven planets. These luminaries lived chastely in a handsome eight-roomed house, one room for each of them and the other for the piano. Social historians and those with a practical interest in the formation of communities have recently been showing interest in the Koreshan model, partly because of the respect and equality for women which featured in it. Elliott Mackle, the leading historian of Koreshanity, paints an attractive picture of life at Estero, as long as Cyrus Teed was there to energize it. The fact that things went so smoothly must largely be attributed to the constant effect of his vision of

New Jerusalem. Potential converts were warned that not everything was yet perfect in the colony, but present hardships were more than made up for by the promise of pioneering the great city of an ideal civilization soon to come. Dr Teed had a magnificent painting giving a bird's-eye view of the future New Jerusalem. Based on the ancient geometers' image of harmony, a square and circle combined, the city's plan extended for miles across the Florida landscape. Broad avenues lined with palatial buildings radiated from its centre far out into the country, symbolizing the world-wide spread of Koreshanity. The streets were to be built on several different levels, separating pedestrians, carriages, passenger railways and commercial traffic. Other practical features included a 'movable and continuous earth closet' conveying the city's organic waste to a distant plant for recycling as fertilizer.

Although it was to be the centre of world commerce and industry as well as culture, New Jerusalem was to be quite free of industrial pollution. Steam and petrol machinery would be made obsolete by the perfection of alchemical science and the discovery of a clean, natural source of energy in the electro-magnetic currents of the earth and atmosphere. Teed anticipated modern ley-line and earth-energy researchers in believing that the ancient sages knew the secrets of manipulating the earth's vital forces, and that these secrets could be rediscovered and made use of in the science of the future. In his prophetic science-fiction novel, *The Great Red Dragon or The Flaming Devil of the Orient,* he foresaw the use of magnetic currents in the atmosphere to levitate 'anti-gravic' platforms from which missiles could be rained down on enemy armies. Also prophesied in the novel is a war in which a horde of anti-Christian orientals, led by the Japanese, sink the American fleet and begin invading the United States. When all seems lost they are routed by the aerial platforms, invented and made at Estero. Inside America the forces of big business are defeated by the masses, inspired by Koreshan ideals; New Jerusalem is built and its founders, implicitly Dr Teed and Mrs Ordway, preside over a regenerate world as instruments of the Divine Motherhood. All this to the loyal Koreshans was no fiction but an inspired prevision of what was soon to come about.

The Koreshans were generally on good terms with their country neighbours, who benefited from their industry and enterprise. They ran a regular service of passenger boats between Estero and the nearest railhead at Fort Myers, where the citizens were also friendly. There was, however, one source of trouble, often encountered by immigrant communities: the natives had a rooted objection to being outvoted at political elections by newcomers. Fort Myers and the surrounding areas of Lee County were controlled by the Democrats. The local party administration was inbred and corrupt, and they resented the Koreshans' practice of block-voting for their own candidates. In politics, as in all their activities, the Koreshans were vigorous and determined. When polls were rigged against them they declared war on the Fort Myers Democrats and allied themselves with the Socialists to form their own Progressive Liberal Party. To support it, they started a weekly newspaper, *The American Eagle*. Composed and printed by the experts at the community press, it was of far better quality than any other Florida paper, and it quickly gained circulation at the expense of its Fort Myers rival, the organ of the Democrats. The Koreshan writers usually did best in the battle of editorials waged between the two papers. Their new party was seen as a threat to the local establishment, and from this there ensued an unpleasant incident which brought disaster upon the house of Koresh.

One afternoon in October 1906 a Koreshan politician was assaulted by a local bully in a Fort Myers street. Dr Teed, who happened to be near at hand with a party of followers, attempted to calm the assailant and was himself attacked, receiving several blows to the head. The town marshal was standing by but made no effort to intervene. The other Koreshans sprang to their leader's defence and were beaten up by the town mob. No one seemed to have been badly hurt, but from that day on Dr Teed's health began to decline. Though often in pain he continued to direct the round of activities at Estero, wrote his novel, travelled extensively on lecture tours and visited other Koreshan properties. Returning to Estero he tried to cure his infirmity by a variety of treatments, from salt-water baths to electro-therapy, but with no lasting results. In 1908, three days before Christmas, he died.

Many of the Koreshans simply could not believe it. They had always assumed that Koresh was immortal, so his apparent death must merely be a trance, a further stage in his progress towards divinity. His resurrection was expected to take place on Christmas Day, and the community watched and prayed over his body until the local health authority ordered its burial. A monumental vault was quickly erected on

Estero Island, and therein were laid the remains of Cyrus Teed. From far and wide Koreshans flocked to the funeral, speculating on the possibility of a miraculous rising from the tomb. No immediate sign was given them, but some years later a violent storm hit Estero Island, the entire vault was washed away by the sea, and no trace was ever found of the body of Koresh. It was said at Estero that he had been transported to some faraway land in continuance of his mission, and that some day he would return home.

Koreshanity today

On the departure of their prophet the Koreshans came under the leadership of Mrs Ordway; but she defected in order to get married, and there followed a succession of leaders, all good people but lacking the inspired genius of the founder. Slowly the community wound down. There were quarrels and schisms, people drifted away and no new converts came forward to replace them. Among the Koreshans were a few married couples, living separately from the main celibate body, but most of their children left Estero when they grew up. One by one the industries closed down until only the printing works were left. They survived until 1949, producing Koreshan literature and *The American Eagle*, which had turned away from politics to become a gardening journal. In that year the print shop was destroyed by fire. From its peak of over two hundred members the community's strength had dwindled to a mere dozen. The final extinction of Koreshanity along with Dr Teed's dream of New Jerusalem seemed imminent.

Unexpectedly a renaissance took place. At the beginning of the Second World War a rare new member joined the group at Estero. Hedwig Michel came to America to escape the Nazis. She had been headmistress of a Jewish school in Germany and had fallen under the influence of a master on her staff, Peter Bender. A former pilot, wounded in the First War, he had taken up the study of mathematics. Certain calculations led him to formulate a hollow-earth theory very similar to Teed's. His *Hohlweltlehre* gained a considerable following in Germany and still has adherents there today. It was only after he had announced his theory that he came across a copy of Teed's *Cellular Cosmogony*. He entered into correspondence with the community at Estero and, when things were looking black for Jews in Germany, he asked them whether they would give refuge to his fellow-believer, Miss Michel. The Koreshans sent her an invitation to come and live with them. Bender, who by that time had grown to fancy himself a reincarnation of Koresh, stayed on in Germany, was arrested by the Nazis and died in a prison camp.

When Hedwig Michel arrived at Estero she found the colony in a sad state of decay. Its remaining members were no longer the bustling Yankees of the early settlement. In appearance and speech they were now indistinguishable from the locals and they had adapted to the easy-going pace of Southern life. Their riverside park was overgrown and many of their buildings were empty and derelict. In the best manner of a German headmistress Miss Michel took things in hand. She had the most useful houses repaired, organized the finances, revived education and generally put new heart into the community. *The American Eagle* was relaunched in 1965, this time as a journal of ecology. Through her efforts the future of the Koreshan Unity was assured.

In 1967 the board of the Unity struck a bargain with the State of Florida, presenting their village and some of the land round it for use as a public park, in return for which the State agreed to rebuild the settlement as it was in its prime and to restore its ornamental gardens. The Koreshans seem to have done well out of the deal. A visit to Estero in April 1983 was rendered delightful by guide Louis Cureton, an expert on Koreshanity and an obvious sympathizer. His lecture at the Art Hall was illustrated with relics from the days of Koresh, preserved there by the State, including his charts demonstrating the hollow earth, his picture of New Jerusalem and instruments of the community orchestra and brass band. All that is missing is the Rectilineator, the surviving section of which is now in a museum at Fort Myers. Having secured protection by the State for their principal shrine, the Koreshans have turned to education. They no longer emphasize the hollow earth doctrine, but other aspects of Koreshanity are studied at their new college, located a few hundred yards from their original settlement. The whole place is still pervaded by the spirit of Dr Teed. His plan for New Jerusalem has never been forgotten at Estero, and the land on which he meant to build it is still largely in Koreshan hands. It is now extremely valuable real estate. Towers of luxury apartments throng its neighbouring coastline, but the only development which will be permitted at Estero is the construction of New Jerusalem.

THE DIEHARD PRIEST
WHO OPPOSED CAPITALISM

The small place in history occupied by Father Jeremiah O'Callaghan commemorates his brave rearguard action against the capitalist system and its basis in usury. As properly defined, usury means charging interest on the loan (*usus*) of money or commodities, but the true meaning has been betrayed by lexicographers with their new interpretation: lending money at *excessive* interest. Father O'Callaghan took the word in its literal sense, and was persecuted accordingly.

During the early part of his career, as a country priest in south Cork, he had paid little attention to usury, accepting it like everyone else as part of normal business practice. It was not until 1819, when he was thirty-nine years old, that it began to trouble him. At a local priestly conference an elderly Father, Daniel Burke, spoke out against the growing custom, contrary to Christian doctrine, of taking interest on loans. He was opposed by a more worldly cleric, William O'Brien, and the Vicar General of the diocese ordered a debate on the subject at the next Synod. O'Brien argued his case before the Synod with energy, but poor Father Burke, a doddering eighty-year-old, 'was not able even to read his scribbled long list of Canons and Fathers which he held in his trembling hands'. The debate went against him, but on later reflection O'Callaghan decided that the old man was right. The further back he read in the history of ecclesiastical law, the more firmly he found it stated that usury of any sort was contrary to the word of God. One day he was called out to administer last rites to a local corn-dealer who was known to charge interest on monies owed to him. O'Callaghan refused to absolve him until he had restored to each of his debtors the interest he had taken. His eloquence caused the man to repent, and he ordered repayments to be made by the executors of his will.

The other businessmen of the district, fearing they had a fanatic in their midst, complained to the authorities, and Bishop Coppinger of Cloyne and Ross sent O'Callaghan a letter of rebuke, moved him from his post and put him under the supervision of another priest. He was forbidden thenceforth to withhold the sacraments from usurers, and pressure was put on the man he had converted to revoke his will. He refused to do so, however, being persuaded by O'Callaghan that he would do better to give expense to his heirs than to lose his place in Heaven.

Finding himself barred from exercising his proper function as a priest, Father O'Callaghan opened a Catholic school at Ross Carbery in Cork and then made a trip to France where, he noted, the practice of usury was ecclesiastically frowned upon. Returning to Ireland, he attempted to re-open negotiations with the Bishop, but Coppinger was unyielding. Lending at interest was now the custom and, although the Church was officially against it, enthusiasm on the subject was tactless and unwelcome. When O'Callaghan persisted in being strictly orthodox, Coppinger disallowed him from saying Mass and promised to use his influence to prevent any other bishop from employing him.

The boycott was effective. O'Callaghan wrote to the Vatican, stating the facts of his case, requesting guidance on the question of usury and accusing Bishop Coppinger himself of being a usurer. Receiving no reply, he took ship in 1823 for America, landing at New York. The Bishop there seemed sympathetic, but when he heard of Coppinger's ban he refused to accept O'Callaghan's services, even though he was short of priests. O'Callaghan was told that the hierarchy in Canada took a firm line against usury, so he began his long journey north, suffering terrible discomforts including sea-sickness on Lake Ontario. He found that in Canada usury was indeed discouraged, but when he applied to the local bishop, revealing his record, he was again turned down flat. 'Thus,' he wrote, 'was frustrated in a moment my journey of seven hundred miles, though forests, rivers, lakes: under frost, rain and snow; God's will be done on earth, as it is in heaven.'

The winter in Canada was hard. O'Callaghan fell ill, ran out of money and had to live on the alms of other priests. One of them sheltered him in his house in Montreal, where he wrote a book, *Usury or Lending at Interest... Proved to be Repugnant to the Divine and Ecclesiastical Law and Destructive to Civil Society*. When spring came he made his way back to

New York, found a publisher for his book and took with him sixty copies of it on a ship to Ireland. Arriving back in his own country, he found his reputation as a troublemaker well established; the police and customs refused to let him off the ship until enquiries were made, and it was ten days before he could land.

The main reason for his return home was that, while in Canada, he had at last received an answering letter from the Holy See. It instructed him to go humbly to Bishop Coppinger and make peace with him. No firm ruling was given on the question of usury, but enclosed with the letter was a summary of Vatican policy towards it, cunningly designed to allow the tempering of principle with expediency.

Armed with this letter, O'Callaghan went for an interview with Bishop Coppinger, who remarked on reading it: 'You are commanded to come to me, but I am not commanded to receive you!' – and refused any dealings with him. His appeals to higher authorities went unheard.

In despair of finding justice from anyone but the Pope himself, O'Callaghan set off for Rome. On the way he passed through London, and on happy impulse left a copy of his book at the Fleet Street office of William Cobbett, that prodigious defender of popular rights against all usurpers. By December of 1824 he was in Rome, where the Vatican officials made him a small allowance for his keep while enquiries into his case were made of Bishop Coppinger. It took five months before the reply came from Ireland, and when it did — 'What stuff!' exclaimed O'Callaghan. He had cause for exasperation. Coppinger evaded the issue by accusing his former priest of slandering him, defended himself against the imputation that he had ever practised usury and, as a final bombshell, informed the Vatican that Father O'Callaghan was a notorious parasite. He had heard that Cobbett had published a new edition of the book on usury, and its author was no doubt enjoying rich royalties from it while living at the Vatican's expense.

In vain O'Callaghan protested that he knew nothing of Cobbett's edition and had received no royalties. The Vatican people were tired of him. His insistence on upholding the orthodox doctrine, after the Church had tacitly dropped it, was causing embarrassment in high places. They cut off his allowance and he had to leave Rome.

William Cobbett in London was delighted with the book left in his office. He had never heard of O'Callaghan and his stand against usury, but he agreed with everything he had written. At that time he was preparing for press the first monthly part of his *History of the Protestant Reformation*, showing how 'that old wife-killer, Henry VIII,' had impoverished the country by seizing common and Church lands under the pretence of suppressing Catholic superstitions and abuses. In fact, said Cobbett, the Reformation 'was engendered in lust, brought forth in hypocrisy and perfidy, and cherished and fed by plunder, devastation, and by rivers of innocent English and Irish blood'. Although not himself a Catholic, Cobbett denounced the Reformation as the source of all the evils he fought against: official usury, the National Debt, the funding system and the sapping of local and individual independence to the advantage of central banks and government. In O'Callaghan's book he found some useful quotations on traditional Church doctrines and the demoralizing effects of loans and money-lending on the Irish peasantry. He borrowed them for his own work, and made generous restitution by re-publishing *Usury* in 1825 at his own expense. Not knowing of its author's whereabouts, he advertised for him in his publications, promising to pay his royalties whenever he cared to claim them. Thus, when O'Callaghan appeared in London, penniless and in debt, having had to borrow from fellow coach-passengers to pay his fare from Rome, Cobbett greeted him with a handful of sovereigns and an invitation to dine with his family. There are many anecdotes to illustrate Cobbett's nobility of spirit, but as an example of timely, tactful aid given by one author to another, his treatment of O'Callaghan is uniquely attractive.

Reconciliation with the Bishop was now out of the question. Coppinger had taken great offence at the complaints about himself published in *Usury*, and he would not even consider O'Callaghan's request to be restored to his priestly duties until he had published a full retraction and apology. Since this required the suppression and denial of facts, O'Callaghan would not do so. The Bishop's new stipulation, he said, was merely an attempt to conceal the truth of the matter, that he had been sacked for teaching the words of Christ, clearly stated in St. Luke's Gospel (6.35): 'Lend, hoping for nothing again.' But the rights and wrongs of the affair counted for nothing. Coppinger had power over his former priest and he used it crushingly. True to his promise, he prevented O'Callaghan from obtaining a post in his or any other diocese, and his victim had no money to sustain his protest.

Once more Cobbett saved the day, inviting the rejected priest to become classics tutor to his sons. In 1828 he brought out another edition of *Usury*, containing its author's own account of the adventures and persecutions he had undergone for the sake of true religion. Cobbett's contribution as publisher was an extraordinarily violent attack on the Quakers, with whom he was quarrelling at the time. They were, he said, the very worst type of usurers, waxing 'sleek as moles' at other people's expense while never doing a stroke of work in their lives. He obtained from O'Callaghan a long list of Irish sacred places destroyed at the Reformation, and printed it at the end of his *Protestant Reformation* which appeared in two volumes the following year.

O'Callaghan never forgot the influence of Cobbett, remaining to the end of his days a keen polemical pamphleteer. Seeing no future in Europe, he emigrated to America and finally, in Boston, found a bishop who would employ him. He was sent out as a missionary to Vermont, where his talents were well exercised in religious arguments with the natives. He built a church at Burlington, and when enemies burnt it down he built it up again. After a long, active career, preaching and writing against Protestantism, seeking converts for his own faith and shepherding his rustic flocks far from the centres of usury, he died in 1861 at Holyoke, Massachussetts, aged eighty-one.

Mainly through Cobbett's publicity ('It ought to be read by every man, and especially every young man, in the kingdom', he declared in advertising it), O'Callaghan's book had a good sale and some influence, but it is evident that neither of the two men had much success in their stand against capitalism and usury. Cobbett lived in daily expectation that the system of loans and paper money would reach its limits and burst like a bubble, leaving people to look after themselves again by agriculture and local crafts. He looked forward to that day as the occasion when rural prosperity and popular culture would be renewed. On hearing that a bank in his home town had gone bankrupt, he gave a public dinner of celebration in the streets. But he underestimated the ingenuity of the new financiers and the ability of the new economics to adapt and expand, nationally and world-wide. Nor was he able, any more than modern historians are able, to put his finger on the source and origin of usury and suggest a means of controlling it. Its practice has apparently been known, dreaded and legislated against from the earliest times, though it has commonly been regarded as only fair that, for instance, a farmer who lends seed-corn to another, having provided the borrower at his own risk with the means to obtain a harvest, should be entitled to a share in the yield. Once this is allowed it is difficult to know where to draw the line.

The Mosaic law on the subject, found in Deuteronomy 23.20, is firm and precise: 'Unto a stranger thou mayest lend upon usury; but unto thy brother thou shalt not lend upon usury.' Jews are therefore forbidden to take interest from their own people, though they may from others, and as money-lenders they made themselves unpopular in Norman and Angevin England from which they were expelled in 1290. The whole affair was wrapped in hypocrisy, because the rulers of the time made use of the Jews as unofficial tax-gatherers and public scapegoats, regularly confiscating their wealth and goods while blaming them for all the ills of the kingdom.

As Cobbett perceived, the abolition of old customs and traditional institutions at the Reformation, and the growth of central, secular power which followed it, weakened the native inhibition against usury. By the time O'Callaghan came along to challenge it, the practice of taking interest on loans had become so rooted in society that to preach against it was little more than a waste of breath. He was one of those people who are in the right, and know it and can prove it, but have the bad luck to be born in an age when no one wants to hear about it.

A MOST CONSERVATIVE M.P.
AND THE
ROYAL BOYCOTT OF LINCOLN

At the British parliamentary election of 1826 the successful candidates at Lincoln included a forty-three-year-old retired army officer and Peninsular War veteran, Colonel Charles de Laet Waldo Sibthorp, standing as a Tory. He was a member of an ancient family, well known and influential locally, and the Lincoln seat was under its control. It had not therefore been necessary for Colonel Sibthorp to explain his views in speeches to the electorate. His politics were unknown, and when the time came to declare them, on the day of the poll, he was unable to do so, having been knocked unconscious by a brickbat hurled from the crowd.

Previous to his election, however, he had dropped a significant hint as to the way he proposed to represent Lincoln. He had been asked whether he would support the cause of parliamentary reform, and a record had been made of his impressive answer: 'On no account would I sanction any attempts to subvert that glorious fabric, our matchless Constitution, which has reached its present perfection by the experience of ages, by any new-fangled schemes which interested or deluded individuals might bring forward, and those who expect any advantages from such notions will find their visions go like a vapour and vanish into nothing.'

During his many years in the House of Commons, Colonel Sibthorp made his name as the most conservative Member of Parliament ever known, setting a standard of reaction, nationalism and xenophobia unrivalled in parliamentary history. He opposed every change and innovation, regarding even the mildest reform as a fundamental attack on his idol, the English Constitution of his youth. It was his misfortune to live through an age of radical reforms and social changes, but it brought him one compensation. As his indignation flourished, so did his powers of oratory. His emphatic speeches against everything new or foreign delighted the House of Commons and made him their popular favourite. The things he disapproved of were always 'Humbugs', and his repetitions of this and other familiar terms of abuse were greeted with roars of parliamentary laughter. His dress was as old-fashioned as his opinions, usually consisting of a bottle-green frock-coat and wide white trousers hoisted high above his top-boots in the Regency manner. His wispy beard, tall white hat and antique quizzing glasses on a cord distinguished him from all other Members. This naturally endeared him to caricaturists, and his frequent appearances in the political cartoons of *Punch* and other papers brought him national fame. The people of Lincoln grew proud of their eccentric M.P. When he lost his seat in 1833, due to the passing of the Reform Bill, the ladies of the city presented him with a costly diamond ring, and the following year he was returned to Parliament on a popular vote which was repeated at every election up to his death in 1855.

An idyllic childhood in the pre-industrial English countryside left Charles Sibthorp with a glowing memory of the old order of things and a constant determination to maintain and restore it. He was one of five brothers, the eldest of whom died in 1822, making him heir to the rich family estates. One of his younger brothers, Richard, also became notorious when, as a Church of England clergyman, he defected to Rome. Later he returned to the English Church, then again became a Catholic priest and changed his faith in all five or six times. Charles, of course, was a dyed-in-the-wool Protestant, detesting the Roman Church and vigorously opposing in Parliament every stage of the Catholic Emancipation Bill. It might therefore be supposed that Richard's endless flirtations with Catholicism would have led to family friction. But that was not so. Charles Sibthorp had a clear vision of his own duty, performed it without rancour towards others and, though he wept and prayed for him, remained on excellent terms with his saintly, tortured brother. Throughout his career he is said to have made only one lasting enemy, and that was Queen Victoria.

Colonel Sibthorp was obviously very loyal to the Monarchy, but in his eyes Queen Victoria had committed one terrible blunder: she had married a foreigner. He always referred to such people as 'hypocritical foreigners', implying that they were not merely unfortunate but in some way sinister through having been born outside Britain. Prince Albert, he allowed, had some admirable qualities, but his character was permanently impaired by the fact of his foreign birth. Thus, on the eve of the royal marriage, when the motion to allow the Consort an annuity of £50,000 a year was formally presented to Parliament, Sibthorp opposed it, suggesting that £30,000 was quite enough for a foreign prince. Sir Robert Peel, seeing a chance of defeating the government, unexpectedly supported him and his amendment was carried. The Queen was so furious that as long as Colonel Sibthorp was M.P. for Lincoln she refused to visit the city.

He did not do so well in a later brush with the Prince Consort, over the Great Exhibition of 1851, which he denounced as 'one of the greatest humbugs, one of the greatest frauds, one of the greatest absurdities ever known'. He prayed God to smash it down with hailstones or lightning. It was designed to bring waves of foreigners to England's shores, and these creatures always had the basest motives. 'Take care of your wives and daughters, take care of your property and your lives!' he warned the nation. The immoral aliens were coming to rape Englishwomen, burgle English houses, spy out the national defences and undercut English traders with their cheap, shoddy, foreign merchandise. Sibthorp noticed that in Hyde Park English trees were being cut down to make way for the Crystal Palace, that 'palace of tomfoolery', that 'unwholesome castle of glass' as he referred to it in Parliament. The sacrificed trees became his symbol of the national calamity which he foresaw issuing from the Great Exhibition. Its stages were: the corruption of morals by foreigners, the desecration of the Sabbath, political disunion, an increase of poverty and the collapse of trade leading to national bankruptcy. The Colonel himself never visited the Crystal Palace because it was against his principles to do so, but he heard tales of country folk being seduced into travelling to London, pawning their clothes for the fare and ending up naked, destitute and demoralized. The House of Commons listened to his rantings with tolerant good humour, even when he hinted that Prince Albert had an interest in importing his fellow-foreigners to Britain to subvert the national economy.

Bankruptcy of the nation was the disaster most commonly predicted by Colonel Sibthorp, which was odd at a time when expanding trade and empire was making Britain the most prosperous of countries. His first objection to all social or constitutional innovations was on the grounds of cost. The state, he believed, could not afford the Royal Commissions investigating possible reforms, nor could it afford to pay British diplomats abroad, who should give their services for nothing. For the same reason he opposed the building of the National Gallery, suggesting when it was nearly completed that it should be pulled down to avoid further expense. Yet he himself was a connoisseur of painting and cherished a fine collection of classical antiquities at his Lincolnshire mansion.

Behind all his campaigns was the notion that foreign conspirators and their agents in Britain were ceaselessly plotting the downfall of his country. One of these agents, he imagined, was Lord John Russell, the architect of Catholic emancipation and the Reform Bill, and he observed with suspicion everything that Russell did. Even when a mild reduction in the manpower of the Militia was proposed, Sibthorp divined treacherous motives. Picking on one detail of the Bill (the 'sweeping and, I will say, revolutionary measure to do away with all drum-majors'), he thundered to the House of Commons: 'Are the people of this country to be told in the nineteenth century that drum-majors are to be treated in this way? Is it to be borne, or can it be supposed that drum-majors will respect the institutions of their country if the laws afford drum-majors no protection? The noble lord began his democratic career by destroying what he was pleased to call the rotten boroughs; he then endeavoured to subvert the corporations – and then, looking round for further prey it suddenly struck him – "The Militia! – another great constitutional body – I'll have a touch of that!"'

In his very last speech to Parliament, in 1855, Sibthorp accused Russell of fiddling his expense account while on a mission to the Continent.

The coming of the railways provided Colonel Sibthorp with the subject which grew obsessive during his later years. Beginning with the announcement that he had no intention of ever riding in the 'steam humbug', he opposed all railway bills in principle and detail. The new 'degrading form of transport', he foresaw, would bring all sorts of disasters to its patrons, from moral ruin to wholesale slaughter. He kept an eye on the newspapers for reports of railway accidents, and accused the steam companies of playing down the gory details of crashes, underestimating the number of casualties they caused and even falsely denying that they happened. He informed the House that not one railway accident in ten was ever brought to public knowledge. One of his few successes was in preventing the Great Northern Railway from extending its line through Lincoln, to the distress of the town's more ambitious citizens.

Whenever Sibthorp spoke of railway proprietors it was to denounce them as 'public frauds and private robbers', but the day came when, for lack of alternative transport, he was forced to go back on his vow and travel in their humbugs. Yet he retained to the end of his life the firm conviction that railways were a mere nine-day wonder. In one of his later speeches he expressed himself 'of the decided opinion that these nefarious schemes would ere long appear before the public in their true light – that all the railway companies would be bankrupt and that the old and happy mode of travelling the turnpike roads, in chaises, carriages and stages, would be restored'. Christopher Sykes, who has written affectionately about Sibthorp, says that Dostoievski used to read English parliamentary reports, and took Colonel Sibthorp as his model for Lebedev, the character in *The Idiot* who proclaimed that the network of railways spreading across holy Russia was the baleful 'star called Wormwood' prophesied in the Book of Revelation.

Although generally considered about a hundred years behind his time, in one way Colonel Sibthorp was ahead of it. In exposing the machinations of alien Jews, Jesuits, bankers and industrialists, and discovering their secret agents among highly placed people in his own country, he anticipated the conspiracy view of history which began flourishing soon after his death. And at least one of the measures he proposed later came to pass: that foreign travel should be curtailed by limiting the amount of currency that could be taken abroad. It is possible also that his vision of an England freed from railways will one day be realized. One feels that if Colonel Sibthorp were alive today he would be active in the railway preservation movement.

THE FIRST LADY
OF CONSPIRATOLOGY

A memory from schooldays is of being warned by the history teacher against something called Conspiracy Theory. Certain deranged individuals, he told us, believed that the entire course of history had been determined by an hereditary group of hidden plotters, whose purpose was to destroy all the civilized institutions and values which blocked their path towards world-domination. The conspirators, said our teacher, were a figment of perverted imagination, and belief in their existence was both a symptom and a cause of insanity.

We were impressed by this news and took the warning to heart, though some of us could not repress the thought that, if there really was a world conspiracy, our eminent teacher was no doubt part of it. A form of conspiracy theory was already well established among us, thanks to government propaganda. It was during the Second World War and spy mania was raging. The public had been instructed to watch out for mysterious strangers, lights, signalling and other indications of enemy espionage. This call was most warmly responded to by schoolboys. A popular tale in magazines of the time was of brave boys unmasking a German agent, and a spy-catching craze swept the boarding schools of Britain. The authorities, not being readers of boys' comics, had no idea what was going on. Thus many odd incidents passed unexplained. At Wellesley preparatory school in Broadstairs it became obvious to the pupils that their Latin master was a German spy. He bore a peculiar resemblance to an obnoxious gauleiter depicted in *The Hotspur*, and a skin ailment had given his face the colour and texture of putty. It was therefore assumed that he was wearing a mask. Little Heathcote Williams, future poet and playwright, took on the task of exposing him. During Latin class he rose from his desk, ran up to the master and began scrabbling at his face. Even as he did so, the absurdity of the whole thing became suddenly apparent to him, but it was too late to turn back. The rest of the class urged him on with cries of 'Spy!' until the master lost his nerve and bolted for the door. The headmaster was unable to make sense of what had happened so no one was punished.

Not all conspiracy theorists have escaped so lightly. As our history teacher pointed out, the notion of sinister aliens in our midst, secretly plotting the downfall of society, is an illusion that can lead to madness and has been the cause throughout history of innumerable witch-hunts, pogroms, lynchings and mass murders. Hitler's persecution of the Jews, and his suppression of masonic and esoteric groups in Germany, has been traced (in Norman Cohn's *Warrant for Genocide*) to the influence of the most potent of conspiracy documents, the infamous *Protocols of the Learned Elders of Zion*, which purports to be the programme for achieving power over the whole world, drawn up by a council of Jewish masonic elders. In horrendous detail *The Protocols* spells out the method by which this is to be done, involving the systematic corruption of religion, education and politics, the destruction of all decent standards of conduct and the spreading of atheistic revolution to every country. Its anonymous compiler had a truly Manichean insight into the operations of an evil deity in this world, producing an effect of occult horror which has rarely been equalled in literature. People have been made ill by reading it; its English translator, Victor Marsden in 1920, was so distressed by its diabolical spirit that he could not work on it for more than an hour at a time, lost his health and died soon afterwards. Promoters of conspiracy theory are notoriously prone to spells of sickness and ill luck, followed in many cases by extreme paranoia. It is not surprising, therefore, that among them are to be found some of the most outrageous specimens of eccentric thinkers and maniacs.

Conspiracy theory was pioneered and popularized in Britain by a lady of genteel Victorian upbringing, Nesta Webster. The peak of her influence was during the 1920s and 1930s, between the Bolshevik revolution in Russia, which tended to confirm the idea of an international conspiracy, and the Nazi holocaust which demonstrated the dangers and extreme consequences of that type of obsession. She was a natural mystic with a fascination for the occult, but her parents and family were strict Protestants, and she inherited their distrust of cults and secret societies. The true purpose of these organizations, as she saw it, was to undermine religion and bring about the downfall of our civilization.

Her father was Mr Robert Bevan, a rich banker of Trent Park, Hertfordshire. Nesta, the youngest of his large family, was born in 1876 when her mother, Bevan's second wife, was almost fifty. In her first volume of autobiography, *Spacious Days*, Mrs Webster looked back on her early years as a golden age. On her father's beautiful estate she had the company of her brothers and sisters, the numerous friendly staff, pets and ponies. Every summer the family with servants would migrate to another of their houses, Fosbury Manor on the Wiltshire downs, and then to their London house overlooking Hyde Park. Life was simple and assured and, for a little girl, full of entertainment. But as Nesta grew older certain drawbacks became apparent. Her mother, the daughter of a bishop, joined the gloomy ranks of the strict Plymouth Brethren, withdrew from worldly company and took to the study of Biblical prophecies. Robert Bevan was also religious and the only company received at Trent, apart from members of the family and visiting preachers and missionaries, consisted of parties on church or hospital outings. The children were thus left with few opportunities for making friends, and matters became worse when their father fell ill and doctors persuaded him to move abroad, to Cannes, where Nesta was cut off from all congenial company. Frivolous games, novels, amusements and parties were forbidden by her mother, whose only friends were grim Protestant ascetics.

The Bevan family were all clever and learned, and Nesta took every opportunity of educating herself, reading whatever books were permitted her and learning French, German and Italian. The family's annual visits to Trent were her greatest pleasure, but when her father died these came to an end. The rest of the family grew up and left home, and Nesta and her mother wandered about Europe in search of unsociable hotels where Mrs Bevan could study her fanatical literature in peace.

It was not the custom in those days for young ladies to go to school, but Nesta saw it was the only way to escape her mother; and in response to her pesterings Mrs Bevan finally let her go back to England, to a school near Stroud in Gloucestershire, kept by an old lady of undoubted religious probity, Miss Winscombe. At this school, Brownshill Court, Nesta had her first experience of the mysteries and conspiracies which underlie the world of normal experience.

There was something odd about the school. Every night the girls heard a horse approaching and stopping outside it, and the house was full of whispers, creaks and the sound of stealthy footsteps. One of them saw a man crawling along the floor of her dormitory, who ran off when challenged. Most of the sounds came from the basement which the girls were forbidden to enter, but one night two of them opened the door leading to it and heard the sound of men's voices and hammering. Miss Winscombe evidently had some guilty secret, for when she heard the girls talking about the disturbances she swore them to secrecy on the Bible. Nesta suspected that something supernatural was afoot, and since she was terrified of ghosts she determined to leave the school as soon as possible. Later she decided that Miss Winscombe was sheltering a gang of false coiners. The mystery of Brownshill Court was never finally resolved. Many of the other girls were made nervous and persuaded their parents to let them leave at the end of term, and the school closed down.

At the age of eighteen Nesta was allowed to spend two years at Westfield College in Hampstead reading for a degree. Her lack of formal education made it hard work, but she enjoyed the intellectual freedom of college. Exposure to modern philosophy undermined all her religious convictions; there was a time of crisis when her faith and happiness seemed threatened, but she saved them by attending a Quaker meeting house, where preachers spoke as the spirit moved them and Nesta came to recognize that the ruling principle in this world is the God of love. The strength of this belief sustained her sanity throughout her forty years of investigating and exposing the machinations of Evil.

A legacy from her father made her independent at the age of twenty-one, and soon afterwards she began an adventurous series of travels. Wherever she went, in Egypt, India, Ceylon, Burma, Japan, Australia, the United States and Canada, she entered as far as possible into the lives of the natives, learnt their languages and wrote comments on their various societies and customs. Finally, in 1904, while visiting a remote part of India, she met a district police superintendent, Arthur Webster, a quiet, middle-aged bachelor whose main interest was gardening. They quickly became engaged and returned to England for their marriage. Her husband, she noted, answered almost exactly to the prophetic description of him given two years earlier by a London fortune-teller.

The Websters settled in Surrey where for ten years they enjoyed a peaceful country life, gardening, farming and raising a family. During that time Mrs Webster had a strange experience which determined her future career. She happened to read an essay about the Comtesse de Sabran and her lover, the Chevalier de Boufflers, at the time of the French Revolution. As she read, the feeling came over her that she had once known these people and taken part in the events described in their correspondence. Now she realized why certain parts of Paris had always seemed familiar, sometimes filling her with dread; it was because she herself, in a past life, had witnessed the procession of tumbrils bearing aristocrats to the guillotine. Nesta Webster had once lived as the Comtesse de Sabran. That seemed the most likely explanation for her extraordinary sense of identity with the life and times of the Comtesse. Others occurred to her, such as the possibility of an ancestral memory or telepathic thought-messages from someone living or dead, but she was more inclined to the theory of reincarnation. An acquaintance of hers was Miss Jourdain, one of the two ladies who had caused a sensation with their book, *An Adventure*, describing how, on a visit to Versailles, they had been transported back to the eighteenth century and the court of the Sun King, Louis XIV. Mrs Webster felt that the same sort of thing had happened to her, though less dramatically. Her book on the old French lovers, *The Chevalier de Boufflers*, was informed not just by literary research but, so she believed, by personal memory of their lives. She was delighted to hear that a Frenchman, whose grandfather had been guillotined, commented, 'No one could have written that book who had not lived at the Court of Marie-Antoinette.'

While studying the history of the French Revolution, Nesta Webster became more and more convinced that at every stage it had been engineered by malevolent conspirators and that the ordinary French people had neither instigated nor wanted it. The conspirators included the sinister Duke of Orleans, disaffected politicians, Prussian agents, atheists and Freemasons, but behind all of these she detected the guidance of a Hidden Hand. The Revolution was not created by any of the characters who played active parts in it, nor had any of its episodes occurred by chance. The entire course of events had been directed by an occult power, loosed on the world in 1776 by one Adam Weishaupt.

On May the first of that year, Weishaupt, a former Jesuit lawyer turned occultist and Freemason, founded the sect of the Illuminati in

Bavaria. His philosophy resembled those of Rousseau and the Romantics in glorifying the natural state of primeval humanity in contrast to the corrupt state of civilization. The idea of a golden age in the remote past and the belief that human nature manifested its best qualities in times before civilization were not, of course, invented by Weishaupt. They have been held by radicals and revivalists throughout history, and they have always been opposed by people of a conservative cast of mind such as Nesta Webster.

In Adam Weishaupt she perceived the evil genius of the modern age and the author of all its ills. Indeed, all that is known about the man does make him seem rather extreme. He was one of those people who are not content with adopting or formulating their own brand of social theory, but feel called upon to impose it on everyone else. Weishaupt became the sworn enemy of civilized order and pledged his followers to work secretly for its destruction. Their task was to corrupt society on all levels, infiltrating the institutions of education, culture, religion and politics and taking every opportunity to spread confusion and chaos. Established beliefs and authorities were everywhere to be discredited and revolutions were to be encouraged, leading to the collapse of all civilized standards and clearing the way for the Illuminati to take control of the world. These things were to be done in the name of the people, who would thus become the instruments of their own oppression.

The anti-social ambitions of the Illuminati were discovered by the Bavarian authorities a few years after the foundation of the sect, which was then officially suppressed. The legend of how they were exposed is that one of their couriers was riding from Germany to Paris when he and his horse were struck by lightning and reduced to cinders. His documents survived unharmed, and among them were found all the details of the Illuminatus conspiracy. Discredited in public, Weishaupt's followers went underground and continued operations through masonic and secret societies. In the opinion of Mrs Webster, they have been responsible for every subsequent revolution, from the French to the Bolshevik, for the spread of atheism, rationalism, communism and capitalism, and for all other plagues and problems of the modern world.

This theory has the obvious attraction of explaining at one stroke the entire development of recent history. Mrs Webster was a powerful writer, and her controversial statements were supported by numerous quotations from the works of earlier authorities. Most reputable historians are agreed that the Freemasons and members of secret societies played a significant part in the French Revolution. One can also find conspiracies behind almost everything that happens in life. The behind-the-scenes account, given in Nesta Webster's *The French Revolution*, was therefore somewhat plausible; the book was widely reviewed and had large sales. Yet its author was not content. Not all the reviews were favourable, and some critics dismissed her entire thesis out of hand. She detected a literary plot against her. It was to be expected that Continental writers would attack her work, since they were heavily under the influence of the Illuminati; but she had hoped that it would open the eyes of British and American readers, alerting them to the revolutionary forces that threatened them and establishing her own reputation as a true and timely prophet. Its failure to cause any great sensation made her suspect that the Illuminatus conspiracy had taken hold in Britain also, particularly in the academic world. Far from discouraging her, this realization caused her to become ever more strident in her denunciations of society's enemies.

The opportunity for some active field-work in her battle against alien conspirators came with the outbreak of the First World War. The Websters were living near Chanctonbury Ring in Sussex, a high, lonely spot ideally situated for spies signalling to the enemy. It was rumoured locally that something of the sort was happening, and the authorities called upon the police experience of Mr Webster, asking him to investigate. He and his wife entered into the spirit of the thing, and Webster sent in voluminous reports about 'mystery flashes seen at night, carrier pigeons intercepted and other happenings of a highly suspect nature'. In her autobiography Nesta described how together they 'traced out on an ordnance map the points at which these phenomena occurred and a curious line of communication could be traced out between Aldershot [army headquarters] and the sea'. This was taken seriously enough for two officers to be dispatched from London to make further inquiries. One of them was the novelist and espionage expert Mr William Le Queux. He arrived with the very latest aid to spy-catching, a wireless. The apparatus had only just been invented, and was so cumbersome that it had to be carried on a large lorry, attended by a staff of naval ratings. They erected its mast in a field and the whole party sat around it, listening for radio messages from enemy agents. Late at night they contacted a German, broadcasting in code, and arranged to meet him near the house, intending to shoot him down when he turned up; but he never appeared. Next night they all drove to a high spot at Hindhead gibbet and sent flashlight signals far and wide, hoping that an agent would be tricked into responding, but again with no luck. Nesta remained convinced that the whole country was riddled with spies and traitors, some of whom had achieved high positions within the government. It surprised her that the war was eventually won.

The chief components in the universal conspiracy were identified in Mrs Webster's *Secret Societies and Subversive Movements* as 'Grand Orient Masonry, Theosophy, Pan-Germanism, International Finance and Social Revolution', but behind all these she detected a greater influence, 'an Occult Power at work in the world'. In the characteristic manner of conspiracy-hunters she proclaimed herself the champion of Christian civilization in opposition to the powers of darkness. The Adversary, she now realized, had been active from the earliest times, long before the foundation of the Illuminati, perverting the teachings of initiates and esoteric groups in order to corrupt and destroy all true religious systems, whether Christian, Jewish, Muslim or Buddhist.

Readers were thrilled by the mystical nature of her crusade and its air of high moral righteousness, which distracted attention from the weak points and improbabilities in the details of her thesis. In the period of turmoil and revolution following the war, conspiracy theory was rife, and the notion of a central anarchistic command, secretly directing anti-social operations throughout the world, flourished in high places. The British Foreign Office in 1919 published a report stating that Bolshevism was the product of a conspiracy centred on Germany and 'carried out by international Jews' for their own economic advantage. The following year *The Protocols* appeared in its first English edition under the title *The Jewish Peril*, and Winston Churchill wrote a sensational article for a Sunday newspaper, citing Nesta Webster's *French Revolution* as evidence for his belief in an international Jewish-Bolshevik conspiracy. Her writings acquired an influential following. In 1920 she began a series of lectures to officers of the Artillery, the Brigade of Guards and the Secret Service, informing them about the history and intentions of the forces behind World Revolution. It has been claimed, though never proved, that she was working hand-in-glove with the British Secret Service at the time, and that they were the sponsors of her next book, *World Revolution: The Plot Against*

Civilization. In it she declared that Britain was the last bastion in the battle to defend humanity against Illuminism and the powers of evil.

The conspiracy books of Nesta Webster are particularly fascinating to readers who enjoy horror stories and occult mysteries, offering an exciting glimpse at the esoteric forces which operate below the surface of history. Unfortunately for her later reputation, many of her ideas were similar to those of politicians in Europe who took them seriously and were in a position to act upon them. Hitler believed, or affected to believe, that *The Protocols of the Learned Elders of Zion* was a genuine document, outlining a Jewish plot for world domination. This was no part of Mrs Webster's thesis; she considered it to be a restatement of Weishaupt's Illuminatus manifesto, of German rather than Jewish composition. Her cast of conspirators did include many of Jewish origin, such as international financiers and 'apostate Jews who have thrown themselves into the revolutionary movement', but she insisted that these types represented as great a threat to Jewish culture as to that of all other peoples. Thus she was no blind anti-Semite, as her detractors, as well as many of her followers, have represented her. Nevertheless, she became an early member of the British Fascists and wrote numerous articles for the right-wing journal, *The Patriot*, published by her patron the Duke of Northumberland. She admired Mussolini more than Hitler, but her hatred of Communism led her to support the National Socialist regime, and in 1938 she even denied that Jews in Germany were being unfairly persecuted, dismissing all evidence to the contrary as a product of conspiratorial propaganda.

German imperialism (Pan-Germanism) was one of her chief bugbears. It was responsible, she believed, for sending Lenin to Russia as 'the agent of the great German-Jewish conspiracy that hopes to rule the world'. Thus Bolshevism was a creation of Pan-Germanism, and in the tortuous mind of Nesta Webster the two movements were somehow allied. In Hitler she discerned a staunch opponent of Bolshevism and Pan-Germanism alike. But in this, as in many other of her opinions, she was proved wrong, her faith being shattered in 1939 when Hitler signed his pact with Stalin.

As she grew older Mrs Webster became more and more pessimistic about the chances of saving humanity from the universal government of the Illuminati. Having trained herself to detect conspiracies in history, she began to find them all around her in daily life. She took to answering her doorbell with pistol in hand. Yet to the year of her death, in 1960, she kept up fierce literary battles with her critics and enemies, real and imagined. The last book she wrote was the second part of her autobiography, *Crowded Hours*, covering the period of her most notable activities. No publisher could be found for it during her lifetime, but in 1972 it was accepted by the right-wing Britons Publishing Company in Devon. But *Crowded Hours* has never been published, and never will be. As if in direct confirmation of its author's belief in conspiracy, the manuscript, the only copy, was mysteriously abstracted from the publisher's office by an American visitor whose identity has never been disclosed. He could have been an agent of the Illuminati, belatedly suppressing the last of Mrs Webster's revelations; or perhaps the reason for the theft was to protect the reputations of former Nazi sympathizers named in her reminiscences.

The United States is the country where Mrs Webster's theories have found their best market. This is not surprising as the Americans have a long tradition of being wise to the machinations of the Illuminati and their like. In 1790 there was a violent outbreak of hysteria in New England when word went round that Adam Weishaupt's followers occupied high positions in government and were about to take over the Republic. A similar mania in the 1850s, this time directed mostly against Catholics, gave rise to the briefly influential Know Nothing Party, so called because the policy of its members if questioned was to say that they knew nothing about anything. One thing, however, they did claim to know: that the Pope was trying to take over America by flooding it with Irish and Italian immigrants. The Know Nothings set up a counter-conspiracy, forming secret societies and allying themselves with politicians who were for denying immigrant Americans equal rights with the established population. Some years later Ignatius Donnelly, the many-talented hero of a later chapter, founded his Populist Party on the belief that an international conspiracy of bankers, with ambitions for world rule, were deliberately ruining farmers in the Midwest by manipulating agricultural prices from their headquarters in London.

Nesta Webster's books thus had a familiar ring to many American readers, and their success has carried on into the present. Those of them in print today are published by a Christian fundamentalist press and distributed through the powerful John Birch Society. The Birchers have inherited the main features of her awesome world-view, and have added some thoughts of their own, one of them being that the corruption of American youth is due to the baleful influence of those sinister aliens, the Beatles.

The Plot against Civilization and the other titles in the Webster canon seem tame and conventional by the standards of conspiracy literature today. That much-honoured American institution, freedom of the press, allows anyone's idea of who is really behind the current fiasco to be displayed in print, and the results can be literally incredible. The conspiracy market is serviced by a host of small magazines, each with its own angle on the subject and its own peculiar suspicions. Some of their writers are earnest and informed, while others are so wild and erratic that one's first inclination is to dismiss them as out-and-out cranks. These days, however, conspiratology is big business, and the most sensational publications are those which achieve the best circulation. *Spotlight,* the magazine connected with the highly conservative – to use a mild term – Liberty Lobby, sells 350,000 copies weekly by its headlined revelations of 'Soviet Spy in White House', that 'The Diary of Anne Frank is a Fraud' and that 'Rockefeller is Named Dope Overlord'.

The Rockefellers are the particular enemies of *Spotlight,* which charges them weekly with a fresh series of bizarre misdemeanours. They are said for instance to be promoters of Communism and to be behind the suppression of laetrile, an alleged cancer cure which appeals for some odd reason to people with extreme right-wing views. In 1972 David Rockefeller of Chase Manhattan Bank set up the Trilateral Commission, thereby setting up a target which *Spotlight* and other conspiracy writers have found irresistible. The Commission's declared aim is to bring together the 'best brains in the world', meaning bankers, industrialists, professors and politicians from America, Japan and Europe, with the idea that they should privately form a 'conceptual framework of foreign and domestic foreign policies' – whatever that means. British members have included Reginald Maudling, Edward Heath, Denis Healey and Lord Harlech, whose names have thus become familiar to readers of conspiracy journalism, but it is the leading American Trilateralists who are most commonly exposed in *Spotlight.* In 1976 the magazine was found guilty of unfair play, and its publishers were penalized by the Federal Election Commission for boldly alleging 'Jimmy Carter's Cocaine Connection'. Another former member, Vice President George Bush, had to contend during his 1980 election campaign with the rooted conviction among Midwest farmers that the Trilateral Commission was yet another bankers' conspiracy to put them out of business.

Conspiracy theory has the effect of completing a circle and bringing the left and right extremes of political opinion into conjunction. Parallel publications to those of the Liberty Lobby come from a purportedly Marxist organization called the US Labor Party (not at all associated with the correspondingly named party in Britain). Not that the US Laborites would value such association, for in their view the British are the main villains of the piece. London bankers and aristocrats, led by the Royal Family whom they always refer to as The Guelphs, are, they say, the secret rulers of the world. In league with anglophile liberals of eastern America, the Guelphs run the heroin racket and promote religious cults to weaken the spirit of America's youth. Among their agents are the Ku Klux Klan and, of course, the insidious Beatles.

The US Labor Party is strongly in favour of nuclear energy and technological progress, declaring that the whole environmentalist movement is promoted by British Intelligence with the object of ruining American industry and plunging the world into a dark age of ignorance and slavery under the British feudal system.

Details of the shadowy figures in the conspiracy publishing business are given in *The Conspiracy Peddlers,* the author of which, Robert Eringer, specializes in anthropological research among groups of conspiracy-hunters and other eccentric theorists. One of the perils he has encountered in his profession is familiar to infiltrators and secret agents: that through affecting zeal for whatever cause is being promoted one is liable to rapid promotion and to end up running the organization one set out merely to investigate. G. K. Chesterton's *The Man who was Thursday* gives an extreme example of that situation.

The game of hunting out subversives was once played exclusively by professional teams from each country's Secret Service. Nesta Webster broke their monopoly by taking a hand in it herself. Now it is open to all comers, bringing forth a confusion of theories and suspicions which may well reflect the value of the game on any level. The world is full of crazy schemers, official and amateur. Every group of conspiracy-theorists believes that its rivals have been set up or infiltrated by the CIA, KGB, Mafia, Rockefellers or whatever; and Heaven knows! they may sometimes be right. Perhaps it is no bad thing that the freedom of the printing press allows anyone's fears and foibles to be aired openly alongside everyone else's. The resulting display of competing obsessions enriches the human comedy and brings a welcome note of levity into the dire subject of conspiracies – brilliantly deployed in Robert Anton Wilson's satirical *Illuminatus* trilogy.

Our history master at school was certainly right in warning us against the blandishments of conspiracy-theorists. Yet a small dose of their doctrines, as administered here, is the best prophylactic against infection by them. Another point in favour of giving some consideration to the 'conspiracy' school of history, made by Gary Allen in *None Dare Call it Conspiracy* (though he dared and got away with it), is that it serves as a useful corrective to the prevailing 'accidental' school. If accused of paranoid thinking, one can find consolation in a remark of Socrates, that the gods give us paranoia so that we may occasionally glimpse something of the truth.

THE MAN WHO GOT
LETTERS FROM STATUES

In 1847 the little Fox sisters of New York State heard strange rapping noises in their family house. One of the girls rapped back in a code of her own devising, and the phantom rapper responded in kind. Their story sparked off the great spiritualist craze, which swept America and soon spilt over into Europe. The clergy spoke out against it, but to no avail. Throughout the social order, from housemaids to aristocrats, people were eager to join in the new sport of necromancy. Wherever a few were gathered together, tables were made to spin and dance and rap out oracles. Distinguished scientists joined in, dignifying the proceedings with grave theories of etheric phantasms and invisible magnetic fluids, and in response to the demand there sprung up a host of mediums for hire. Opponents of spiritualism also flourished, attacking from two quarters: the Church issued professional warnings about the dangers of laymen meddling with spirits, while the priests of scientific materialism denounced the whole thing as hoax and fraud.

The first spiritualist circle in Paris, formed in 1850, met at the house of Baron Ludwig de Güldenstubbé. He was a lover of ancient mysteries and the occult, and some years earlier had investigated a happening on the Estonian island of Saare Maa where a poltergeist had run amok in a family vault and hurled coffins about.

Spirit-rapping and table-turning were all very well in their way, but de Güldenstubbé was not always content with mediums and craved a more direct form of communication with the unseen world. In the Old Testament are recorded two instances of supernatural writing: the engraved tablets of law which Moses brought down from Mount Sinai and the digital apparition on the wall of King Belshazzar's dining room. These reports, together with the well-attested habit of the statue of

Memnon in Egypt of emitting a mysterious musical cry at sunrise, persuaded de Güldenstubbé that it was not unreasonable to try for similar effects in the modern age.

His first experiment, in 1856, involved locking a pad of blank paper and a pencil into a box and awaiting results. After several disappointments he one day opened the box and found some marks on the paper. That same day other messages appeared, one of them in the Baron's native language, Estonian. He found that even if he left the box open the writing continued, and he could watch it happening, the letters forming spontaneously on the paper without the help of the pencil. The scripts were short and of no apparent significance, consisting of a few scrawled words or a rough drawing. But it was the medium rather than the message which fascinated the experimenter. The new phenomenon of direct spirit-writing would establish the claims of spiritualism beyond further question, or, as he put it: 'The hour is about to come when materialism and the sceptical rationalism of our so-called modern savants will be utterly routed.'

One drawback to the experiment so far was that there was no way of identifying the authors of the spirit messages. De Güldenstubbé then had the bright idea of communicating with specific characters of the past through the medium of their statues. With various reputable friends, led by the Comte d'Ourches, he visited the Hall of Antiquities at the Louvre, the Basilica of Saint-Denis and churches and cemeteries throughout Paris, leaving sheets of writing paper and visiting-cards by the statues and tombs of the famous dead. The results were astounding. When he returned to the monuments he found that most of his chosen correspondents had accepted his invitation and come through with some kind of message. Always they wrote in their native languages. Thus the paper from the statue of Mary Stuart was scrawled on in English; Plato, Socrates and St Paul managed a few Greek words, and Cicero, Virgil and Julius Caesar wrote Latin. Mostly they confined themselves to hinting at their own identities, adding little else of interest.

During his period of inspiration de Güldenstubbé communicated with most of the notable statues of Paris, as well as of Versailles and Fontainebleau. By the end of it he had accumulated over five hundred messages in twenty different languages. Many of them were published in facsimile in his book, *Positive and Experimental Pneumatology: The Reality of Spirits and the Marvellous Phenomenon of their Direct Handwriting*, where he defended spiritualism by showing how prevalent and respectable it had been throughout the world's history.

The public response to this book was of stunned amazement. It was hardly possible to accuse the Baron and his lordly friends of cheating, though some suggested that they had been duped by a charlatan medium. But the prospect of statues being subjected to a regular course of questioning on all details of past and future history was almost too awesome to contemplate. Somehow the matter was never followed up. It might be added to the list of odd experiments, described in this book, which deserve a revival. A useful start could be made at the statues of Bacon and Shakespeare.

Our last sighting of Baron de Güldenstubbé is in London, where he was living in 1867. He had reverted to séances, and to his house came the famous medium, Miss Nichol, later Mrs Samuel Guppy. She became best known for a performance in 1871, the so-called Transit of Venus, when she levitated from her rooms in Highgate and was teleported to a house three miles away where a spiritualist group was in session. Her sudden descent into the midst of the gathering made a strong impression, for she weighed 17 stone (240 pounds). At the Baron's house she did a few primitive levitations and delighted his family with some charming manifestations. In one of her dimly-lit séances Mademoiselle de Güldenstubbé found herself inexplicably crowned with a wreath of flowers and ferns, and Miss Nichol then proceeded to conjure up a variety of delicious things, such as grapes and other fruits, live eels, lobsters and shellfish. De Güldenstubbé may have found these products of spiritualism ultimately more satisfying than scrappy notes from old statues.

TWO UNUSUAL LANDOWNERS

Lord Rokeby's rural economy

Matthew Robinson-Morris, later to become Lord Rokeby, was born in 1713, read law at Cambridge, travelled in fashionable company on the Continent and then became M.P. for Canterbury.

He was a man of high principles and radically democratic views. The House of Commons, he believed, should be an assembly of independent delegates, voting by conscience and faithfully representing the interests of their constituents and country. He abhorred corruption and party politics, declaring that any Member who pledged himself to any particular group or leader was a traitor.

Anticipating the modern ideal of a conscientious M.P., Robinson-Morris became personally acquainted with most of the electors of Canterbury, visiting them in their shops, factories, markets and clubs. He was the rarest type of Englishman, able to converse on natural, friendly terms with people of all sorts, from royalty to working folk. In the House of Commons, however, he regarded himself as a failure. The system was so rotten and the ministers so wily that it needed a more capable man than himself to reform and correct them. For that reason, he told the people of Canterbury, he could no longer represent them, and despite their eagerness that he continue he retired into private life.

He had inherited from his mother a fine estate at Monks Horton near Hythe in Kent, and there he began the system of management which made him notorious. The land was fertile and well farmed, but Robinson-Morris put a stop to all cultivation, allowed no tree or hedge to be chopped or trimmed within his boundaries and left the fields to wilderness. Throughout his acres, even in the ornamental and walled gardens, cattle, sheep and horses were free to roam at large.

The result was much admired by lovers of the picturesque, but the neighbours complained, particularly since the roads through the estate were also untended and became overgrown. The family coach was left to rot in the decaying coach-house as its owner did most of his travelling on foot. It was said of him that he could outwalk a horse.

One day he received a visit from his kinsman, to whom he was heir, Lord Rokeby, Archbishop of Armagh and Primate of Ireland. It was a Saturday and Robinson-Morris suddenly realized that next day the Archbishop would certainly want to go to church. The difficulty was that the church, churchyard and road leading to them were in ruins. He himself never went near the place, believing that God was to be found in nature and that clergymen were not only useless but actual impediments to religion. But he also believed that everyone should be free to do as they pleased, and if the Archbishop wanted to go to church, so he should. He therefore summoned from Hythe and the neighbouring villages all available carpenters, paviours, furnishers, gardeners and labourers, who rose to the occasion by putting the church and its surroundings in worthy shape for the Archbishop's attendance. Next day Robinson-Morris saw his kinsman into his pew. That was the last time he ever entered a church.

By adopting systematically the style of classical simplicity, Lord Rokeby (as he became in 1794) made himself an object of popular curiosity. His pecularities were legendary. He would eat nothing but local produce, substituting honey for sugar and experimenting with burnt peas and beans in place of coffee. Wheat he dismissed as an alien and he would touch nothing fermented. Yet these idiosyncrasies were purely expressions of his own taste and he never tried to impose them on others. Guests at his house could order whatever they wanted to eat and drink, but on one condition, that they would not object to the host eating whatever and whenever he wanted. If people tried to tease him by giving him, say, a piece of pie, and then telling him it had sugar in it, he would merely smile and say, 'Where is the man that lives as he preaches?'

Water was Lord Rokeby's favourite element. He drank nothing else, apart from his favourite beef-tea, and was accustomed throughout his life to bathe several times a day. As in many other things, he was ahead of his time in constructing a solar-heated bath house, quaintly thatched. In it he spent much of the latter part of his life, emerging only to wander about a nearby grove, meditating on philosophy. Sometimes he would walk to the beach near Hythe, where he kept a hut for the purpose of sea-bathing. On these outings he was followed by a carriage, not for his own use but for that of the attendant servants, in case they were tired or it came on to rain.

With the idea of extending the benefits of water to others he ordered a large number of fountains with stone basins to be erected alongside the local public roads. If in the course of his rambles he saw anyone drinking from them he would hand out rewards from a supply of half-crowns which he kept in his pocket for that purpose.

Despite his simple, solitary way of life on his overgrown estate, Lord Rokeby could never be said to have vegetated. He was an active and accomplished scholar, a great reader and much respected for his clear intellect and grasp of principles. Also admired were the political pamphlets he occasionally published, criticizing government policy in North America and the conduct of the war there or calling for the dismissal of Pitt. In all his opinions he was remarkably firm, particularly in one which became almost an obsession with him, that the Bank of England would very shortly fail. This conviction grew stronger as he grew older and he would insist upon it in almost every conversation. It led to a bet with a local banker, the terms being that if the Bank had not broken by the time of Rokeby's death his executors would pay the banker £10. If the Bank did break £10 was to be paid to Rokeby. On one occasion, when the Bank of England was forced temporarily to suspend payment, Lord Rokeby called at the banker's house in Maidstone and demanded payment. The other man, however, disputed the terms of the wager and the matter was left unsettled.

In an age when fashion was against whiskers, Lord Rokeby sported a forked beard, growing its natural length down to his waist. In association with his tall, awkward figure this made him a unique spectacle. He was said to be the only bearded peer, and possibly the only bearded gentleman, in Britain or Ireland. During one of his travels he was besieged at an inn by rustics who thought he was a Turk. Rumours at the time depicted him as a sort of wild man, even a cannibal, and it was prophesied that his savage way of life would lead to the ruin of himself and his estates. This was far from the case. To everyone's amazement his estates prospered under the system of natural management. The cattle of the wild woods and pastures did well and grew fat, the tenants, whose rents were never raised, were thus able to pay them regularly and in full, and Lord Rokeby accumulated many guineas which, since he did not trust banks nor approve of usury, he kept mostly at home. Yet he would occasionally deposit money with private bankers, even in France where he lost some of it during the Revolution. From his income he was able to buy more land to add to the wilderness of his estate, and the nephew who succeeded him came into a good fortune.

At the age of eighty-seven, when death was near, Lord Rokeby received a visit from this nephew, who left a record of his uncle's attitude to the medical profession. When his last moments came, said the old man, the nephew was on no account to call a doctor. If he did so, and if by some accident the doctor failed to kill him, Lord Rokeby promised to use his last strength in cutting the nephew out of his will.

Lord Rokeby's ideas would have accorded well with those of a patrician old Roman, and many of them – on diet, hygiene, exercise, egalitarianism, solar heating and the conversion of his land to a nature reserve – would seem fairly unremarkable in modern times. But the tide of his own eighteenth century was against him. The growth of centralized state and economic institutions was inimical to the style of independence he cultivated, and his contemporary reputation was merely that of a noble oddity.

Lord Rokeby.

An extremely kind landlord

If Henry Lee Warner of Walsingham Abbey had a fault, it was excessive kindness. Everyone said he was too kind, even the tenants and locals of his Norfolk estate who took advantage of it.

At the end of the eighteenth century a literary traveller, the gossipy Mr Samuel J. Pratt, passed through Walsingham and was astonished at what he saw and heard. The estate had apparently been laid waste. Once it had been famous for its fine timber, but now there was hardly a tree standing. The reason was that whenever villagers wanted firewood or building material they came and chopped them down. The squire could not bear to reprove them, nor would he allow his servants and agents to do so.

The people not only stole his timber, they took whatever else they needed. If anyone wanted a horse for ploughing or a journey, they went up to the Abbey stables for one and borrowed a saddle and harness to go with it, returning them whenever they pleased. Mr Lee Warner said nothing. He seemed genuinely unconcerned about the loss of his property. Only once did he show distress, when he saw his favourite landmark, a venerable chestnut tree, being cut down. He sent word to the choppers asking if they would mind sparing it. They said they would do so only if the squire himself told them to. But Lee Warner could never bring himself to deny anything to anybody, so the tree was felled.

The children used to steal the swill from the troughs beneath the snouts of his pigs, so Lee Warner gave up pig-keeping for fear that the animals might starve. But he would not kill or sell the survivors; they were freed to join wandering bands of ducks and chickens that roamed at large through his gardens and orchards. These creatures never slept or roosted until late at night, when their owner rose to give them their breakfasts before having his own. He would then walk in the dark about his estate. If he caught people stealing from him, he would greet them pleasantly and tell them to take care of themselves.

One of his tenant farmers, who was lazy, drunken and never paid rent, came and told him that even with a free farm he could not make a living for lack of capital, and that he would have to surrender his tenancy. Lee Warner begged him not to disturb himself, lent him whatever he needed and even had his own men work the land on behalf of the tenant, who enjoyed the proceeds of their labour in the local inn.

Mr Pratt was so struck by this state of affairs that he took lodgings in Walsingham and went about the village collecting detailed instances of its proprietor's unbridled benevolence. A local favourite was the story of his kindness to a fly. It had been caught by a spider in the squire's dining room, and he kept guests waiting while he carefully released it, taking care not to harm the web, and laid it on his handkerchief until it recovered. In one of the cottages Mr Pratt met a family who spoke indignantly about the wanton cutting-down of trees, how Mr Lee Warner was too long-suffering and should put a stop to it and so on. These righteous folk, he later heard, were actually the worst offenders.

The opportunity of meeting this rare character was too good to miss, so Mr Pratt sent his card up to the Abbey and at eleven o'clock that evening received an invitation to call on the squire – at midnight. He found an elderly man, dressed in the formal clothes of an earlier age, who invited him to have supper while he himself breakfasted. They talked on all manner of subjects, the host was charming and intelligent, and they dined together at dawn. Pleased with each other's company, they spent several nights together in the same way. The visitor, of course, was eager to question Lee Warner about his curiously tolerant system of estate management, but whenever he tried to raise the subject his host avoided it. There are no other accounts of his life, so no one knows when and why he began living entirely by night. Perhaps he wanted to see as little as possible of how he was being treated by his neighbours.

His death at the age of eighty-two was noticed in the *Gentleman's Magazine* of July 1804. The writer said that Mr Lee Warner's mind 'was tinctured by peculiarities which separated him from a comparison with almost any other human being'. He gave instances of his exceptional kindness and observed that, despite all it had cost him, Lee Warner had died extremely rich. His heir, a nephew, discontinued the permissive system, and the country round Walsingham is once again noted for its picturesque woodlands.

THE CONSOLATION
OF A JILTED LATVIAN

Frustrated love has been the incentive for many great works. One example is the Industrial Revolution, which was made possible by the development of the canal system in the eighteenth century. Canal building in England was pioneered by Francis Egerton, third Duke of Bridgewater. At the age of twenty-one he proposed marriage to the beautiful Duchess of Hamilton, but the engagement broke up and the young Duke retired from social life, diverting his energies to the management of his estates. These contained large deposits of coal, but the mines were far from any port and transport by horse and cart was difficult and expensive. By digging canals from the mines to Manchester and other cities, Bridgewater made available both the fuel and the lines of communication on which the Industrial Revolution was founded. The compensation for his disappointment was an interesting, active life, by the end of which he had become enormously rich. Had he been a more successful lover he might have let well alone, and there would have been no necessity for the modern ecology movement.

Just as impressive in its way, and without the lamentable side-effects of Bridgewater's effort, was the feat of compensatory building carried out some years ago by Edward Leedskalnin in Florida. Even in America, the land of the weirdest modern architectural follies, it is an outstanding oddity. In the early 1920s Leedskalnin emigrated to America from his native Latvia, seeking to forget his broken romance with a sixteen-year-old girl who left him on the eve of their marriage. He spent some time in California and Texas, taking odd jobs and looking for somewhere to live as far away from other people as possible, and finally settled near the southern tip of Florida. The local rock there is a very hard form of coral, but Leedskalnin managed to work it with primitive tools, mostly made from parts of an old Ford car. First he built himself a coral and timber house, and then started the amazing project which occupied the remaining thirty or so years of his life.

It is hard to describe exactly what he built. It was a kind of allegorical temple or an expression of his peculiar mentality. Working alone and in secret, using the simple devices which he made from timber and scrap metal, he quarried blocks of coral weighing up to thirty tons, rather more than the average weight of the pillars in the sarsen circle at Stonehenge. The site of his works was enclosed by a massive stone wall so that he could proceed unobserved. Over the years he carved out a series of bizarre objects, both whimsical and scientific. Among the latter were huge stone instruments for observing the heavens: shadow-throwers, holed stones for sighting the Pole Star, monuments to various planets and a 25-foot tall obelisk.

Other works included a large stone slab, carved in the shape of a map of Florida, with twelve stone rocking-chairs around it. Leedskalnin's idea was to invite the Governor of the State and his council to hold a meeting there. In designing his furniture he never forgot the lost bride in Latvia. Bedroom fittings were all made from coral; two carved stone beds stood side by side, and there was a cradle and small beds for children. All was made ready in case the girl should decide to join him after all, or for her possible replacement. The stone furniture was never put to use, but in later life the sculptor would invite parties of children to his domain and delight them with his marvels, one of which was a Grotto of the Three Bears equipped with all the items mentioned in the fairy story and, in the centre, a great coral porridge bowl.

The main entrance was through a lintelled gateway in the wall, blocked by a nine-ton coral slab which was so delicately poised on its centre of gravity that it opened like a swing door at the touch of a finger. Engineers are still puzzled as to how Leedskalnin found the exact point of balance on which this great stone pivots. It is one of the site's many mysteries. Just how Leedskalnin worked the coral is another. His rock furniture bears no chisel marks and looks almost as if it were shaped by nature. There is also the question of how he moved and manoeuvred the gigantic stone blocks he used for building. The rectangular, two-storey tower in which he lived and worked is made of squared rocks weighing up to nine tons, yet the man himself was only four feet eight inches tall and of slight build. When asked to explain his methods he would hint at having rediscovered the secrets of stone-working and leverage which were known to the Incas and the Pyramid-builders of ancient Egypt.

In the course of time his desire for solitude waned and he was ready to exhibit his works to visitors. Finding his original site too inaccessible, he hired a truck with a driver and moved his home and rocks to a more public spot near the main highway about twenty-five miles south of Miami. How he loaded, unloaded and reassembled his sculptures is again a mystery. He did it, like everything else, single-handed and unobserved. Rock Gate, later renamed Coral Castle, was completed in its new setting, where its eccentric marvels are now on view to tourists.

Clues to Leedskalnin's working methods may be found, by those qualified by knowledge of physics to understand them, in some of the odd papers and booklets he published. While labouring at his constructions he was also studying the nature of electricity and magnetism. The earth appeared to him to be a giant magnet, producing positively and negatively charged particles through its north and south poles respectively. These particles gave cohesion to matter and produced through their interactions all life and motion. His experiments were simple affairs, conducted mostly with car batteries and his stone instruments of astronomy, but they confirmed for him his view of the world and all its phenomena as effects of polar magnetism. He believed that scientists were fundamentally wrong in their explanations of electricity, animal and plant growth and the movements of the planets, the cause of which was the same cosmic force, the flow of magnetic particles. To these particles he attributed sight, taste and the other animal senses and even the functioning of the brain, believing human thought to be an automatic response to universal magnetism. His was a mechanistic world-view, rather like that held by Lucretius and the old Greek atomists. As a practical demonstration of his theory he constructed a 'perpetual motion holder', a dynamic model of the earth as a self-regulating magnetic organism. Its workings were revealed in a pamphlet which he sold for one dollar together with a folder of other publications on the magnetic nature of the universe. They were written in homely style and a personal form of English. An example is his summary on magnetic particles, which he called magnets:

'Magnets in general are indestructible. For instance you can burn wood or flesh. You can destroy the body, but you cannot destroy the magnets that held together the body. They go somewhere else. Iron has more magnets than wood, and every different substance has a different number of magnets that hold the substance together. If I make a battery with copper for positive terminal and beef for negative terminal I get more magnets out of it than when I used copper for positive terminal and sweet potato for negative terminal. From this you can see that no two things are alike.'

Those who can understand what he was talking about might be able to relate Leedskalnin's experiments with natural energies to his success in manipulating giant stone blocks. There are suggestions in his writings that the two were connected, but he was never explicit, and if he really did discover the esoteric arts of the ancient pyramid-builders the secret was lost again at his death.

Finally Leedskalnin published his simple book of philosophy and advice to the world, entitled *A Book in Every Home*. Much of it is extremely practical and down-to-earth. Few readers can fail to benefit from the maxims set out in the chapter on domestic conduct. The last of these reads:

'Everyone should be trained not to go out anywhere before someone else has examined them to see if everything is all right. It would save many people from unexpected embarrassment.'

The main part of the book is a discourse on the principles to be followed in rearing young girls. Some of the advice is good common sense. 'Don't raise the girls too big by over feeding them and [or?] too curved by neglect', the writer warns. Other items are more controversial. He stood firm against the American cult of the wide grin. Children should be taught not to smile too much, because it distorts the mouth and leaves ugly wrinkles. 'I have seen moving picture stars, public singers and others with their mouths open so wide that you would think the person lacks refinement, but if they knew how bad it looks they would train it out.'

The book's first chapter, 'Ed's Sweet Sixteen', is about the Latvian maiden who turned him down and the ideal qualities to be looked for in a sixteen-year-old girl. Above all she should be pure, chaste and faithful. To preserve her in that condition is the prime duty of the mother. There are bound to be problems, the author admits, with 'fresh' boys, and he proposes an interesting solution: 'In case a girl's mamma thinks that there is a boy somewhere who needs experience, then she, herself, could pose as an experimental station for that fresh boy to practise on and so save the girl. Nothing can hurt her any more. She has already gone through all the experience that can be gone through and so in her case it would be all right.'

A Book in Every Home has a unique feature: every other page being left blank. The reason for that is given in an Author's Preface: 'Reader, if for any reason you do not like the things I say in this little book, I have left just as much space as I used, so you can write your own opinion opposite it and see if you can do better.'

Edward Leedskalnin died in 1951. For years he had lived on a sparse diet of sardines and crackers, and during his last series of experiments with magnetic current he forgot to eat at all. The cause of his death was starvation. It was a sad end to a life of disappointment, but his monument to that life is an enduring delight. It just seems a shame that no loving couple has ever occupied the stone beds and populated the stone cots in the rock-furnished bedchamber of Coral Castle.

The loss of his sixteen-year-old sweetheart in Latvia caused Edward Leedskalnin to emigrate to America and begin his life's work of solitary building. In a remote part of Florida he made castle walls out of huge coral blocks and filled the courtyard with fantastic sculptures, including astronomical instruments and, below, a stone map of Florida surrounded by rocking-chairs. The secret of how he manipulated the great rocks died with him in 1951. (18, 19)

Lord Monboddo (right), caricatured in 1784. The picture on the wall behind him, of dancing men with tails, is a reference to his belief that chimpanzees and orang-outangs would be recognized as members of the human race were it not for their low culture. Thomas Love Peacock played on this notion by introducing in one of his novels the artistic and noble ape, Sir Oran Haut-ton (above). The character, above right, is Peter the Wild Boy, found in the woods and adopted by a farmer's family. Monboddo visited Peter and others of his kind, believing them to represent a primitive type of humanity, allied to the apes. (20, 21, 22)

CONTEMPLATION.

Francis Galton, the distinguished Victorian scientist, whose evolutionist beliefs and studies of heredity led him to propose that only the upper classes should be allowed to breed. To assist his anthropological researches he invented composite portraiture, taking photographs on the same plate of a number of individuals from the same family, race, profession or other distinct group, and thus obtaining their common likeness. Below is his plate of composite images, illustrating 'the Jewish type'. (23, 24)

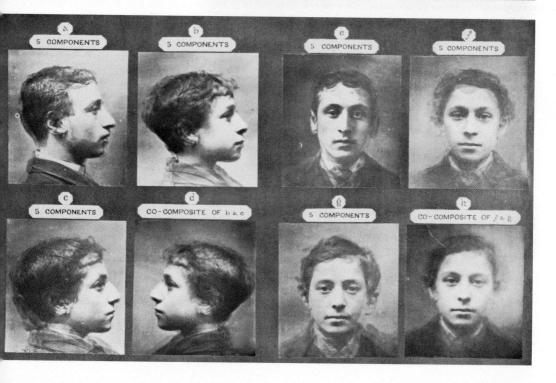

Geoffrey Pyke's imaginative schemes for winning the Second World War included the construction of unsinkable giant ships made of ice, designed to serve as mid-Atlantic bases and assault-craft for attacking enemy ports. Below is an artist's view of an ice-ship, as it would have

A GIGANTIC AIRCRAFT-CARRIER MADE OF ICE: "H.M.S. HABBA

DRAWN BY OUR SPECIAL ARTIST, G. H. DAVIS, WITH OFF

A PROPOSED "SECRET WEAPON" IN THE WAR AGAINST U-BOATS: THE "HABBAKUK" PROJECT – ISLANDS OF ICE

One of the most remarkable schemes produced during the war has just been revealed by the Admiralty. This scheme envisaged the building of gigantic aircraft-carriers made of a mixture of ice and wood-pulp, called "Pykrete," which were to cruise about the Atlantic and act as advanced airfields in anti-submarine warfare. The project, originated in September 1942, was put forward by Mr. Geoffrey Pyke, then acting as Director of Programmes at Combined Operations Headquarters. Such importance was attached to the project that the Prime

Minister, Mr. Winston Churchill, and Lord Cherwell were consulted, and the former commented as follows: I attach the greatest importance to the examination of these ideas. The advantages of a floating island or islands, if only used as refuelling depôts for aircraft, are so dazzling that they do not at the moment need to be discussed. There would be no difficulty in finding a place to put such a stepping-stone in any of the plans of war now under consideration. As a result, a directing committee for research and development of the "Habbakuk" project,

as it was called. on ice would be Subsequently it for building a ve ice was produce of concrete a work was carrie

appeared, dwarfing a conventional aircraft-
carrier. (25)
The lower of the two portraits, right, shows Pyke
on honeymoon with his wife, Margaret, his
partner in a scheme for the ideal education of
children. (26, 27)

PARED WITH H.M.S. "INDEFATIGABLE."

ATLANTIC – ABANDONED OWING TO OUR MASTERY OF THE U-BOATS.

at that large-scale experiments
only be carried out in Canada.
insufficient strength as material
rporating a binding substance,
he same order as the strength
ing the early months of 1943
anada and the United States.

Progress was so rapid that an order was placed with the Canadian Government
for one of these craft for the season 1943-44. The final design was for a craft
made of ice reinforced with wood-pulp, 2000 ft. long, 300 ft. wide and 200 ft. deep,
weighing approximately 2,000,000 tons, covered with an insulating skin and kept
permanently frozen by means of refrigerating machinery. An experimental model
of the proposed icedrome, 60 ft. long by 30 ft. wide, had already been successfully
produced on Lake Patricia, Jaspar, in Canada. This was built up with square
Continued overleaf.

Dr William Price, the revolutionary Welsh Druid, in his ritual outfit of scarlet merino wool with green silk letters in the bardic alphabet he discovered. His famous cremation, and illustrations of his domestic life, are shown in the commemorative print, right. Below is the Pontypridd Rocking Stone as it appeared in 1893, surrounded by the stones of the 'serpent temple' erected by Welsh Druid revivalists. Dr Price was one of a succession of Archdruids who performed ceremonies there through the nineteenth century. (28, 29, 30)

DISTANT VIEW OF LLANTRISSANT AND THE CREMATION

OR PRICE'S HOME, LLANTRISSANT.

THE CREMATION OF DR PRICE JANY 31ST 1893.

CHILDREN IESU GRIST AND PENELOPEN.

INTERIOR OF HOUSE.

DR PRICE,

ARCH DRUID.

GWEN LLEWELLYN.

THE FUNERAL AT EARLY MORN.

IN MEMORIAM. 1893.

Comyns Beaumont, the Fleet Street editor, whose writings included books on Bacon as the author of Shakespeare and on ancient catastrophes on earth caused by the fall of comets. In his later works he claimed that Jerusalem was not originally in Palestine but at Edinburgh, and he produced a revolutionary world history, in which every famous event and site was located in the British Isles. This map, from one of Beaumont's books, shows his discovery of ancient Egypt and the Holy Land in Somerset. (31, 32)

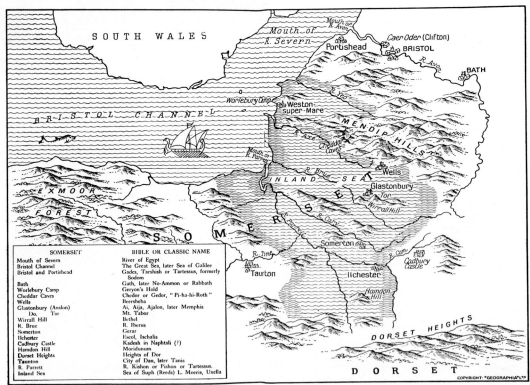

SOMERSET	BIBLE OR CLASSIC NAME
Mouth of Severn	River of Egypt
Bristol Channel	The Great Sea, later Sea of Galilee
Bristol and Portishead	Gades, Tarshish or Tartessus, formerly Sodom
Bath	Gath, later No-Ammon or Rabbath
Worlebury Camp	Geryon's Hold
Cheddar Caves	Chedor or Gedor, " Pi-ha-hi-Roth "
Wells	Beersheba
Glastonbury (Avalon)	Ai, Aija, Ajalon, later Memphis
Do. Tor	Mt. Tabor
Wirrall Hill	Bethel
R. Brue	R. Iberus
Somerton	Gerar
Ilchester	Escol, Ischalis
Cadbury Castle	Kadesh in Naphtali (?)
Hamdon Hill	Moridunum
Dorset Heights	Heights of Dor
Taunton	City of Dan, later Tanis
R. Parrett	R. Kishon or Pishon or Tartessus.
Inland Sea	Sea of Suph (Reeds) L. Moeris, Uxella

COPYRIGHT: "GEOGRAPHIA" LTD

THE JUDGE
WHO VISITED WILD MEN

An attractive character in Thomas Love Peacock's novel of 1817, *Melincourt*, is Sir Oran Haut-ton, a baronet and a Member of Parliament. He is tall and strong but somewhat uncouth-looking, and due to the circumstances of his early life he has never learnt to speak. Despite that, he is fully accepted in fashionable society, being rich and titled, and is popular on account of his excellent manners and good fellowship. The Honourable Mrs Pinmoney, who is looking for a husband for her daughter, is struck by Sir Oran's remarkable ugliness, but on hearing about his position in the world she changes her tune. 'A Baronet! and M.P.! Well, now I look at him again, I certainly do not think him so very plain: he has a very fashionable air. Haut-ton! French extraction, no doubt. And now I think of it, there is something very French in his physiognomy.'

Sir Oran was not, however, French. His early history is told by his inseparable companion, Mr Sylvan Forester, the hero of the novel. He was caught when very young in the woods of Angola and brought up in the household of a native family, where 'he acquired the practice of such of the simpler arts of life as the degree of civilization in that part of Africa admits'. At the age of seventeen he was sold to a passing seaman, Captain Hawltight, and they both retired to a cottage in Devon where they spent convivial evenings together, the Captain singing nautical ballads over his grog, accompanied by Oran on the French horn. Mr Forester, on a visit to his old friend Hawltight, was so enchanted by his companion that he rented a house in the neighbourhood and, when the Captain died, took charge of Oran and proposed to educate him. Oran was sensitive, and if anyone laughed at him he was likely to die from chagrin, so it was necessary to introduce him to the best society where people were too polite to comment on his grotesque appearance. Mr

Forester gave him an estate and bought him a baronetcy and a seat in Parliament. During their adventures together, Sir Oran distinguished himself in valour and sagacity, and when his benefactor married he settled in with the family, entertaining them with his music and drawing.

Peacock's authority for all these details of how a domesticated orang-outang might be expected to behave in polite society was the Scottish judge and philosopher, Lord Monboddo. Footnotes in *Melincourt* justify each one of Sir Oran's acts and accomplishments by quotations from Monboddo's *Origin and Progress of Language* or *Ancient Metaphysics*. Large parts of the combined twelve volumes of these works are devoted to proving that orang-outangs and chimpanzees are true men with all the human attributes except the habit of speech; and that deficiency, so Monboddo believed, was caused merely by their primitive culture.

Monboddo's writings deal at great length with the weightiest matters of science and philosophy, and at the same time they are remarkably entertaining. Their intended gravity is constantly mitigated by the touches of high craziness which so appealed to Peacock. During Monboddo's lifetime, from 1714 to 1799, the Age of Reason was marching ahead, but he was never in step with his contemporaries. He turned his back on Locke and Newton and constructed a modern world-view on the philosophy of the ancient Greeks. In the manner of classical authors he collected indiscriminately the stories about mythical creatures and monsters related by travellers down the ages. From the ancients he learnt about dog-headed men, tribes which hopped on single legs and people with one eye in the middle of their foreheads or faces on their chests. More recent travellers told of lands inhabited by giants and wild people. He saw no reason for disbelief in any of these reports, and quoted them extensively as evidence for his theory of evolution. Every type of creature that can possibly be imagined to exist, he thought, probably does exist or has only recently become extinct.

The accepted belief in Monboddo's day was that the human race had been gifted from the time of Creation with speech and language. This he disputed, maintaining that in the primeval state of nature men could make sounds like animals but were unable to communicate ideas. They banded together for defence against wild beasts and later formed settlements as the first steps towards civilization. It was only at that stage that languages became necessary. Like civilization itself, they were not innate but were invented in different countries as the need arose. From the various centres of original culture, such as Egypt, they spread almost universally.

Not all races had yet adopted a language, however. The proof of Monboddo's theory, as he saw it, would be found in remote parts of the world where people might still exist in their natural condition, uncorrupted by civilization. They would be much taller and stronger than ourselves, with vegetarian diets and simple human virtues, but speechless. Looking through his collection of travellers' tales, Monboddo found many references to such people. 'Not only solitary savages,' he wrote, 'but a whole nation, if I may call them so, have been found without the use of speech. This is the case of the Orang-Outangs that are found in the kingdom of Angola in Africa and several parts of Asia.'

Linnaeus, Buffon and most other naturalists classified these beings as mere animals, but Monboddo had a store of anecdotes which contradicted that judgment. By selecting those which suited his thesis, he built up a charming picture of the innocent orang-outang nation. Captain Hawltight was a fair representative type of his informants. In mariners' logs he found stories of apes who had learnt to play musical instruments, shown aptitude for drawing and displayed such peculiarly human qualities as affection, grief and shyness at being seen naked. Some of them had sat at table, eating and drinking wine like the rest of the company. One specimen, which Monboddo saw stuffed at Versailles, was said when alive to have had 'as much of the understanding of a man as could be expected from his education, and performed many little offices to the lady with whom he lived'. Another, described by Buffon, 'gave him his hand to visitors who came to see him, walking with them gravely like a person of society'.

Even in their own countries, far removed from civilized influence, orang-outangs, pongos and similar tribes behaved like natural men. Monboddo was informed that 'Chimpanzees live together in communities, build little towns or villages, are governed by a king that does not work, and have their games and pastimes as well as the negroes.' They walk erect, carrying sticks as weapons, and it is well known that the orang-outang 'has a very great inclination to copulate with the black women, and frequently ravishes them'.

From his records of cyclopses, mermaids and dog-headed men, Monboddo concluded that the human body could take all kinds of forms. Orang-outangs were well within the range of what had been reported. If only they could speak, as no doubt they would do when their social development required it, their human status would be plain to everyone. The same might possibly be said of beavers, who enjoy family life, conduct wars and mutual enterprises and own slaves. In Monboddo's system these creatures stood on the borderline between two types of consciousness: the rational which has been achieved by modern man and the instinctive or animal state of mind from which it evolved. Below the animal, and linked to it by intermediary forms such as molluscs, is the vegetable state, and the lowest type of consciousness is the mineral.

The existence of universal consciousness was the main tenet in Monboddo's philosophy. In opposition to Newton and the idea of a mechanical universe, he held that every type and instance of motion is caused by mind. The falling to the ground of Newton's apple was not due to gravity or any external cause, but came about through the vegetable consciousness of the apple which caused it to seek the earth when its stem broke. Other effects of the vegetable mind are the movements of a plant's root towards water and of its leaves towards the light. In the orbiting of planets Monboddo saw the operation of mineral mind. This was in accordance with Plato's belief that the heavenly bodies are living creatures, but Monboddo went further by attributing mineral mind to all inanimate objects. Its highest form, where it most nearly approached the level of vegetable mind, was in magnetism. Another of its products was the tendency of a rounded stone to roll downhill. This, Monboddo insisted, was a motion initiated by the stone's own mineral mind. He rejected on philosophical grounds the Newtonian belief that it was caused by outside influences. Newton's mathematical account of the solar system was all right as far as it went, but it was a description rather than an explanation and, by implying that the universe worked automatically, it opened the way to atheism. Newton's first law of motion laid down that a body in motion would proceed endlessly in a straight line if it were not for the influence upon it of other bodies. To account for the orbital paths of planets he had to bring in centrifugal forces and gravity. Monboddo objected to the straight line idea and the introduction of hypothetical forces. He saw no reason why planets should not move in circles of their own accord, if that was the way their mineral minds were designed to work; and his image of a universe directed by Divine Intelligence through the four different levels of consciousness appealed to him as simpler and more comprehensive than the Newtonian model. It did not conflict with the evidence of modern science and it was fully in accordance with the traditions of classical philosophy.

The author of these lively ideas was a brilliant advocate, born James Burnett, the son of a small landowner at the village of Monboddo in Kincardineshire. He was lucky enough in his early career to become involved in the celebrated Douglas case, a dispute to the title to vast estates which dragged on for years to the great benefit of the lawyers. It made Burnett's name and earned him promotion as a Judge of Session in Scotland with the title of Lord Monboddo. He could have risen even higher, but that would have meant neglecting his main interests, study and writing. He was recognized as a profound scholar, especially in Greek, which he claimed no one but he knew how to pronounce correctly. As an author he was justly praised by the most discerning critics, but one fatal mistake ruined his entire literary reputation. The effect of his beautiful prose, his noble philosophy and his acute criticisms of Locke, Hume and Newton was destroyed by this one error. He discovered men with tails.

The discovery came about through a reference in the works of Linnaeus to a seventeenth-century Swedish sailor, Koeping, who had seen some curious things while serving in the Far East. Monboddo wrote to Linnaeus for more details, and the great taxonomist replied in Latin, giving the title of Koeping's book and recommending its author as apparently honest. It was in Swedish, but Monboddo had parts of it translated and learnt that on one of the Nicobar Islands Lieutenant Koeping and his shipmates on a Dutch East India Company vessel had encountered a savage tribe with tails like cats who had captured and eaten some of their crew. Monboddo researched further, found other mentions of tailed folk and published his conclusion that most people in Borneo and many in the Philippines and Formosa were born with tails. Nearer home he uncovered further examples, such as the late Mr Barber of Inverness who was found after death to have a tail six inches long. He began to suspect that most babies had tails but midwives everywhere conspired to conceal that fact.

This was too much for Monboddo's readers. Classical monsters such as one-legged or one-eyed people were fair enough, being evidenced by the best ancient authors, but men with cats' tails were a complete novelty. The humour of a great earnest metaphysical system being based on such a ridiculous notion was appreciated by every wag. The learned judge found himself the butt of a thousand poor jokes. James Boswell, his former disciple, turned spiteful and went around spreading mockery of Lord Monboddo and his tail. In his *Tour of the Hebrides* he quoted Dr Johnson's comment: 'Other people have strange notions, but they conceal them. If they have tails, they hide them. But Monboddo is as jealous of his tail as a squirrel.' The *Edinburgh Review* wanted a caricature of 'my Lord Monboddo in his quadruped form' to illustrate a satirical notice of his first book, and a rival author, Lord Kames, scored a hit by insisting on Monboddo taking precedence over him, saying, 'You must walk first that I may see your tail.' This may have been unfair, but Kames was merely levelling accounts, for at a previous meeting he had incautiously asked Monboddo whether he had read his latest book, and was told, 'I have not, my lord. You write a great deal faster than I am able to read.'

The tailed men haunted Monboddo for the rest of his days, and his posthumous fame rested on the legend of his eccentric notions and habits rather than on the merit of his works. His life, like his philosophy, was modelled on the ancients. At his country house he bathed every morning at six o'clock in cold water from a stream, took an 'air bath' in the evening and anointed himself with oil. In Edinburgh he held philosophical dinners in the Roman style, with the table and wine jug garlanded with roses. He was a tiny figure, less than five feet tall, with thin, pointed features, but he was conspicuous for his dandified dress, sometimes wearing a suit of white velvet at official functions. Every year he rode from Scotland to London and back, following the ancients in disdaining the use of a carriage even in his extreme old age. Dressed in a long scarlet cloak and attended by his black servant riding behind him, he ambled along on an old horse, peering at a pocket Homer which he held a few inches from his nose. The pair became a familiar sight on the northern highway. King George III liked to see him in London and used to tease his cavalry officers by contrasting their effete mode of travel, in carriages, with the spartan habits of the old judge.

In his youth Monboddo was fond of the theatre, and he seems to have been a natural though involuntary comedian, because not only his writings but everything he did made people laugh. One of the many stories told about him was that in 1785 he was seated on the King's

Bench as a guest of the London judges when part of the floor gave way. Thinking that the roof was about to come down, the Englishmen rushed for the door, leaving Monboddo, who was deaf and short-sighted and had probably not noticed anything, alone on the Bench. When asked why he had not escaped with the others, he said that he had supposed the running out of court to be an ancient annual ceremony performed by the English judges, which did not concern him as a Scotsman.

In an age when most other people were excited about progress and the promise of science, Monboddo held the unfashionable view that the world was running down and would soon come to an end. This seems to contradict his evolutionary ideas, but he believed that the human frame had reached the peak of its condition in ancient times, when men were giants, since when it had been steadily deteriorating. He calculated that Achilles was about fourteen feet tall and that the builders of Stonehenge were of at least that height, citing the evidence of a giant's bones from a barrow nearby. He interviewed seamen about giants they claimed to have seen on their voyages. In 1764 Commodore Byron and his officers found that some of the natives of Patagonia were eight or nine feet tall. A skeleton of one of these giants, said to measure over twelve feet, was acquired by M. de Guyot, the captain of a French trading ship, who tried to bring it back to Europe. During the voyage a storm arose, and the Spanish Archbishop of Lima who was a passenger on board insisted that the pagan's bones be thrown into the sea to propitiate the Deity. Monboddo was furious at the Archbishop for losing him the opportunity of proving his thesis, and 'wished that he had been thrown overboard sooner, and then the bones of the Patagonian would have arrived safely'.

Also unfashionable were Monboddo's views on economics. Unlike many of his neighbours who were increasing their incomes by turning people off their lands and letting them to one tenant, he encouraged a large population on his small estate in Kincardineshire. The land was divided up between numerous tenants who in turn supported cottagers, and the community could thus provide its own labour and craftsmen. As a measure of the number of people maintained on his land, Monboddo said that one of his holdings of less than eight acres provided a living for four families. One of his proofs of modern degeneracy was that the population of the country had noticeably declined in his own lifetime, and he believed that to be so all over the world. The total rent he took from his tenants was no more than £300 a year, and in *Ancient Metaphysics* he said he could well have doubled it by letting it all to a modern farmer, but 'I should be sorry to increase my rent by depopulating my part of the country; and I keep these small tenants as a monument to the way in which, I believe, a great part of the lowlands of Scotland was cultivated in antient times.'

At harvest time Monboddo was always at home, dressed as a farmer and working in the fields with his men. In the ancient style he ploughed with oxen rather than horses. Dr Johnson did not approve of these rustic manners. On his journey to the Hebrides with Boswell he visited Monboddo and was critical about the old house and his host's simple dinner. The two men had obvious interests in common and admired each other's scholarship, but they were of such different casts of mind that it was impossible for them to agree. Boswell's attempts to reconcile them came to an end when he received a letter from Monboddo advising him not to waste his time in writing the life of a schoolmaster.

In extreme old age, having outlived his family and most of his contemporaries, Monboddo still rode every year to London while the volume of his writings increased. He had been inspired by a vision which occurred at the crisis of an almost fatal fever in 1778. A beautiful woman appeared before him and gave him a long lecture in French about philosophy. She apparently confirmed the ideas he had already, and the experience cured him and increased his confidence. After a marriage of eight years his wife had died, and so had their son. One of the two daughters eloped to an unsatisfactory marriage, but the younger, the beautiful Eliza Burnett admired by Robert Burns, remained devoted to her father. Her early death was a sad blow in his old age. After the vision he tried to marry again, proposing to several of the young bluestocking ladies whose company he enjoyed in London. They all turned him down but he was philosophical about it. After he had been refused by Miss Hannah More, who was about half his age, he told another of his lady friends, Mrs Garrick, 'I am very sorry for this refusal: I should have so much liked to teach that nice girl Greek.'

Monboddo has been called a forerunner of Darwin, but although he disbelieved in the fixity of species, his ideas had more to do with the evolution of consciousness. Darwin, who was mean with his acknowledgments and poorly credited even his own grandfather, made no mention of Monboddo. Yet he had cause to be grateful to his Scottish predecessor for exhausting all the jokes that could possibly be made about ape-men and people with tails. Darwin's opponents tried to treat him like Monboddo and laugh away his theories by caricaturing him with a monkey's tail, but the humour by that time was stale. The notion of human descent from the same stock as the orang-outang was already familiar and now came into its own, though its triumph was seventy years too late to gratify its true pioneer.

Insofar as Monboddo is read and appreciated today, it is for the very part of his work which brought about his downfall and neglect. With his collection of monsters and prodigies he included some first-hand accounts of interviews with the type of people whom Linnaeus classified as *Homo sapiens ferus*, the Wild Man. Representatives of this class had been sighted or taken alive in forests, living alone or with animals in a state of savagery. Monboddo was fascinated by wild men and would go miles to see a specimen. Those who survived capture could be educated to some extent in civilized manners, but they could rarely be taught to speak more than a few words. This was evidence for one of Monboddo's main points, that language was not inherent in human nature and could rarely be acquired after a certain age, which was why the orang-outang nation remained dumb.

In Paris he called on Mademoiselle Le Blanc, the famous Wild Girl of Songi, who had been caught at the age of about ten in the woods of Champagne. She had been protected by a local landowner, Vicomte d'Epinoy, and other notables including the Queen of Poland had taken an interest in her. When Monboddo saw her in 1765 she had been trained out of her feral ways, lost her teeth and grown fat. She had also managed to learn French, and Monboddo discovered that she was not originally wild but had been abducted as a child from some unknown country which he identified as the region of Hudson Bay. In the West Indies she had been sold as a slave and then shipped to Europe, where she survived a shipwreck off the French coast and took to the woods together with a black girl. When caught she was armed with a club, said to have some writing on it, with which she had earlier laid low her companion. It was preserved in Epinoy's country house, and Monboddo made a journey to inspect it, but the Vicomte was not at home when he called. He engaged his clerk to make a translation of a pamphlet about the Wild Girl and added his own comments in an introduction.

A later excursion was to Berkhampstead in Hertfordshire where a wild man was lodging with a farmer's family. This was Peter, who had been captured in 1724 in Hanover. King George I had brought him to London where he became a popular spectacle, and after his novelty waned had pensioned him off with the farmer. When Monboddo visited him, Peter was about the same age as himself, over seventy, and he was still fairly wild but had developed a great liking for drink. Monboddo thoroughly examined him, noting that he had originally been a vegetarian and could articulate nothing but his own name and a few other sounds he had been taught to imitate. Yet he was apparently no idiot. In Monboddo's *Ancient Metaphysics*, Peter the Wild Boy was an important figure as exhibiting the same level of cultural development as the orang-outang.

A previous book by Robert Rickard and the present writer, *Living Wonders*, deals with the subject of cryptozoology, the study of lake monsters, wild men sighted in the mountains of Asia and America and other such creatures which may or may not exist in remote corners of the earth. In the annals of that science Lord Monboddo has an honoured place as one of its great pioneers.

A CRUSADER FOR
THOROUGHBRED PEOPLE

In the latter part of the last century a respectable-looking gentleman could be seen walking about the cities of Britain, gazing intently at young women. He always had one hand in his pocket, and every time he passed a girl in the street the hand would make a slight twitch. There was a perfectly innocent explanation for this: the pocketed hand belonged to Sir Francis Galton, the great man of science, and the purpose of his urban rambles was to gather material for a Beauty Map of Great Britain. Also in his pocket was a piece of paper divided into three sections. Each woman he saw was categorized as either beautiful, middling or ugly, and the judgment was recorded on the appropriate part of the paper by pricking it with a needle mounted on a thimble. No detailed results of these researches were ever published, but Galton's general conclusion was that the prettiest girls are found in London and the worst-looking in Aberdeen.

The Victorians' worship of science, which became almost a millennial movement at the end of the nineteenth century, is fully illustrated by the career of Francis Galton. He was the founder, priest and prophet of a scientific cult which he offered the world as a new universal religion. In the oddity of his ideas and the enthusiasm with which he propagated them, Galton was the equal of any of the strange theorists described in this book. But no one in his own time ever called him a crank. His long life (1822-1911) was crowned with academic awards, honorary degrees and finally a knighthood. According to his leading disciple, Karl Pearson, author of a massive, four-volume *Life of Galton*, he was a greater man than his cousin, Charles Darwin, because he found a practical use for the theory of evolution.

In common with most other educated people of his time Galton assumed that the civilized white races were the highest form of humanity, that men were inherently more intelligent than women and that the grades of human merit could be established by scientific measurement. Today he is best remembered as the pioneer of eugenics, intelligence-testing and theories about the natural superiority of particular classes and races.

He was an expert in many subjects and intervened widely in others. Among his contributions to learned journals were papers on meteorology, navigation, surveying, anthropology, archaeology, painting, photography, the use of spectacles by divers, ultrasonic whistles, diet fads, currency reform, visions, corporal punishment, the ideal length of rope for hanging people, the flashing of signals to Mars and dozens of other topics. Almost as numerous were his inventions, ranging from advanced scientific instruments to gadgets for personal convenience. At the age of thirteen he designed a steam flying machine, followed by an hour-glass speedometer for bicycles and, in later life, a periscope for seeing over the heads of crowds. It was used for viewing processions, of which he was particularly fond, in conjunction with a wooden brick, wrapped in cloth and tied to a string so that it could be lowered to the ground for standing on.

One of his pet subjects was the identification and treatment of criminals. He was among the first to recognize the value of finger-printing, causing it to be adopted by the police forces of Europe. Another of his ideas was that judges should sentence offenders to so many 'units of pain' rather than specifying a penalty. Galton's argument was that some criminals were literally hardened and did not feel pain as much as others. The condemned man should therefore be examined by skilled anthropologists to assess his degree of sensitivity, the amount of chastisement he received being graded accordingly.

Composite photography was among the most interesting of Galton's inventions. To capture the essential likeness within a family or any other group of people, he obtained portraits of all its members, taken from an identical angle, and photographed them one after another on the same plate, allowing a fraction of the total time of exposure to each portrait. A hope raised by this invention was that sociologists would be enabled through its use to recognize the face of a natural criminal type. They were disappointed when, after the villainous features of frauds or poisoners had been superimposed on each other, all that emerged was a sad but ordinary-looking human face.

The most imaginative use of composite photography was for historical research. Galton collected as many profile portraits of Alexander the

Great as he could find, reduced them to the same size and obtained a likeness of the king as the average view of all the artists who had depicted him. He tried the same thing with lunatics, but their features were so irregular that no satisfactory composite appeared. There were also practical difficulties in that line of study. At Hanwell lunatic asylum he lined up the inmates to have their portraits taken by his photographer. One of them, who believed that he was a royal personage and that he had not been given proper precedence, waited until the photographer had bent down to put his head under the camera cloth, and then ran behind him and took a vicious bite at his 'unprotected hinder end'. The photographer insisted on being allowed to back into a corner of the room if he was to complete the work.

Galton's father, a Birmingham banker, left him a fortune which made him independent for life. After leaving Cambridge with an education in medicine and mathematics, he took full advantage of his youth, health and income by spending his time hunting and travelling. He became a renowned sportsman and then made his name as an explorer. At the age of twenty-eight in 1850, he was encouraged by the Royal Geographical Society to go to South-West Africa, where he led a large expedition deep into uncharted territory. In his trek through the wilderness young Francis Galton showed the extreme force of character for which he was always noted. When warring tribes stood in his way, he called them to order by browbeating their chiefs and imposing laws and treaties upon them.

On returning to England he found himself an acknowledged expert on Africa. Exploration at that time was all the rage. The Royal Geographical Society's man in Africa, Dr David Livingstone, had not been heard of for over two years, and public concern forced the Society to send a relief expedition. Before they could reach their man he was found by another explorer, Henry Stanley. The Society was jealous and put it about that Stanley was a mere jumped-up journalist who had really been found and rescued by Livingstone rather than the other way round. When Stanley came to England and addressed a meeting of the British Association for the Advancement of Science, Galton who introduced the speaker tried to snub him by meanly inviting him to declare his true origins. Stanley, who claimed to have been born an American, was in fact a Welsh bastard of American adoption. Galton's bid to discredit him was defeated by Queen Victoria, who ignored Stanley's birth in favour of his merits and graciously received him. The Society then felt obliged to present him with its highest award, but Galton kept up his campaign against Stanley. Not without justification, he accused him of slaughtering his way across Africa, and questioned whether a private journalist was entitled to make war on tribesmen in their own territory.

For some years Galton wrote and edited travel books. He published *The Art of Travel*, containing useful hints on how to survive in the wilds. An example of his pragmatic fieldcraft is his account of the best method of fording a river with the aid of a horse. One should walk the animal along the bank, then suddenly push it into the water, dive in after it, grab its tail and steer it by splashing the left or right side of its face. The British Army was impressed by the book and hired Galton to give lectures to officers preparing for the Crimean War on how to make soap, light fires, avoid the spring of a wild beast and other useful skills for life under canvas.

His life-long obsessions were counting, measuring and the analysis of statistics, including the vital ones of women. He wrote admiringly about the fine figures of African women, but misunderstandings arose when he tried to record them with a tape-measure, so he devised a way of measuring their hips and busts from a distance by the use of a sextant. Any kind of statistical information was grist to his mill. One of his papers gave 'The weights of British noblemen during the last three generations'; another described 'Three generations of lunatic cats'. The pocket thimble and pricker with which he had gathered data for his Beauty Map was constantly in use for noting the colour of eyes and hair and other features of everyone he met. Personal surveys of human types told him, for example, that the finest men came from Ballater in Scotland. He also tried to measure the levels of honesty obtaining among different nations, discovering from reports of legal proceedings that the most reliable witnesses were British, while 'the centre of gravity of lying' was at Salonika in Greece.

Galton's own marriage was childless and, by all accounts, not particularly affectionate, but he was ever fascinated by the phenomenon of sexual attraction which, like everything else, he believed he could measure. Assuming that people who were either too like or too unlike each other were not mutually attractive, he tried to make a graph showing the ideal amount of difference between couples. Then he remembered that people in love were said to be 'inclined' to each other.

This gave him the idea of measuring the degree of their inclinations. At dinner parties in his London house he put pressure-gauges under the chairlegs of the guests, recording the extent to which they leant sideways and thus how heavily they inclined. Another of his useful inventions was for judging the quality of a lecturer by the extent to which he bored his listeners. He observed that the heads of an attentive audience are still and upright, while a dull speaker causes them to roll around. Thus by a version of the inclination-gauge it should be possible to assess the lecturer's attraction. This was found difficult in practice, so Galton hit on another method, the counting of fidgets. At scientific meetings he recorded the number of times the audience fidgeted, while keeping simultaneous count of his own heartbeats as a measure of time.

One of Galton's oddest papers, his 'Statistical inquiries into the efficacy of prayer', was published in 1872 and caused furious debate. His statistics showed that monarchs, whose good health and longevity is constantly wished for in the prayers of their subjects, enjoy on average a slightly shorter life-span than other rich men. The nobility, who are also prayed for, are notoriously prone to insanity, and eminent divines are less healthy and long-lived than lawyers and doctors. If there were any material advantages to be gained by prayer, they would long have been observed by those sharp-eyed men who calculate insurance risks. Yet Galton could point out that insurance companies do not reduce their rates for missionary ships, which are no less liable to sink than slavers; nor do doctors report a higher incidence of recoveries among their pious or prayed-for patients. As a final blow to the clergy, he said that if they really believed what they preached they would not need to put lightning conductors on churches.

Soon after his return from Africa Galton became interested in spiritualism, attended some seances and was impressed when the medium addressed him in the style and language of a chief of the Damaras, a tribe with whom Galton had had many dealings during his travels. He was the only European who spoke Damara, so the medium must either have been transmitting a genuine message from a deceased member of the tribe or reading Galton's mind. He returned to the subject in the 1870s, when the spiritualist craze was at its height, and witnessed some performances of apparent miracles by D. D. Hume and other famous mediums at meetings arranged by Sir William Crookes, the scientist who incurred the mockery of his colleagues by his brave stand for fair investigation of alleged spirit phenomena. Charles Darwin was also interested, but in an aloof manner, avoiding personal involvement in seances while encouraging Galton to send reports. These for a time were enthusiastic until Darwin's scepticism and the hostility of T.H. Huxley and other influential men finally discouraged him. Hume was never exposed, but his reputation and that of Crookes were slandered away, and Galton joined his peers in setting his face against the world of spirits.

His anti-clerical outbursts and denial of the power of prayer to bring material benefits were not, as his critics charged, due to flippancy, but to the opposite cause, his extreme earnestness and practicality. Later in life he recognized that prayer had psychological value, so he restored family prayers in his household and formed the habit of praying every time he wrote an article. In fact he was strongly religious, but the only type of worship that appealed to him was the spontaneous variety he had seen among the Africans. He considered that their chants, dances and fetish worship expressed the genuine religious spirit of the natural man. As usual, he put that belief to practical test. Looking round for the least worshipful object he could find, he hit upon the comic figure of Mr Punch, and forced his mind into believing that it possessed divine powers. The experiment succeeded. He came to experience 'a large share of the feelings that a barbarian entertains towards his idol', and for a long time he was unable to look at Mr Punch's grotesque features without a feeling of reverence.

Outlandish inquiries into the human faculties were a speciality of Galton's. From an early age he had been curious about the automatic functions of mind and body and whether they could be controlled by the will. One of his experiments was with breathing. He concentrated on drawing breaths by will alone. Having succeeded, he then tried to resume breathing automatically, but found he was unable to do so. He was convinced that if he stopped taking deliberate breaths he would asphyxiate, and it was only after thirty minutes of agonizing mental struggle that he was able to breathe normally again.

A similar type of experiment was with madness. Galton observed that one of its classical symptoms was the feeling of being spied on. To understand that delusion he had to experience it personally; so one morning he left his London house at Rutland Gate and walked eastwards towards Piccadilly, willing himself to believe that every person and object he passed was looking suspiciously at him. Once again the experiment was almost too successful. He quickly became certain that he was the object of universal attention and when he reached Green Park he nearly panicked on seeing the horses on a cab-rank pricking up their ears and staring at him.

His cousin's *Origins of Species* had turned Galton away from the dogma of the Church and provided him with a new object of worship. Natural selection, identified by Darwin as the process through which all species have evolved in harmony with their environment, became the guiding principle in Galton's philosophy. Its operation, as he understood it, was towards the perfection of every race by giving advantage to its strong, adaptable members and weeding out the poorer specimens. Yet for all his admiration of natural selection, Galton believed that he himself could do its work better. He proposed 'to further the ends of evolution more rapidly and with less distress than if events were left to their own course'. The way to do this was to apply the skills of horticulturists and animal breeders to the cultivation of human stock. For that purpose he invented a new science to which, having tried and rejected 'viriculture', he gave the name of 'eugenics'.

Galton's ambition was to implant the aims and principles of eugenics in every branch of science and education. After a few generations the notion of breeding people for their good points, as one breeds horses and dogs, would be accepted as common sense, while people who suggested that couples should be allowed to marry and produce children according to their own preferences would be dismissed as cranks. Eugenics would become a religion, proclaiming taboos against unsuitable marriages, sanctifying unions between human thoroughbreds and offering the hope of racial salvation through the emergence of a higher species of man. Galton's Superman was to be as different from ourselves as we are from our supposed apish ancestors.

The first step, or most obvious stumbling block, in developing eugenics is to decide what sort of people should be encouraged to breed. As a general guide, Galton listed their qualities, including 'health, energy, ability, manliness and courteous disposition'. It is no coincidence that these were the very qualities displayed by Galton himself. In creating eugenics he made it in his own image. The Galton family were mostly rich and industrious Quakers with a line of ancestors made up of scientists, scholars, merchants and professional men. They epitomized the type of family which Galton proposed to favour through his new science. His studies in heredity had shown him that the virile qualities that raise men to eminence in their professions are passed down to their descendants. From the families of these men should therefore be selected the breeding-stock of the nation. Their choice progeny should be encouraged to wed each other at an early age, thus giving them a head-start in the race to produce children. Undistinguished specimens from ordinary families might be allowed to mate around middle age, while idiots, criminals and other worthless types were to be secluded in humane labour camps and rigorously barred from procreation.

Galton respected the House of Lords, because many of its members married the daughters of millionaires, thus passing on shrewd business talents to their descendants; but his aristocracy of the future was to be drawn from a human bloodstock book, a Register of Superior Families in place of *Burke's Peerage*. In his lectures to learned societies he urged them to collaborate in making up the Register, but with no success. Fellow-savants were interested in his ideas, but quailed at the thought of issuing certificates to the public, specifying whom and when each person might marry. Even Darwin, who was generally favourable to the idea, felt it was utopian and impractical. H.G. Wells objected to Galton's inclusion of criminals among those to be forbidden from breeding, pointing out that they were often the most energetic and intelligent members of their communities. In reply to critics who thought he was being unrealistic, Galton produced a long list of marriage customs in different societies, each with prohibitions against particular types of union, such as those between close relatives. His proposals were therefore nothing new. All he wanted was to reform existing customs, instituting taboos based on rational, scientific principles against unsuitable marriages. Matters were simplified by one of his followers who suggested that marriages should be arranged by doctors.

As a means of interesting the public in eugenics, Galton set up an Anthropometric Laboratory in the South Kensington Science Museum. For an entrance fee of threepence customers were weighed and measured and given written assessments of their strength, physical senses and overall rating as human specimens. One of the visitors was the Prime Minister, W.E. Gladstone, who drew Galton's attention to the size of his head of which he was very proud. He went on to say that if he ever found a man with a nobler head he would make him a member of his cabinet. Galton's measurements showed that the Prime Minister's head was not all that exceptional and, according to the story he told his great-great-nephew Hesketh Pearson, he replied that he did know of a better head – his own. Gladstone took the news well, but refrained, wisely no doubt, from inviting Galton to join his administration.

As he grew older Galton became more and more active in spreading the doctrine of eugenics. At the age of eighty-two he set up and endowed the Eugenics Laboratory and Records Office as a department of London University. It had the benefit of the vast hoard of human statistics he had collected over a lifetime, and when he died it inherited the bulk of his large fortune. His final work was a utopian novel, describing the adventures of an English traveller in a strange country where society is ideally regulated by eugenics. In the lives of its people examinations loom large, for everyone's future depends on the marks they obtain in tests of their physique, personality, literacy, family background and so on. Those who do well live happily and innocently in fine houses with allotments, visibly improving their stock with each generation. The unfit disappear into exile or forced labour camps. In a visionary manner the novel summarized the whole of Galton's philosophy, but unfortunately only fragments of it have survived. On the advice of his niece, who objected that its love scenes were absurdly unrealistic, its author destroyed it.

Galton's idea of breeding a Super-race was taken up by Friedrich Nietzsche, became politically tainted and fell into discredit. In principle, eugenics is a worthy and interesting subject, and has been considered so since before the time of Plato – but in principle only. It is easy enough to enumerate agreeable human qualities, health, beauty, intelligence, courage, good temper etc., and everyone wants to see such things in their children and future generations. But how one sets about locating these and all the other necessary attributes of human nature is a problem that defeats every dispassionate inquirer. Galton's conclusions, though well buttressed by statistics and scientific proofs, were blatantly derived from his own prejudices and those of his age. At the root of every system of eugenics lie somebody's personal beliefs and preferences. In that case, the safest and most satisfactory method of breeding the human race appears to be the one now commonly in force, of putting everyone in charge of their own eugenics programme and letting them mate or marry whomever they feel most inclined to.

THE INVENTOR
OF FROZEN BATTLESHIPS

Geoffrey Nathaniel Pyke (1894-1948) was a fine example of that ever-popular class of eccentric character, the Professor Branestawm type of absent-minded inventor. He was never widely famous because few of his ideas and ambitions ever came to anything. Thus his biographer, David Lampe, titled his book *Pyke the Unknown Genius*. It would have been a different matter had he succeeded in any of his grand projects, which included the prevention of the Second World War, then quickly winning it, and then solving the economic and other problems of its aftermath.

His father, a lawyer, died when Geoffrey was five years old, and his mother sent him to Wellington, the public school which specializes in the sons of army officers. He was dreadfully bullied there, partly because he was a Jew, the first in the school, and partly because his mother insisted on his having a special diet and wearing slightly different clothes from the other boys. After two hellish years at school he was mercifully removed and given a private tutor, and then went up to Cambridge to study law.

When war broke out in 1914, Geoffrey Pyke approached the *Daily Chronicle* with a scheme for sending dispatches direct from the German capital. He was taken on, managed to reach Berlin undetected and sat about in cafés listening to people's conversations. But before he could write anything he was arrested and told he was to be shot as a spy. In the end the Germans took pity on his youth and innocence and sent him to an internment camp instead. He and another English inmate determined to escape, and Pyke devised a scheme. He had noticed a store-hut in the camp grounds where the afternoon sun shone through a window directly into the eyes of the guard who inspected it. Pyke reckoned that two men crouching in the hut at that time would not be seen; and so it proved. At night they climbed over the wire and made the long walk to the Dutch frontier.

The *Daily Chronicle* was delighted by the adventures of its reporter and made much of them; Pyke found himself a hero. He wrote a book about his escape and gave lectures. One of them was at Wellington, where Pyke told the boys that even at the worst period of his imprisonment in Germany, when he thought he was going to be shot, he had never been so miserable as when he had been at school there.

One day Geoffrey Pyke was standing by the Stock Exchange, watching the brokers going in and out. He was struck by how stupid many of them looked. This made him think he would do well in business, so he rented an office and started dealing in the commodities market. His speculations succeeded, and he was soon on the way to making a fortune.

The money he earned was devoted to a scheme for revolutionizing the education system. Pyke was married by that time and was living in Suffolk with his wife and infant son, David. His concern was that David should grow up free of inhibitions, and that meant that the child was never to be checked or frustrated in anything he wanted to do. Pyke believed that children should be treated like foreign dignitaries ignorant of our customs. If they threw their food around or in any other way, according to our standards, misbehaved, the proper way to correct them was by example. They should never be reproved. He took a large house in Cambridge and started the Malting House School to prove his point.

Theories of liberal education were fashionable at that time, but Pyke's experiment was the most radical of all. Studios and laboratories were fitted out with the best modern equipment for crafts and science, and the children were allowed to use these as they wanted. An important instrument in the carpentry shop was a double-handled saw from which they would learn the principle of co-operation. If they wanted to dig up the plants in the garden to see how they were growing, they could do so, and thus they would find out for themselves that plants are best left alone. If a pet animal died the children would dissect it to see how it worked and what had gone wrong. Teachers were regarded as 'co-investigators' of the world together with their charges, and they were never to force instruction upon a child. They had merely to see that the pupils did not hurt themselves and to help them with whatever they decided to study. Everything the children said or did was written down for later analysis.

The carefully picked staff were directed by a woman psychologist whom Pyke engaged to run the school. Unfortunately he would interfere, and this caused dissension. Otherwise the school went well. An observation gallery was opened from which visitors could watch the children learning while playing. Many were impressed and the Malting House School was favourably discussed in the educational press. Rated most successful was Pyke's scheme for giving children an interest in learning reading and arithmetic by letting them write down what they wanted to eat, up to a certain sum, from a priced menu.

In 1928 Pyke suddenly lost everything. His speculations in commodities had grown enormous, and he thought he had discovered an infallible way of making money through certain charts he had devised. By predicting fluctuations in prices he had been able at one time to control a third of the world's supply of raw tin. But despite the large profits, which he used to finance the school, he was always in debt, always buying on margin, and when his charts failed to predict a turn of the market he was ruined overnight. His Malting House experiment was cut short, his wife had to find work, David was sent to a more ordinary school, and Pyke retreated to a cottage in Surrey.

For the next few years he was furiously at work on schemes to improve the world by education and other means. He formed a world union of Christian leaders to denounce Hitler's racial policies and to challenge the myths behind prejudice of all sorts. When the Spanish Civil War broke out, he organized Voluntary Industrial Aid for Spain, working with the trade unions to send equipment to the Spanish Loyalists. One of his deals involved buying up a cheap lot of Harley-Davidson motorcycles and fitting them with specially designed side-cars for use as mini-ambulances or for bringing hot food to the troops at the front. He was a constant inventor and advocate of machinery based on simple principles, easy to operate and requiring little energy. Thus he suggested to the Spanish that they should use pedal power to shunt their trains.

In 1939, when war was imminent, Pyke planned to avert it by presenting Hitler with the results of a public opinion poll showing that the majority of Germans did not want to fight and were against the persecution of the Jews. Such a poll could not be conducted openly in

Germany, so Pyke had to take it in secret. He advertised for adventurous students, and those who answered and were found suitable he sent off to Germany disguised as golfers. Preliminary results showed that most Germans were unwilling to follow Hitler into war, but its actual outbreak aborted the scheme and the students with their golf clubs barely escaped in time to avoid internment.

Pyke's inventiveness was particularly useful in wartime. Admiral Mountbatten, the chief of Combined Operations, took him on his staff as part of a group of scientists and original thinkers whose task was to produce bright ideas for winning the war. Pyke's untidy habits and odd appearance – he was very tall, bearded and always scruffily dressed – were distasteful to his military colleagues, but he made a close friend of Mountbatten who saw to it that even his wildest ideas were given a fair hearing.

One of his early schemes was addressed to the problem of how to destroy the Romanian oil-fields. It was possible, he was told, to land a small force of commandos under cover of a bombing raid, but it would be difficult for them to approach the strongly guarded installations. Pyke's first idea was to send the commandos in with dog-teams, whose baying would be mistaken by the guards for the howling of wolves, scaring them away. Then he thought of training dogs to approach the guards with bottles of brandy tied to their necks, thus making them drunk; alternatively they might be immobilized by sending women to seduce them. All these proposals had obvious drawbacks, but Pyke finally hit on the perfect answer. If the bombers could start a few small fires among the oil-wells, the British commandos could charge freely about if they dressed up as Romanian firemen in replicas of their fire-engines. But instead of putting out the fires, the fake firemen would stoke them up further by spraying them with water mixed with fused incendiary bombs. The idea was much applauded, but no one was rash enough to try it out.

Another project was to use a few specially trained troops to tie up a large enemy army in Norway, where the Germans had essential factories and power stations. These were to be attacked by small military groups, travelling across the snow on mechanized sledges which Pyke undertook to invent. They would tow smaller sledges bearing torpedoes, and if they were pursued uphill by German armour the small sledges could be released to run back on their own tracks and explode among the enemy.

Pyke's first idea was that the vehicle should be designed to carry three men, two to plant bombs and one to guard it while they were away. It then occurred to him that, if the vehicle were so disguised that no German or native civilian would dare to investigate it, a guard would be unnecessary and only two men need be carried. One idea was to present it as a secret Gestapo death-ray device, with a German notice on its side forbidding anyone to touch it. Even better, he thought, might be a notice saying, 'Officers' Latrine. For Colonels Only'. That surely would be effective in preventing German soldiers, noted for their obedience, from entering the vehicle.

The scheme was approved, and trials were started in America of types of snow-going machines such as Pyke needed. He went to Washington with a military mission, but the American army authorities were as disgusted by his dishevelled appearance as the British had been. They kept him as far as possible away from meetings and ignored most of his advice. In consequence the vehicles were not developed until it was too late for them to be used in the war.

The most sensational of the projects which Pyke submitted to Mountbatten was code-named Habakkuk. Pyke in America had been investigating certain properties of ice and had developed a material, 'pykrete', made from a mixture of ice and wood pulp, which was far stronger than pure ice, more stable and less inclined to melt. A ship made of pykrete would be unsinkable; a torpedo would make only a slight dent in its side, quickly repaired. Pipes circulating cold air within the hull would keep it permanently frozen, and Pyke had worked out how the ship was to be powered and steered and other details.

He also knew how the invention should be used to cut short the war. Huge ice ships, clad in timber or cork and looking like ordinary ships only much larger, several times the length of the *Queen Mary*, would serve as transports and aircraft carriers, while smaller versions could be adapted to attack enemy ports. Shrugging off bombs and torpedoes, they would sail in and capture enemy warships by spraying them with super-cooled water (reduced to below freezing point but not allowed to congeal), encasing them in ice and so forcing their surrender. Huge blocks of pykrete would then be unloaded and put together to form a frozen barrier round the port, making it an impregnable fortress, and from there special teams would infiltrate the countryside, spraying railway tunnels with super-cooled water to seal them up and paralyze

German communications. In the end, presumably, Hitler could be sealed up alive in his bunker.

Mountbatten was so excited by the idea that he rushed off to see Churchill, found him in his bath and dropped a block of pykrete into the steaming water to demonstrate its resistance to melting. Churchill in turn went off to exhibit the material to President Roosevelt, while Mountbatten showed it to the allied chiefs of staff in Quebec. Drawing his revolver he fired at a lump of pykrete to prove its resistance – so successfully that the bullet ricocheted and narrowly missed the assembled admirals and field marshals, compelling their admiration for the new material. Operation Habakkuk went speedily ahead. A prototype pykrete ship was built on a Canadian lake and lasted through a hot summer with no sign of melting. The Normandy landings, however, made the use of ice ships unnecessary, and they played no part in the war. The invention of the atom bomb made them obsolete, because a nuclear explosion would turn them into huge radio-active masses. Even though they would be much bigger and cheaper to build than conventional ships, no one seems to have explored their use for civilian purposes.

For the rest of the war Pyke continued to ply Mountbatten with original ideas. One of his inventions was a pipeline for pumping equipment and even soldiers from ships to shore or across difficult country. Like most of his ideas it was never implemented. After the war ended he turned his attention to the problem of reconstruction. Energy was scarce in Europe, but manpower was plentiful, so Pyke recommended forms of simple technology such as the pedal-powered vehicles he had earlier wished upon the Spanish. He worked out how rows of pedallers could move lorries, tractors and trains, wrote papers about it and urged the idea on important people. This was years before the notion of 'intermediate technology' for under-developed countries became fashionable, and Pyke was widely mocked, even by his natural allies the Fabians and *New Statesman* socialists. Grandiose revolutionary schemes for saving the world were more popular at the time than practical ideas for improving it.

Pyke's last days were spent in a room in Hampstead. Often he worked in bed so as not to waste time by getting up and dressing. This was a habit begun in wartime, when Pyke would summon military chiefs to bedside conferences in his flat among piles of papers, old bottles and other debris. His work in Hampstead was a government commission to solve the problem of staffing the National Health Service. It led him to investigate the world economy and the principles for a humane civilization in the future. He was eager as ever to introduce his ideas to influential people. He broadcast and wrote articles. But the more he studied the possibilities for a better world-order, the more hopeless and pessimistic he became. In earlier years he had decided that the reason why people rejected his ideas on education was that they did not really want children superior to themselves. Against him was that aspect of human psychology which distrusts innovations. Frustration and the pervading gloom of post-war England finally overwhelmed him. One winter evening Geoffrey Pyke shaved off his beard and swallowed a bottle of sleeping pills, and next morning his landlady found him dead.

THE LAST OF
THE OLD WELSH DRUIDS

The bards and Druids of ancient Britain were supposed to have been suppressed at the time of the Roman invasion, but eighteen centuries later, in 1789, a letter in *The Gentleman's Magazine* bore the exciting news that their tradition was still alive and flourishing in South Wales in the person of a humble stonemason, Edward Williams. He was described as a sober vegetarian and a hermit, careless of worldly matters, who had never gone to school but had been apprenticed to a bard of the ancient order and properly initiated into the mysteries of his craft at a secret congress of the bards of Glamorgan. Only in that county, said the letter, had the genuine lore of bardism been preserved from prehistoric times, and Edward Williams was the last of his line.

This was not entirely accurate. Edward Williams – better known by his bardic name, Iolo Morganwg – was by no means a hermit but a great lover of company. He had friends in every part of Wales, in cottages, manor houses and inns, whom he often visited in the course of his long pedestrian rambles in search of bardic relics and ancient Welsh documents. These visits were much enjoyed by his hosts, for Iolo was a grand talker and would entertain the household with poems and anecdotes while drinking endless cups of tea stiffened with opium which he took, so he said, to relieve his asthma. That complaint prevented him from ever lying down, so he would sleep upright in a chair before continuing his journey at daybreak.

Iolo Morganwg was known as the most learned man in Wales, and he had the greatest influence in the preservation and revival of the ancient Welsh culture; but ever since his time scholars have been divided about the nature of his achievement. All over the country he rummaged through neglected libraries, and his transcriptions of the manuscripts he found there, many of which later vanished or were destroyed, have been the prime material of all subsequent studies in Welsh literature. But as a bard himself, sharing the same tradition with those he copied, he felt justified in adding his own compositions to the genuine bardic fragments he collected. Exasperated academics, trying to sort out the ancient from the modern among Iolo's texts, have called him a forger; but poets have generally been less fastidious, recognizing in his writing a true expression of the mystical philosophy of the ancients. His greatest admirer, the English Poet Laureate, Robert Southey, encouraged a friend of the bard's old age, Elijah Waring, to publish his *Recollections and Anecdotes of Edward Williams*, a compilation of excellent stories to illustrate Iolo's character.

He was born in 1747 in a cottage at Flimstone, a hamlet near Cowbridge, Glamorgan. His father was a stonemason who taught him the craft by which he later lived, while his mother, who had three other sons, made Edward her darling, decided he was too delicate to go to school, and educated him herself. She was a member of an old local family whose fortunes had come to ruin, and to her son she passed on her love and knowledge of country legends and romantic antiquities. In the secluded hills and valleys of Glamorgan, the ancient Siluria, he became acquainted with the native bards, whose traditional language and music, having survived centuries of English repression, were rapidly succumbing to the puritanism of Welsh fundamentalist zealots. He organized bardic assemblies and continued throughout his life to study and extol the principles behind their ancient doctrines, which he found identical with those of primitive Christianity.

When his mother died in 1770 he left home and began his wanderings, first to North Wales to collect subscriptions for his book of poems, and then with his three brothers to London. The brothers were also stonemasons. They later emigrated to the West Indies and worked there so successfully that, when they died, Edward became heir to a valuable estate. He was always in need of money, but refused to profit by the inheritance because he knew that his brothers had owned slaves. As the self-styled Bard of Liberty he opposed all forms of exploitation, earning himself the reputation of a dangerous radical. Once when he was in Bristol he heard the church bells ringing out in celebration, he was told, of the defeat of Wilberforce's bill to abolish slavery, and he was so disgusted that he walked rapidly out of the city and literally shook the dust from his shoes as he left its limits. Later in life, while trying unsuccessfully to earn a living from a small shop in Cowbridge, selling books and groceries, he boycotted sugar from the slave plantations and sold only the East Indian variety, which he advertised in the window as 'Uncontaminated with human gore'.

After a spell in London, where he met the leading Welsh scholars of his time and made copies of old manuscripts in public collections, he moved first to Kent and then to other parts of southern England, as far afield as Devon and Cornwall, plying his craft as a stonemason. Wherever he went, travelling always on foot, he collected items of local folklore and visited ancient sites, including Stonehenge and Avebury which he recognized as temples of his Druidic predecessors. Returning to Wales, aged thirty-four, he married a farmer's daughter who had inherited £1,000. Her fortune did not last long, because Iolo lost it all in various trading and farming ventures, and four years after their marriage the destitute couple with their small daughter had to flee across the Bristol Channel to avoid their creditors. The stratagem did not work, and Iolo was arrested and had to serve a year in the debtors' prison in Cardiff. This was no great tragedy because it gave him the opportunity of arranging his papers for publication. Meanwhile his wife gave birth to their son, Taliesin, a dutiful boy who took after his father, was initiated by him into the bardic mysteries and later succeeded him as Archdruid.

Leaving his wife and family to shift for themselves, Iolo in 1791 made another journey to London, where he found everyone excited by a traveller's tale from the American Mid-West. It was said that two Welsh missionaries had been captured by a tribe of Indians, and were about to be put to death when one remarked to the other in Welsh what a shame it was that their mission had ended so disastrously. Hearing this the Indians exclaimed in surprise, also speaking Welsh which turned out to be their native language, apologized to the captives and released them. The theory was that these Welsh-speaking Indians were descendants of the party led by Prince Madoc of Wales, who had set sail westwards in the twelfth century and had never been heard from since.

Iolo became a vigorous supporter of that theory and sought backing for an expedition to America to reclaim the lost Welshmen. In preparation for what he imagined America would be like, he took the dramatic course of withdrawing from civilization, sleeping rough in the open air under hedges and trying to live off the land. He had done something like that once before when he and a friend, meaning to recapture the primitive simplicity of ancient bardic life, had spent a day living off raw plants in the fields – or 'grazing' as they called it. By evening they had become so hungry that they went to an inn for bread and cheese. The second experiment was ended by a severe attack of rheumatism, and of this Iolo made an excuse for backing out of the expedition. It went ahead without him, however. One of his young followers, John Evans, sailed off for America and up the Missouri River, and after hair-raising adventures died in New Orleans without locating the Welsh Indians. No official contacts have ever since been made with that interesting tribe.

While in London Iolo became a friend of Richard Brothers, the crazy prophet. Brothers had been a naval officer, but became a pacifist, resigned his commission and proclaimed himself the King of the Jews. He was the first British Israelite, believing that he and his followers had been divinely chosen to lead the Jews back to the Holy Land and lodge them in a splendid New Jerusalem. He drew up detailed architectural plans for the ideal city, which were finely engraved by his disciple, William Sharp, and published in books and pamphlets. His visionary experiences included a sighting of the Devil walking down a London street and a visit at his lodgings from two angels. These beings encouraged him to denounce all worldly thrones and powers. The Government decided that Brothers had gone too far, and anticipated modern practice by holding him a political prisoner in a lunatic asylum. Iolo had his own theory on the matter. He believed that the angels had really been a pair of revolutionary French ventriloquists in disguise, who had duped Brothers into making his inflammatory statements. He visited Brothers to tell him so, but the prophet refused to be persuaded. Iolo wrote to the Prime Minister, William Pitt, informing him of his suspicions. Pitt seemed very interested in the ventriloquist theory, invited the bard to call on him and received him kindly. Brothers, however, was finally committed to Bedlam.

Pitt had evidently taken a liking to Iolo, for he showed him favour on another occasion, when he was in trouble with the police. He had made an enemy of another Welsh bard, Edward Jones, who was court harpist to the Prince of Wales. Jones had been greatly influenced by Iolo, followed his example in reviving bardic assemblies (*eisteddfodau*) in Wales and deplored with him the activities of 'fanatic imposters or illiterate plebeian preachers' who had persuaded many of the native harpists to abandon their craft. The result, said Jones, is that 'Wales, which was formerly one of the merriest and happiest countries in the world, is now become one of the dullest.' But the court bard and the Bard of Liberty were natural rivals. Jones disapproved of Iolo's radical associates, such as Tom Paine, and denounced him to the police, who raided his lodgings and seized his papers. Iolo was called to see Pitt, who looked through his writings, found them innocuous and told him he could take them home. This was not good enough for Iolo. He replied that since the police had carried away his property it was they who should carry it back. Pitt agreed, and the police were instructed to replace the papers where they had found them.

An attractive feature of Iolo's campaign on behalf of the ancient Welsh culture was its freedom from narrow nationalism. He proclaimed that English, equally with Welsh, was a bardic language, and in 1792 he held a Druidic moot in London, on Primrose Hill, which featured chants, ceremonies and the bestowing of bardic degrees. The police suspected that it was something to do with the French Revolution and put a stop to it. They also intervened in Wales, when Iolo held a *gorsedd* on top of the Garth mountain near Cardiff. The Druids were suspected of signalling to a French fleet in the Bristol Channel.

Throughout all his years of collecting and copying ancient Welsh texts and publishing them together with his own bardic contributions, Iolo still kept up his other life as Edward Williams the journeyman mason. His craft was always his stable livelihood. Walking far and wide in search of work, he became a familiar figure on the roads of South Wales. That country, he believed, was well suited for the cultivation of tea, so wherever he went he scattered seeds of the tea plant, hoping to ruin the East India Company's trade. Elijah Waring described the bard in his later days as '. . . an elderly pedestrian, of rather low stature, wearing his long grey hair flowing over his high coat-collar, which, by constant antagonism, had pushed up his hat-brim into a quaint angle of elevation behind. His countenance was marked by a combination of quiet intelligence, and quick sensitiveness; the features angular, the lines deep, and the grey eye benevolent but highly excitable. He was clad in rustic garb; the coat blue, with goodly brass buttons, and the nether integuments good homely corduroy. He wore buckles in his shoes, and a pair of remarkably stout well-set legs were vouchers for the great peripatetic powers he was well known to possess. A pair of canvas wallets were slung over his shoulders, one depending in front, the other behind. These contained a change of linen, and a few books and papers connected with his favourite pursuits. He generally read as he walked, "with spectacles on nose," and a pencil in his hand serving him to make notes as they suggested themselves. A tall staff, which he grasped at about the level of his ear, completed his travelling equipment.'

As an example of his powers as a walker, Waring tells how Iolo left home early one morning, after breakfast, and walked forty-seven miles into Bristol. There he had some tea and bread and butter, did the business he had come on, slept the night in a friend's chair and, next morning, set off for home, arriving just as his wife was putting on the tea kettle. He had walked ninety-four miles within thirty-six hours, eating only twice away from home, both times just bread and butter with tea.

The Bishop of St David's once persuaded Iolo to lend him some precious manuscripts, but was careless about them and they were inadvertently sold and dispersed. Their owner, hearing of this, immediately set out on a long trek through Wales in order to recover them. He was over seventy, and his son, Taliesin, insisted that he take a horse for the journey. Iolo never rode, but he agreed that the horse could come with him as a companion. He drove the animal in front of him, paid its toll-gate fees, but neither mounted it not trusted it with his wallets containing the regained manuscripts. He complained that it was very tiring having to walk with a horse.

One of Iolo's most significant acts took place in 1819, when his friend the Bishop invited him to Abergwili Palace for an *eisteddfod* at the nearby Ivy Bush Hotel. On the ground before the hotel the aged bard laid out a ring of pebbles to represent a stone circle, following a design he had discovered in an old document. In the circle he held a ritual bardic *gorsedd*. Ever since, despite opposition from academic authorities who claim that the *gorsedd* ritual was Iolo's own invention, it has been a popular feature of the Welsh *eisteddfod*. Early this century, the great astronomer-archaeologist, Sir J. Norman Lockyer, recognized Iolo's *gorsedd* pattern as characteristic of Welsh megalithic circles, which are designed to indicate the sunrise on the mornings of the Celtic feast days.

The last years of Iolo Morganwg were spent in his cottage at Flimstone. He dwelt mostly within his own imagination, stimulated by large doses of opium. All around him were papers, his manuscripts, notes and transcriptions, and everything was in the wildest disorder.

When he died in 1826, the dutiful Taliesin carefully sorted through these documents, publishing some of them and arranging sales of others to libraries. Enough were preserved thereby to give employment to generations of Welsh scholars. The controversy about which of them are genuinely ancient and which are of Iolo's writing is still brewing, but that question has never much troubled the bard's admirers. If, as he claimed, Iolo was the anointed heir to an unbroken succession of bards going back into prehistoric times, the content of his writings is as relevant to the study of ancient philosophy as are those of his early predecessors whose style he adopted. That most perceptive of writers on the Celtic and eastern religious systems, W.Y. Evans Wentz, cites Iolo's manuscripts as the authority for his account of the Druidic belief in the after-life. He is aware that the antiquity of these documents has been disputed, but comments that 'since no one questions their Celtic origin – be it ancient or more modern – we are content to use them'.

Iolo's influence has been lasting. The Welsh, who lost their independence to England in 1282, had long been conditioned to accept their own cultural inferiority. Iolo revealed to them the nobility of their ancient traditions and the sublime universal philosophy upheld by their Druid ancestors. Symbols of this philosophy, such as the sword which is never unsheathed and the stones of the *gorsedd* ring, representing the twelve tribes of Israel and the Ark of the Tabernacle, are retained to this day in the national *eisteddfod* ceremony. Nor was he the last of his bardic line. Taliesin, initiated by his father, became the next Archdruid. He was succeeded by a line of extraordinary Welshmen, whose colourful performances in the cause of Druidic revival diverted their countrymen over the next hundred years.

Dr Price at the Pontypridd Rocking Stone

The ritual centre of nineteenth-century Welsh Druidism was a boulder on the common at Pontypridd called the Rocking Stone. It may once have rocked on the natural stone platform that supports it, giving forth oracular creaks, but now it stands firm. Geologists say that it was deposited there by the action of glaciers, while others claim it as an ancient Druid temple. Iolo Morganwg held a ceremony at the Rocking Stone in about 1815, marching up to it in a bardic procession with banners and bearing the State Sword of Wales. His son, Taliesin, kept up the tradition and presided there as Archdruid over several gatherings of bards. When he died in 1847, the inheritance of his title was disputed. The legitimate claimant was the Pontypridd bard, Myfyr Morganwg, but the most vigorous was a local medicine-man, William Price.

In any history of Welsh eccentricity Dr Price would surely play the leading part. His everyday costume was that of an ancient Welsh Druid of the shamanic department. His hair was long and plaited, and over it he wore the head of a fox, its skin and tail hanging down behind and its legs dangling like tassels in front of his face. He dressed in a white tunic with a scarlet waistcoat and green cloth trousers. Thus clad he would visit his patients, treating them wherever possible with herbal remedies, and these together with his startling appearance were generally effective. He earned a great reputation as a healer. Though a qualified doctor, he despised most of his profession, accusing them of heartless exploitation of the sick, dealing in dangerous drugs and prescribing pills which suppressed symptoms of a disease without curing it. He never operated except, as he once confessed, when he needed the money. He was known, however, as a brilliant surgeon. One of his feats, long remembered, was grafting a bone from the leg of a calf onto the crushed leg of a coal-miner.

Born in 1800 into a large family of an inactive literary clergyman who neither preached nor published, William Price drew attention to himself at an early age by walking about the country naked. For that he was denounced by the local clergy, whose anathemas he returned with interest. His life was spent in constant opposition to every form of authority – clergymen, doctors, lawyers, politicians, landlords, mine-owners and all their works and institutions – and he did all he could to discredit them. The only apparent god, and the only ruler he recognized, was nature. That had also been the doctrine of the old Druids, of whom Dr Price considered himself the lineal descendant. This idea was so firm in his mind that he engaged in an expensive lawsuit, claiming possession of a certain Welsh estate on the grounds that it was traditionally a Druid property. His evidence was his own affidavit, 725 pages long, which affirmed not only his right to the estate but 'Authority invested in the primitive bard to govern the world'. A prosaic High Court Judge disallowed his claims.

Usurping from Myfyr the title of Archdruid, Dr Price conducted pagan rituals at the Pontypridd Rocking Stone, which consisted largely of him baying at the moon, watched by a crowd of astonished locals. To augment the natural power of the stone, he proposed that a hundred-foot tower should be built over it, to serve also as a bardic museum. The Rocking Stone was to be 'the banner of our heritage, around which millions, yet unborn, shall assemble to learn the language and music of our people'. The project was to cost £1,000 and a number of subscriptions were received, but Price suddenly lost interest and allowed the matter to drop.

His veneration for the old Welsh Druids was so extreme that he once declared (in a letter signed Lord of South Wales): 'All the Greek books are the works of the Primitive Bards, in our own language!!!!!' and, 'Homer was born in the hamlet of E Van near Caerphilli and built Caerphilli Castle.' In imitation of the ancients he drank local cider, lived as a vegetarian and faithfully upheld the doctrine of free love. Marriage was the institution he most consistently opposed, associating it with the puritan morality of the chapels which had stifled the Welsh spirit. He was a great lover of young women and fathered a long series of children, the last when he was ninety years old.

The reason why Price abandoned the Rocking Stone project was that he became involved in Chartism, the popular movement for extending the franchise and other reforms. He became the most radical of Chartists. It was not mere reforms he wanted, but the abolition of all tyrannies, religious, political and economic, that oppressed the working people of Wales. In 1839 he was elected leader of the Pontypridd Chartists, at a secret, torch-lit meeting, and made an inflammatory speech lasting over two hours. 'We must strike with all our might and power,' he declaimed, and ended: 'I am with you all the way, I, Doctor William Price!'

The meeting was highly impressed, and some of the Chartists took him at his word by planning a national insurrection, beginning with an attack on the town of Newport. An army of four thousand miners, rustically armed with pikes, clubs and old muskets, entered the town, but the authorities were prepared and met them with a force of soldiers and special constables. At the Battle of the Westgate Hotel, the Chartists were routed with heavy casualties. Price, who was deeply implicated in the affair, had to flee for his life, so he disguised himself as a woman and managed to board a ship at Cardiff bound for Liverpool. The captain recognized him and tipped off the police, and at the next port of call, Milford Haven, Price who had gone ashore without disguise for a glass of cider found himself in the company of a special agent. A warrant for his arrest had been applied for, but before it could arrive he was back on board and the ship had put to sea again. As soon as they had left the harbour, Dr Price summoned the captain and harangued him with menaces for his treachery. On reaching the safety of Paris, by way of Liverpool and London, he wrote to the captain with the promise that sooner or later he would take revenge on him.

He spent seven years in Paris, meeting many literary people, including the great poet, Heinrich Heine, who was impressed by his Druidic philosophy. He also met a sixteen-year-old girl, but after her parents found that he had been taking her into the country for nude picnics, they deprived him of her company. Back in Wales he entered into a prodigious number of law-suits. Litigation became his new mania. One of the methods he used to make courts and lawyers look foolish was to bring his infant daughter to the courtroom and introduce her as his 'learned counsel'. In order to prove that his father had been mad in disposing of a certain estate, he had the family grave opened and examined his father's skull. According to him, the skull gave evidence of its late owner's insanity; but other doctors who inspected the relic thought that it showed old Mr Price to have been mentally normal. The exhumation was considered the height of sacrilege, and once more the chapel elders thundered against the impious Dr Price. When another law-suit went against him and he was about to be arrested for debt, he once more fled to France, this time in a trunk of old clothes which his daughter smuggled down to the port.

During his first stay in Paris he had discovered in the Louvre a precious stone, inscribed with an image of 'the primitive bard addressing the moon' and a number of hieroglyphs which no one had been able to read. Price recognized them as characters in the Druid script and, having translated them, found that the message they contained was addressed to him. It was from an Archdruid of two thousand years earlier, appointing Dr Price his successor in office and prophesying that he would one day sire a son who would restore the Druid system in all its ancient glory.

At the age of eighty-five Price was presented with a son by his young woman friend, Gwenllian, and recognized the fulfilment of prophecy. He named the boy Iesu Grist (Jesus Christ in Welsh), thus further enraging the chapel ministers. But Iesu was not to succeed him as Archdruid, for at the age of five months he died. His father took the body up to a hilltop, lit a great fire and began to cremate it – a proceeding quite unheard of at the time – in the sight of people coming out of chapel. It caused a riot. A crowd stormed the hilltop, seized Dr Price and would have thrown him on his own fire if the police had not intervened. They took charge of the baby's half-burnt body, arrested Price and held him in gaol.

At the trial which followed Price appeared in a costume he had designed for the occasion, consisting of a white linen smock with scolloped collar and cuffs and a huge royal tartan shawl over his shoulders. Unyielding as ever, he conducted his own defence, arguing that cremation was a healthier practice than burial and that no law prevented it. In winning the case he made history. It was the first time that cremation had been declared legal in Britain, and the name of William Price is still famous among undertakers as its pioneer. Even before the trial he had demanded from the police the return of his son's remains and defiantly completed their burning. Throughout Wales sermons were preached against him, and one night a mob attacked his cottage. The aged Dr Price was chased into the hills, while Gwenllian guarded their home with dogs and pistols.

The couple began rebuilding their family when Gwenllian gave birth to a daughter, Penelope, followed by the long-wanted son, also named Iesu Grist. The father was ninety at the time, vigorous as ever and still walking to visit patients in his fox-skin headdress. About two years later he had a fall and had to stay in bed, but patients flocked to him from all parts of the country, and he treated them up to the week before his death in January 1893. He died after drinking a glass of champagne, which he took instead of cider when he felt unwell.

He left a will with precise instructions about the disposal of his body. It was to be a cremation of course, the first ever held officially in Wales, and his ashes were to be scattered to the four winds, 'thus helping the grass to grow and the flowers to bloom'. The news of his death spread quickly throughout Wales, and a crowd of over twenty thousand people assembled to witness the last rites, besieging his shabby old cottage and drinking the pubs dry in the nearby small town of Llantrisant. At seven in the morning the funeral procession approached the field where the pyre had been prepared for the burning. Iesu Grist, wearing a miniature version of his father's fox-skin outfit, followed the coffin, together with his sisters and Gwenllian in traditional Welsh costumes. The huge crowd pressed upon them so eagerly that the police had difficulty in keeping order. The site of the cremation had been chosen by Price and was marked with a sixty-foot pole topped with the image of a crescent moon. The body was consumed there in a great fire, and after the flames had died down the people combed through the ashes for relics of the old magician. In the following weeks thousands more visitors arrived on the scene. Gwenllian issued tickets of admission to the cremation field, and her family did a good trade selling photographs of Dr Price and other mementoes.

The Last Druid

The Pontypridd Archdruid, Evan Davies, or Myfyr Morganwg, whose life-span (1808–88) closely coincided with Price's, was rather overshadowed by his flamboyant rival, but the two of them joined forces on many occasions to promote their common cause. In his book on the Druid philosophy Keith Woolnough pictures one of their meetings:

'At Llangollen railway station in June 1864 there was gathered together the most curious group of Welsh eccentrics imaginable. Dr William Price was clad in scarlet trousers, white shirt and green waistcoat; a great sword was at his waist and in his hand he bore a staff topped with a crescent moon emblem, like an Indian saddhu's Shiva trident. Myfyr Morganwg accompanied him, a Druid's serpent egg suspended on a chain around his neck, wearing his white Archdruid's robes. With them stood the seemingly more conventional figure of the Rev R.W. Morgan (the bard Môr Meirion) whose works on the early British church included *St Paul in Britain*, proving the apostolic origin of British Christianity. These three comprised the organizing committee for the largest, most successful Eisteddfod to date, and they were assembled on the station platform to greet the honoured guests.'

Myfyr was a gentle soul, self-educated like Iolo Morganwg and a profound Druid scholar in the same tradition. He was profound also in his reading and understanding of esoteric literature from the East. Comparing the two branches of ancient wisdom, eastern and western, he concluded that the Druid system had first arisen in Britain, spreading thence throughout the entire world. Eastern religions, he believed, were degenerate forms of the original Welsh model, and their proper reformation was primitive Christianity. Thus he reconciled the Christian nonconformist faith into which he was born with the Druid religion he adopted. This was not good enough for the local chapel ministers, but Myfyr stood firm against their charges of heresy and accused them of having so corrupted the true faith that they were now 'mere fortune-tellers'.

Unlike Price, Myfyr was no great orator or popular leader, but he was punctilious in keeping up the Druid services at the Pontypridd Rocking Stone. It was the centre of his cult, and after the lapse of Price's scheme to encase it in a tower, he and his followers set about improving it according to the orthodox notion of how a Druid temple should look. The model was a plate from William Stukeley's book on Avebury, representing its stone circles and avenues in the form of a giant serpent, symbol of Druid wisdom. In giving Wales an Avebury of its own, Myfyr built one of the strangest megalithic monuments ever conceived. Surrounding the Rocking Stone he erected two circles of standing stones, joined by an avenue to a smaller circle, the serpent's head. The eyes were formed by two other stones, carved with symbols in the Druid alphabet as discovered by Iolo Morganwg.

The serpent temple was used for bardic assemblies by the last of the Pontypridd Druids, Morien. He was a reporter on the *Western Mail* and wrote some remarkable books with titles such as *The Light of Britannia* and *The Royal Winged Son of Stonehenge and Avebury* on the Druid philosophy. He identified the Rocking Stone as an image of Noah's ark and found Welsh locations for the sacred myths of the Greeks and Hebrews. Christianity, he wrote, 'is the venerable religion of the Druids, brought back to the Isles of the Gentiles from the East, under a Greek name.' It is generally agreed that Morien's exposition of Druidism can fully be understood only by an initiate of the Welsh mysteries – and such people are no longer to be found. With the death of Morien in 1928 the Druidic line of succession became extinct.

JERUSALEM IN SCOTLAND
AND OTHER FINDINGS
OF A REVISIONIST GEOGRAPHER

In the winter of 1910 Dr Orville Owen of Detroit (whose exploits in the decoding of Shakespeare are summarized in a later chapter) was engaged in the Great Baconian Treasure Hunt around Chepstow Castle. He was hoping to discover valuable relics concealed there by Sir Francis Bacon, together with documents proving his authorship of the works of Shakespeare. Owen's excavations in the bed of the river Wye became a rallying point for mystics and adventurers and soon attracted the press. Keenest of the journalists was a leading staff-writer on the *Daily Mail*, William Comyns Beaumont. He agreed a contract with Dr Owen for the results of the treasure hunt to be reported exclusively in his paper, and arranged to write a series of articles about the discovery of Bacon's hoard. Beaumont had an advantage over other journalists in being himself a confirmed Baconian. He fell readily under the spell of Dr Owen, developed complete faith in his cipher and, even after the search was abandoned with nothing to show for it, remained a true believer. Years later he wrote a book, *The Private Life of the Virgin Queen*, upholding the established belief among Baconian decoders, that Francis Bacon was the natural son of Queen Elizabeth.

Baconianism, however, was the most conventional of Comyns Beaumont's heresies. None of the other unusual thinkers mentioned in this book can rival him in the number and strangeness of the unorthodox theories he propagated. Like Ignatius Donnelly he believed in Atlantis and in the past destruction of civilization on earth by the impact of a comet; but to these theories he gave peculiar twists of his own, and in the field of speculative geography his imagination outreached even that of the great Minnesotan.

Born in 1873, Beaumont went to public school but avoided university by accepting the post of private secretary to a rich American diplomat. He travelled with his employer to India, America and other parts of the world, meeting many of the important people in politics and finance, and began his career in journalism as foreign correspondent to the New York *Herald*. His next job was at Newcastle, writing for a local paper. There he met the daughter of an old Catholic family from nearby County Durham, and proposed marriage. Her family objected, not because of religion – Beaumont had earlier converted to Catholicism – but on account of his poverty. So the couple married in secret, and immediately parted, the bridegroom going off on a mission abroad while the bride returned innocently to her family. It was three years before they met again, by which time Beaumont had obtained a good position in London, on the *Daily Mail*. The marriage was successful, and so was his career. He became an intimate aide to the newspaper's proprietor, Lord Northcliffe, and made his name over many years in Fleet Street as founder and editor of numerous journals concerned with politics and the arts. As editor of *The Bystander* he was the first to publish a story by Daphne Du Maurier, who was his niece, his sister's daughter.

To the public eye Comyns Beaumont was handsome, talented, worldly, well-connected and the last sort of person one would normally suspect of heresy. Yet in his mind strange ideas were brewing. Some are hinted at in his autobiography, *A Rebel in Fleet Street*, which is mostly an account of his professional career, but also includes warnings about a Zionist plot to subvert the British Empire and a brief outline of his unusual opinions on earthquakes and volcanoes. In 1909 he had been to the scene of a disastrous earthquake at Messina in Sicily, which had killed 200,000 people the year before, and had come to believe that all such upheavals were caused by 'meteoric impacts which in turn are closely related to cometary movements'. That belief was the cornerstone for Beaumont's revolutionary theories of history and geography.

Family reminiscences tell of Beaumont returning from work to his large, comfortable house and, after dinner, retiring to his study for long spells of reading and writing. His main subjects were mythology, early history, geology and ancient astronomical records. In all of them he found convincing evidence that the earth had suffered many cataclysms in the course of its history, the most recent having occurred in about 1322 BC. These were due to bits of dismembered planets striking the earth in the form of giant comets and altering its size and orbit. When his children asked about his writings, he terrified them with tales of collapsing worlds and the prediction that a monster comet would crash to earth in December 1919. The uneventful passing of that date only intensified his belief in the rest of his theories – as is invariably the case with doomsday prophets – and in middle age he published two books on world catastrophes, directing them at geology professors, who unanimously ignored them. It was not until he was retired and over seventy that he undertook the great work of his life, a massive trilogy in which every supposed fact about ancient history was overturned.

In the first of the series, *The Riddle of Prehistoric Britain,* Beaumont identified the British Isles as Atlantis, the original paradise and cradle of the Aryan race by which civilization was spread to all other lands. Some of its members were giants, responsible for building the great rock piles on the tors of Devon and Cornwall, and among them were skilled artificers who invented bombs, firearms and flying machines. Their merchant navies traded as far afield as South America, and everywhere they planted colonies. Nationalistic writers of many different countries have made sweeping claims for their own people as the original culture-bearers; but, in the audacity of his pretensions on behalf of the British, Beaumont surpassed them all.

He stripped the entire ancient world of its history, myths, culture and sacred sites and transferred them wholesale to Britain. Egypt and its Pharaohs were not, as commonly believed, located in North Africa but in western Scotland. Also in that land were ancient Greece, Israel and Babylonia with all their legendary heroes. Mount Olympus, throne of the gods, was really Ben Nevis, the first site of Athens was the town of Dumbarton, the battle of Thermopylae was fought at Glencoe, and Ur of the Chaldees flourished near the Stones of Stenness in the Orkney Islands. From that former Atlantean centre Abraham migrated to Wiltshire and settled near the stone circle at Avebury, which Beaumont identified as Mizpah, Thebes, the dragon's teeth sown by Cadmus, an astronomical temple to Saturn and the image of a destructive comet. Having appropriated the whole of antiquity for Britain, Beaumont had the problem of finding enough British sites to accommodate the cities and landmarks of many different lands. This he solved by giving each of the prominent places in Britain several names from a variety of ancient cultures.

The conspiratorial cast of mind which caused him to perceive a Zionist plot against Britain also revealed to him the extent to which the Old Testament had been tampered with. The Holy Land was not originally in Palestine but in the British Isles and a part of Scandinavia which, in antediluvian times, was separated from Britain by a narrow stretch of water known to antiquity as the Hellespont. The destruction of Atlantis, Noah's flood and similar catastrophe legends all over the world referred to one and the same event, the fall of a huge double comet made up of fragments from a collapsed planet. It landed in Scotland, not far from Edinburgh which in those days was called Jerusalem. The accident was considered a miracle because Jerusalem was then under siege by a colonial army, equipped with superior firearms and led by a brilliant but sinister character whom Beaumont identified simultaneously as Moses, Zoroaster, Silenus and Odin. By the storms, floods and earthquakes which followed the invading host was destroyed, and so was much of Atlantis-Britain. The bulk of the comet increased the size of the earth and knocked it further away from the sun, lengthening the period of its orbit from 360 to 365¼ days and altering its climate. The British Isles, which had previously enjoyed sub-tropical weather, became cold and misty. Many of the surviving population migrated south, founding colonies which they named after districts of their homeland, Egypt, Israel, Greece and so on. Yet the stricken lands of the North continued to be the centre of world culture. Jerusalem was rebuilt on its ancient site in Edinburgh, York flourished as Babylon, Lincoln as Antioch, London as Damascus, Bristol as both Sodom and Tarshish, and Bath as the Philistine city of Gath. The Holy Family settled near Glastonbury, where Jesus was born, and his entire mission took place in Somerset, then known as Galilee.

In the second and third parts of his trilogy (*Britain the Key to World History* and the still unpublished *After Atlantis: the Greatest Story Never Told*) Beaumont closely identified the geography of Somerset with that of the Holy Land. Glastonbury was Bethel, the fortress of Abraham, the birthplace of Christianity and the original site of the Garden of Eden. Its Tor hill was formerly known as Mount Tabor, and it was to this spot that Joseph of Arimathaea sailed from Jerusalem (Edinburgh), navigating the inland waters of Somerset, then called the Red Sea, after passing through the Bristol Channel or Sea of Galilee. On his route was the land of Gadara, situated at Clifton near Bristol, where the Gadarene swine had earlier plunged into the Avon Gorge near the present Suspension Bridge.

The Romans invaded Britain for the sake of its rich minerals, and at about the same time they are recorded as having besieged and destroyed Jerusalem. The Emperor Hadrian, who built the famous wall against the Picts and Scots, was also active in the campaign against the Jews, and several of the Roman generals were said to have served both in Britain and at Jerusalem, even though the journey from Britain to Palestine was long and arduous. In Beaumont's opinion they did not have so far to travel, because Jerusalem in those days was still situated at Edinburgh. This became one of the main pillars of his thesis. Ancient descriptions of Jerusalem, he found, applied far more closely to Edinburgh than to the 'squalid and provincial' city in Palestine. Arthur's Seat, for example, was more worthy to be the true Mount of Olives than the insignificant hill which now bears that name, and Beaumont was gratified to discover that a seaside suburb of Edinburgh, Joppa, had the same name as the traditional port for Jerusalem. The London *Daily News* (13 November 1950) published Beaumont's offer to conduct any qualified archaeologist round Britain and prove to him 'that this island and not Palestine is the Holy Land of the Bible'.

If Beaumont was right, the obvious question is why everyone else should believe that Jerusalem and the Holy Land were always where they are today. Beaumont's answer was that Britain was systematically robbed. Among those responsible was Hadrian, who moved Athens away from Dumbarton, not only in name but physically, transporting some of its finer buildings for re-erection in Mediterranean Greece. But the main culprit was Constantine the Great. According to Beaumont he was a Yorkshireman, by upbringing if not birth, and his mother, Helena, was the daughter of that popular British ruler, Old King Cole. He was thus well aware of the true location of Jerusalem, at Edinburgh, but he found that fact inconvenient. It was too far from his own capital in Asia Minor. He engaged therefore in one of those grand conspiracies so dear to the heart of Comyns Beaumont, tricking his old mother into finding the supposed True Cross in Palestine and announcing that on that barren spot was the Jerusalem of old. He then gathered together the writings of every ancient and contemporary chronicler, destroyed every text that placed the Holy Land in Britain and severely censored those documents he spared. Beaumont compiled a long list of classical works known to have existed but now lost, and suggested that they had fallen victim to Constantine's literary purges because they did not fit in with his new pattern of sacred geography. All that has come down to us of the original early histories is a few doctored fragments.

Religion had no interest for Beaumont personally, since in his opinion all legends of gods and their interventions on earth could be explained in meteorological terms. Successive cataclysms, caused by falls of comets, had traumatic effects on the minds of their survivors and on the human memory over many generations. Stone monuments were first constructed as places of refuge from an elemental upheaval, and later to record the event and placate the gods. Records of the most recent disaster, identified as such by Beaumont, included the ancient Golspie Stone of Sutherland and other monuments of the same period and district, bearing mysterious carved symbols, notably a pair of linked circles which he took to be an image of the double comet of 1322 BC. Cometary impacts were preceded by strange disorders in nature, such as earth tremors and volcanic eruptions, which were remembered in history as portents of divine wrath. Thus he interpreted the Old Testament stories of the plagues of Egypt and the destruction of Pharaoh's host in the Red Sea as references to the great disaster, described in other myths as the ruin of Atlantis and Noah's flood, caused by the fall of a comet on the northern part of Britain.

In deriving all religion, mythology and the history of our era from one single cataclysmic event, Beaumont produced a simplified, materialistic theory of cosmology with the same type of appeal as the belief in extra-terrestrial origins of culture, pioneered by Brinsley le Poer Trench and popularized by Erich von Däniken. Yet Beaumont's reputation and the sales of his books never approached those of the latter author. An evident reason is that he buttressed every item in his thesis with such a large body of evidence that much of his writing, despite its stunning originality, was inclined to be long-winded and tedious. No doubt also the times were against him. Among contemporaries, however, he was not entirely without allies. The psychic archaeologist, J. Foster Forbes, also wrote books showing the British to have been culture-bearers to the world as heirs to the wise Atlanteans, and Beaumont's work found favour among some of the British Israelites, even though his notions on the origins and destiny of the British people were diametrically opposed to their own. But in his lifetime he attracted no significant following, and it is only recently that his works have found a champion, a man prepared to devote his life to the restoration of Jerusalem to Edinburgh.

In 1975 a Comyns Beaumont society was incorporated at Philadelphia, Pennsylvania. Its founder and moving spirit was Mr Robert C. Stephanos, an American psychologist of Albanian descent – which may be significant, in that the Albanians now claim to be the only nation practising pure atheism, having pulled down all their mosques and churches; and because of their traditional associations with Scotland or Alban, evident in the name of their country and their liking for kilts and bagpipes. Stephanos had long been interested in theories of former terrestrial cataclysms and was an early supporter of the most recent catastrophist, Immanuel Velikovsky. When Velikovsky's fortunes were at their lowest ebb, when his writings were boycotted by academic publishers, and college professors refused to permit his fantastic theories to be aired in front of their students, Stephanos came to his rescue. In 1973 he talked the authorities of Philadelphia's Temple University into inviting Velikovsky to lecture. The audience was large and enthusiastic, and Velikovsky followed up with a series of lectures at other colleges, also arranged by Stephanos. The novelty of his ideas, and the reputation he had earned as a martyr through the attempted suppression of his first book, *Worlds in Collision*, were attractive to his young listeners. But as his cult grew, Velikovsky became nervous and suspicious. He quarrelled with Stephanos who, thus deprived of a cause, looked round for another. Velikovsky was mean with his acknowledgments, referring only once, in a disdainful footnote, to his great catastrophist predecessor, Ignatius Donnelly, and not at all to Comyns Beaumont. Yet Beaumont's theory of destructive comets was the same as Velikovsky's in all but some minor details. His books were hard to find, particularly in America, but Stephanos finally succeeded and, having read them, became a convert to Beaumont's entire thesis, his eccentric geography included. After founding The Beaumont Society: Scientific Endeavours Inc., he set off for England to research Beaumont's life.

He interviewed members of the family, including Beaumont's niece, Dame Daphne Du Maurier, and his daughter, Ursula Pike, who lived in Tipperary. Mrs Pike had exciting news, of a kind which all literary researchers dream about, news of an unknown manuscript. As published, Beaumont's trilogy was incomplete. He was known to have been at work on a third part, but it was thought to have been either lost or never finished. Enquiring about it, Stephanos was told that there might still be a copy in existence. He encouraged the whole family in search, and in an attic of one of Beaumont's granddaughters the missing manuscript was found — just in time to save it from the mice nibbling through its margins. Having acquired copyright in the manuscript and Beaumont's other books, Stephanos returned home to arrange publication of them all. Beaumont, he says, is too important a writer to be allowed to languish in obscurity. One may therefore hope that *After Atlantis: the Greatest Story Never Told,* the crowning part of Beaumont's trilogy, will soon be astounding the public as delightfully as it has astounded the few whom Robert Stephanos has kindly made privileged to read it. He himself is planning to retire to Britain and collaborate with the independent Comyns Beaumont Society, flourishing in Edinburgh, in exposing the forgeries by which Constantine the Great convinced everybody else that that city was not really Jerusalem.

THE PEOPLE WITH
HOLES IN THEIR HEADS

Amanda Feilding lives in a charming flat looking over London's river with her companion, Joey Mellen, and their infant son, Rock. She is a successful painter, and she and Joey have an art gallery in a fashionable street off the King's Road. Another of her talents is for politics. At the last two General Elections she stood for Parliament in Chelsea, more than doubling her vote on the second occasion from 49 to 139. It does not sound much, but the cause for which she stands is unfamiliar and lacks obvious appeal. Feilding and her voters demand that trepanning operations be made freely available on the National Health. Trepanation means cutting a hole in your skull.

The founder of the trepanation movement is a Dutch savant, Dr Bart Huges. In 1962 he made a discovery which his followers proclaim as the most significant in modern times. One's state and degree of consciousness, he realized, are related to the volume of blood in the brain. According to his theory of evolution, the adoption of an upright stance brought certain benefits to the human race, but it caused the flow of blood through the head to be limited by gravity, thus reducing the range of human consciousness. Certain parts of the brain ceased or reduced their functions while others, particularly those parts relating to speech and reasoning, became emphasized in compensation. One can redress the balance by a number of methods, such as standing on one's head, jumping from a hot bath into a cold one or the use of drugs; but the wider consciousness thus obtained is only temporary. Bart Huges shared the common goal of mystics and poets in all ages: he wanted to achieve permanently the higher level of vision, which he associated with an increased volume of blood in the capillaries of the brain.

The higher state of mind he sought was that of childhood. Babies are born with skulls unsealed, and it is not until one is adult that the bony carapace is formed which completely encloses the membranes sur-

144

rounding the brain and inhibits their pulsations in response to heart-beats. In consequence, the adult loses touch with the dreams, imagination and intense perceptions of the child. His mental balance becomes upset by egoism and neuroses. To cure these problems, first in himself and then for the whole world, Dr Huges returned his cranium to something like the condition of infancy by cutting out a small disc of bone with an electric drill. Experiencing immediate beneficial effects from this operation, he began preaching to anyone who would listen the doctrine of trepanation. By liberating his brain from its total imprison-ment in his skull, he claimed to have restored its pulsations, increased the volume of blood in it and acquired a more complete, satisfying state of consciousness than grown-up people normally enjoy. The medical and legal authorities reacted to Huges's discovery with horror and rewarded him with a spell in a Dutch lunatic asylum.

Joseph Mellen met Bart Huges in 1965 in Ibiza and quickly became his leading, or rather one and only, disciple. Years later he wrote a book called *Bore Hole,* the contents of which are summarized in its opening sentence: 'This is the story of how I came to drill a hole in my skull to get permanently high.'

The first part of *Bore Hole* is about Joey's earlier life, preceding his conversion to the perforated head movement. He was born within a few days of the outbreak of the Second World War, was educated at Eton College and Oxford University and, at the age of twenty-one, found himself in London, on course for a career as a chartered accountant. The marvellous era of the 1960s was then dawning. New modes of music, combined with the sudden appearance and popularity of all sorts of drugs, were giving rise to radically new styles of thought and fashion. Joey had always been an enthusiast. Following the example of his father, a former Oxford rowing blue, he had become a renowned sportsman during his schooldays, ending up as captain of the Oxford University boxing team. In London, the devotion he had paid to boxing was transferred to drugs, beginning with amphetamines and cannabis. At about that time a book came into his hands called *Wisdom, Madness and Folly: the Philosophy of a Lunatic.* Its author was a manic-depressive, and the insights he recorded were similar to those Joey was experiencing through drugs, persuading him that life at large offered more interest and excitement than could be found in an accountant's office. He abandoned professional studies for life in London's High Bohemia.

The account in *Bore Hole* of its author's career during the 1960s constitutes a valuable record of the peculiar atmosphere of the period. Joey's friends included drug-addict crooks and con-men, as well as many of the young artists and aristocrats of avant-garde society. Among these were Jane Ormesby-Gore and her future husband, Michael Rainey, whose Chelsea boutique purveyed colourful outfits to Beatles, Rolling Stones and others of fame and rank; Christopher Gibbs who provided the same sort of customers with fine English furniture and country houses; Kenneth Anger the mystical film-maker; Sir Mark Palmer, the Queen's page who rose to become an itinerant horse-dealer; Lord Timothy Willoughby who disappeared from his boat in the Mediterranean; and Joshua Macmillan, a grandson of the then Prime Minister and an early victim of alcohol and amphetamines combined. Their favourite resort was Torremolinos in the south of Spain, where Rainey's sister, Shelagh Tennant, had a night-club. She disapproved of Joey's passion for drugs, but liked him enough to bear him a daughter, whom they presented to his mother for adoption. With other friends, the beatniks, bohemians and early hippies of Torremolinos, he enjoyed the life of a free spirit and the diversity of sex and drugs on offer at the time. After an experience of mescalin he decided that he had only one drug problem, how to obtain more of it. Soon the pleasures of Torremolinos became widely famed, waves of fresh hedonists arrived for a share in them, and Joey and his friends were impelled to seek new playgrounds. He found his in Ibiza where, on his first evening, he met Bart Huges and took his first LSD trip.

Many writers have tried to describe the effects of drugs such as LSD, mostly without conveying very much. Joey's effort in *Bore Hole* is at least intelligible: 'I felt brilliant, god-like, able to understand everything. At the same time as being fascinated by the way I could see things as though through a magnifying glass, I could hear all the sounds of the town outside the house as well as those inside, and each perception registered quite clearly, distinct from all the others though related to them, like the various instruments in an orchestra. Now I knew what eternity meant. Time seemed to stop and still everything was moving. I was ecstatic. I kept eating sugarlumps. I could feel that this was the energy I needed to get round this universe in my brain.'

The eating of sugar during the LSD trip was due to another of Bart Huges's discoveries. His explanation for the effects of taking drugs was that they cause constriction of the veins carrying blood from the head back to the heart, thus raising the volume of blood in the capillaries from which the brain takes nourishment. This is in the form of oxygen and glucose, so if there is not enough sugar in the blood, the brain is liable to pangs of starvation, resulting in feelings of unease or horror and, as they say, a bad trip. Those under Bart's influence made sure that they took plenty of sugar, fruit juice and other sweet things with their LSD, claiming that their drug experiences were thereby made delightful and never became frightening.

It was not so with other people. As the powerful acid (lysergic acid diethylamide or LSD) made the rounds of Ibiza, the sensations of awe and ecstasy it first inspired quickly turned to fear. It is a drug which accentuates all perceptions, including self-awareness, and many who took it casually for pleasure were shaken to the core by the images of themselves encountered under its influence. Waves of paranoia swept over the drug-fanciers of Ibiza. Dr Huges diagnosed sugar-lack, and he and Joey did their best to spread the word about sugar-cubes and 'Brainbloodvolume' among the stricken acid heroes. It was in vain. No one seemed to have time or patience for their lectures about the connection between sugar, the brain and LSD. There was a nasty scene when Joey introduced a French woman tourist to acid, insisting that she take sugar with it. She had previously been drinking, and her combined ingestions caused her to vomit and lose control. She fled to her husband who accused Joey of trying to poison her.

Back in London, Joey took on the task of preparing his fellow-countrymen for the coming of LSD. He exhibited the magnificent scroll with coloured diagrams which Bart had designed to demonstrate the mechanisms of Brainbloodvolume, and he also composed an open letter to drug dealers about the advice they should give their clients on taking acid. A notable character in London at the time was Michael Holingshead, who had assumed that name in reference to the mystical third eye, or hole in the head, as a symbol of enlightenment. Holingshead was the original acid guru who had initiated Timothy Leary by giving him his first taste of LSD. His flat in Pont Street, Chelsea, was headquarters of the World Psychedelic Centre where neophytes could enjoy their LSD experience in a pleasant atmosphere with music and soft lights. Joey told him about Bart Huges's discoveries, but the guru was unreceptive to the idea of making a physical hole in his head, maintaining that the third eye should be considered purely as a symbol. But he was won over to the theory of sugar and fruit-juice as an aid to LSD-trippers, and he helped circulate the open letter among acid-dealers. The World Psychedelic Centre became so popular that it attracted the attention of the police, who closed it down and arrested its officials, Joey included. In the Magistrate's Court he spoke eloquently in defence of LSD, elaborating on a text from Bart Huges's writings, 'The evolutionary religion protects the right of the individual to have his own blood in his own brain.' The Court was evidently impressed and fined Joey £20, considerably less than the other defendants.

Early in 1966 money was raised to bring Bart Huges over to London and lodge him in a Chelsea flat. LSD was the sensation of the time, and there were many who believed that the unique experiences and insights it provided were about to revolutionize patterns of thought and behaviour throughout the world. The press was full of the subject, and Bart and Joey were much in demand for lectures and interviews. Inexperienced in the ways of journalists, they had supposed that their theories would be reported as seriously as they were expounded. They were soon disillusioned. After a lecture they gave at the respected bookshop, Better Books, they were approached for an interview by two journalists of the Sunday newspaper, *The People*. Their attitude was sympathetic, Bart and Joey accepted them as genuine seekers after truth and they spent a whole night together in deep study of Brainblood-volume and trepanation. Eager to see how the message had been presented to the world, Joey was out first thing Sunday morning for the paper. In it was a crude article about Bart under a banner headline: THIS DANGEROUS IDIOT SHOULD BE THROWN OUT.

Wild, virulent articles in the popular press about the orgies of drug-fiends were varied by occasional attempts on the part of journalists to present the LSD phenomenon in serious terms. The results were sometimes ludicrous, as when the BBC asked Joey to arrange for their team to televise a group of acid-takers. Recording rational interviews with people on LSD proved no easy task; George Andrews, veteran author and cannabis-smoker, managed to recite some poetry, but nothing coherent emerged about the advantages of sugar and trepana-tion. In the end the BBC had to fill in with shots of some writhing figures, as if suffering from belladonna poisoning, which they presented as victims of a bad LSD trip.

Bart Huges's ideas had their best reception among artists and bohemians. Among those impressed was Heathcote Williams, who published a dialogue between Joey and Bart in the literary *Transatlantic Review* and made a trepanation scene the climax of his award-winning play, *AC–DC*. An important convert was Julie Felix, a world-famous (in London) American singer in the style of Joan Baez. She was eager to promote the doctrine of trepanation and recorded some of the propaganda songs which Joey had composed, including *Brainblood-volume*, *The Great Brain Robbery* and *Sugarlack*.

The time came when Joey felt he had preached enough and that he now had to act. He did not agree with Holingshead that the third eye was merely a figure of speech, believing in its physical attainment through self-trepanation. Support for this can be found in archaeology. Skulls of ancient people all over the world give evidence that their owners were skilfully trepanned during their lifetimes, and many of these appear to have been of noble or priestly castes. The medical practice of trepanation was continued up to the present century in treatment for madness, the hole in the skull being seen as a way of relieving pressure on the brain or letting out the devils that possessed it. By his scientific explanation of the reasons for the operation, Bart Huges had removed it from the area of superstition, and Joey Mellen proposed to be the second person to perform it on himself in the interest of enlightenment.

Bart had become a close friend of Amanda Feilding, and they went off to Amsterdam together while Joey took care of Amanda's flat. This was the opportunity he had been waiting for to bore a hole in his head.

The most gripping passages in *Bore Hole* describe his various attempts to complete the operation. They are also extremely gruesome, and those who lack medical curiosity would do well to read no further. Yet to those who might contemplate trepanation for and by themselves, Joey's experiences are a salutary warning. It should be emphasized that neither he, Bart nor Amanda has ever recommended people to follow their example by performing their own operations. For years they have been looking for doctors who could understand their theories and would agree to trepan volunteer patients as a form of therapy. Strangely enough, not one member of the medical profession has been converted.

In a surgical store Joey found a trepan instrument, a kind of auger or corkscrew designed to be worked by hand. It was much cheaper and,

Joey felt, more sensitive than an electric drill. Its main feature was a metal spike, surrounded by a ring of saw-teeth. The spike was meant to be driven into the skull, holding the trepan steady until the revolving saw made a groove, after which it could be retracted. If all went well, the saw-band should remove a disc of bone and expose the brain.

Joey's first attempt at self-trepanation was a fiasco. He had no previous medical experience, and the needles he had bought for administering a local anaesthetic to the crown of his head proved to be too thin and crumpled up or broke. Next day he obtained some stouter needles, took a tab of LSD to steady his nerves and set to in earnest. First he made an incision to the bone, and then applied the trepan to his bared skull. But the first part of the operation, driving the spike into the bone, was impossible to accomplish. Joey described it as like trying to uncork a bottle from the inside. He realized he needed help and telephoned Bart in Amsterdam, who promised he would come over and assist at the next operation. This plan was frustrated by the Home Office, which listed Dr Huges as an undesirable visitor to Britain and barred his entry.

Amanda agreed to take his place. Soon after her return to London she helped Joey re-open the wound in his head and, by pressing the trepan with all her might against his skull, managed to get the spike to take hold and the saw-teeth to bite. Joey then took over at cranking the saw. Once again he had swallowed some LSD. After a long period of sawing, just as he was about to break through, he suddenly fainted. Amanda called an ambulance and he was taken to hospital, where horrified doctors told him that he was lucky to be alive and that if he had drilled a fraction of an inch further he would have killed himself.

The psychiatrists took a particular interest in his case, and a group of them arranged to examine him. Before this could be done, he had to appear in court on a charge of possessing a small amount of cannabis. The magistrate demanded another psychiatrist's report and remanded him for a week in prison.

There followed a period of embarrassment as the rumour went round London that Joey Mellen had trepanned himself, whereas in fact he had failed to do so. As soon as possible, therefore, he prepared for a third attempt. Proceeding as before, but now with the benefit of experience, he soon found the groove from the previous operation and began to saw through the sliver of bone separating him from enlightenment or, as the doctors had predicted, instant death. What followed is best quoted from *Bore Hole*.

'After some time there was an ominous sounding schlurp and the sound of bubbling. I drew the trepan out and the gurgling continued. It sounded like air bubbles running under the skull as they were pressed out. I looked at the trepan and there was a bit of bone in it. At last! On closer inspection I saw that the disc of bone was much deeper on one side than on the other. Obviously the trepan had not been straight and had gone through at one point only, then the piece of bone had snapped off and come out. I was reluctant to start drilling again for fear of damaging the brain membranes with the deeper part while I was cutting through the rest or of breaking off a splinter. If only I had had an electric drill it would have been so much simpler. Amanda was sure I was through. There seemed no other explanation of the schlurping noises. I decided to call it a day. At that time I thought that any hole would do, no matter what size. I bandaged up my head and cleared away the mess.'

There was still doubt in his mind as to whether he had really broken through and, if so, whether the hole was big enough to restore pulsation to his brain. The operation had left him with a feeling of wellbeing, but he realized that it could simply be from relief at having ended it. To put the matter beyond doubt, he decided to bore another hole at a new spot just above the hairline, this time using an electric drill. In the spring of 1970 Amanda was in America and Joey did the operation alone. He applied the drill to his forehead, but after half an hour's work the electric cable burnt out. Once again he was frustrated. An engineer in the flat below him was able to repair the instrument, and next day he set out to finish the job. 'This time I was not in any doubt. The drill head went at least an inch deep through the hole. A great gush of blood followed my withdrawal of the drill. In the mirror I could see the blood in the hole rising and falling with the pulsation of the brain.'

The result was all he had hoped for. During the next four hours he felt his spirits rising higher until he reached a state of freedom and serenity which, he claims, has been with him ever since.

For some time now he had been sharing a flat with Amanda, and when she came back from America she immediately noticed the change in him. This encouraged her to join him on the mental plane by doing her own trepanation. The operation was carefully recorded. She had obtained a cine-camera, and Joey stood by, filming, as she attacked her head with an electric drill. The film shows her carefully at work, dressed in a blood-spattered white robe. She shaves her hair, makes an incision in her head with a scalpel and calmly starts drilling. Blood spurts as she penetrates the skull. She lays aside the drill and with a triumphant smile advances towards Joey and the camera.

Ever since, Joey and Amanda have lived and worked together in harmony. From the business of buying old prints to colour and resell, they have progressed to ownership of the Pigeonhole Gallery and seem reasonably prosperous. They have also started a family. There is nothing apparently abnormal about them, and many of their old friends agree in finding them even more pleasant and contented since their operations. There is plenty of leisure in their lives, mingled with the kind of activities they most enjoy. These of course include talking and writing about trepanation. They have lectured widely in Europe and America to groups of doctors and other interested people, showing the film of Amanda's self-operation, entitled *Heartbeat in the Brain*. It is generally received with awe, the sight of blood often causing people to faint. At one showing in London a film critic described the audience 'dropping off their seats one by one like ripe plums'. Yet it was not designed to be gruesome. The soundtrack is of soothing music, and the surgical scenes alternate with some delightful motion studies of Amanda's pet pigeon, Birdie, as a symbol of peace and wisdom.

A sixteenth-century trepanation.

BIBLIOMANIACS

Bibliomania, the passionate desire to handle, possess and accumulate books, has been the subject of warnings by many writers, mostly those who have been touched by it themselves. Others, however, have defended it on the grounds that, since as one grows older one's level of insanity inevitably increases, it is best to adopt one of the more liberal forms of madness such as obsession with books.

Some truly horrid examples are recorded of fanatical book collecting, and of those who have been ruined by it, alienated wives and families and even been driven from their own homes by their libraries. Thomas Rawlinson, a collector of the early eighteenth century, stuffed his rooms at Gray's Inn so full of books that he had to sleep in the passage. He then moved into a large mansion which he shared with his brother, and did the same thing there. By the time Thomas died, aged forty-four, there was scarcely a place where the brothers could sit among the books, papers and dust of their collection.

A bibliomaniac of Paris, M. Boulard, bought books indiscriminately until he owned more than 600,000 of them. Shelf space in his house had long given out, so he filled trunks and cupboards with books, and then the attics, cellars, storerooms and the floors of every other room. The weight was so onerous that the house began to collapse, so Boulard bought more houses, six in all, which he filled entirely with books, gradually driving out the tenants before the rising flood of his collection.

Bibliomania is the title of a book published in 1809 by the Rev. Thomas Frognall Dibdin, whose principal subject was the outstanding bibliomaniac of his time, Richard Heber. Dibdin came from a show-business family; his uncle was the writer of such long-popular songs as 'Tom Bowling' and ''Twas in the good ship Rover', later to be parodied by rugger players. With Heber and other bibliomaniacs of the time Dibdin founded the Roxburghe Club, where the first toast was to 'the cause of Bibliomania all over the world', followed by more toasts to famous printers and book-collectors of ages past. It was a time when book prices were low, and Dibdin and his fellows could pick up for a few shillings manuscripts now worth many thousands of pounds. He had a sharp nose for a bargain and, though a clergyman, did not spare even his reverend colleagues when it came to book business. On a visit to Lincoln Cathedral he noticed in the library some rare old volumes, the worth of which was quite unrecognized by the unworldly clerics. Dibdin offered to help improve the library by providing it with up-to-date books by the best authors in exchange for the old ones. The Lincoln clergy accepted, and were delighted with the £300 worth of modern books which the Rev. Dibdin chose for them. Their mood changed, however, when they heard that their benefactor had sold just one of the old books from their library for £1,800. When Dibdin called again, eager to make a further exchange, they shut the door of the library in his face.

Richard Heber was a prodigy of bibliomania. Born in 1774, the son of a rich clergyman at Hodnet in Cheshire, he compiled at the age of eight a catalogue of the library he had already built up, with detailed instructions on how the books were to be bound. Throughout his school days he bought far beyond the limit of his means, becoming a familiar figure at book auctions. His father saw his rectory being overrun by books, followed by accounts from dealers and book-binders, and did his best to curb Richard's frenzy. It was in vain. Richard's magpie career went on unchecked and he became a discriminating buyer of old rarities. He was also that rare type among bibliomaniacs, a scholar, actually reading some portion of the writings he accumulated. When he went up to Oxford he further annoyed his father by editing for publication a classical work which the good clergyman found improper.

When old Mr Heber died, leaving a fine estate and fortune, Richard was freed of his only previous restraint, lack of money. His book-buying exploits became fantastic. It seemed as if he wanted to own every book that ever was, and not just one copy of each. He used to say that every gentleman needed at least three copies of a book, one for his country house library, one for reading and one to lend to friends. But three copies was by no means his limit. Several of his collections of different copies or editions of the same work would have formed a considerable library on their own. He would buy the entire contents of a bookseller's catalogue or collections of many thousands of books in one lot, and he would also make diffficult journeys of hundreds of miles in pursuit of a single coveted volume. Only once was he diverted from his career, and only for a short time, when he contemplated marriage. Not that it really was a deviation, for the wife he almost chose was Miss Richardson Currer of Yorkshire, the most renowned of English women book-collectors. The proposal, in fact, was for a marriage of libraries, but either the couple or their books did not suit each other, for nothing came of the match.

Heber's appetite for books, said Dibdin, displayed 'a rapaciousness of hunger and thirst, such as the world never saw before, and is unlikely to see again'. Holbrook Jackson summed him up as 'a bibliomaniac if ever there was one... a bibliomaniac in the most unpleasant sense of the word; no confirmed drunkard, no incurable opium-eater had less self-control; to see a book was to desire it, to desire it was to possess it; the great and strong passion of his life was to amass such a library as no individual before him had ever amassed.... His collection was omnigenous, and he never ceased to accumulate books of all kinds, buying them by all methods, in all places, at all times.'

Towards the end of his life Heber became a recluse, gloating over his treasures behind the shutters of his London house in Pimlico. In one of its rooms he had been born, and in 1833 he died in it, despairing and alone, shortly after he had sent a substantial order to a bookseller. It was his inner citadel, fabulous among bibliophiles because no one else had ever been allowed to enter it. The inquisitive Dibdin hurried at once to Pimlico to be the first to break in. 'I looked around me in amazement,' he wrote. 'I had never seen rooms, cupboards, passages, and corridors, so choked, so suffocated with books. Treble rows were here, double rows were there. Hundreds of slim quartos – several upon each other – were longitudinally placed over thin and stunted duodecimos, reaching from one extremity of a shelf to another. Up to the very ceiling the piles of volumes extended; while the floor was strewn with them, in loose and numerous heaps. When I looked on all this, and thought what might be at Hodnet, and upon the Continent, it were difficult to describe my emotions.'

From the piles of paper Dibdin was at last able to unearth Richard Heber's will. Like Shakspere's, it made no mention of any books. Indeed, it was some time before the executors could locate the manifold branches of his gigantic library. Two houses in London were found to be stuffed with books, and so was the large mansion he had inherited in Cheshire. Other houses, similarly filled, were located in Paris, Brussels, Antwerp and Ghent, and another in Germany. No one has ever been certain whether these eight repositories housed the entire library of Richard Heber, or whether he had other store-places about Europe where unknown literary treasures may still be lurking.

A monstrous paper collector

At the sale of Richard Heber's manuscripts in 1836 the largest buyer was a Worcestershire landowner, Sir Thomas Phillipps, who went on to become the largest collector ever known of old papers and documents. Born in 1792, he inherited at the age of twenty-six his father's estate at Middle Hill near Broadway, married the daughter of an Irish general and used the influence of his father-in-law to have himself made a baronet. Sir Thomas had a considerable income, all of which, together with all the money he could raise through mortgaging his property, he spent on buying manuscripts.

No individual's life has ever been better documented than that of Sir Thomas Phillipps, partly because he never threw away a scrap of paper, hoarding household bills and drafts and copies of all his correspondence, and partly because of A.N.L. Munby's five published volumes of *Phillipps Studies* (later boiled down to one volume entitled *Portrait of an Obsession*). Described in this work is the amazing series of transactions by which Phillipps built up a collection of ancient and medieval manuscripts, far more extensive than that of the British Museum or any university library. It is the most detailed history of the most extreme of bibliomaniacs. 'Tim' Munby was himself afflicted by bibliomania, but he controlled the disease through its only known antidote by becoming a bibliophile. He collected not only books but curious anecdotes about book dealers and their customers, many of which he published in later years when he was Librarian at King's College, Cambridge. Some of the best were about himself. As a young man, while working for the famous dealer Bernard Quaritch, he had acquired two medieval manuscripts which he then sold to finance a half share in a 1925 type 40 Bugatti. It was a fine vehicle but it was always breaking down, one of its gaskets giving repeated trouble. Munby repaired it with a piece of thick vellum cut from an old book. When people asked him the age of the Bugatti he was thus able to reply, 'Parts of it date back to the fifteenth century.'

There is no record of any such tomfoolery in the life of Sir Thomas Phillipps. He was serious, dry, cross and utterly obsessed. Apart from a few minor hobbies, such as abusing the Pope and issuing violently anti-Catholic tracts, his whole time was spent acquiring books and manuscripts. He would buy whole valuable libraries, booksellers' entire stocks, old records thrown out by government departments and cartloads of waste paper on the way to be pulped. Among the rubbish were many items of worth and rarity, which were thus saved from destruction. Phillipps offered higher prices for collections of old documents than the waste-paper dealers could pay, and thus broke their monopoly of the market. Other collectors followed his example, and preservation of thousands of unique records and historical documents is credited to Sir Thomas's obsession with paper.

It was impossible for any one man to catalogue this continually waxing library, but Phillipps did his best. He pressed his wife, three daughters and their governess into the task of listing manuscripts and copying out those which he thought worth publishing. A succession of resident printers issued catalogues and small editions of texts for the benefit of scholars. These activities were constantly interrupted by the intrusion of creditors . On many occasions Phillipps was so deeply in debt that he seemed on the verge of ruin. Yet he always pulled through, never selling from his library, ever adding to it. His estate buildings collapsed because he refused to spend money repairing them, and his family were forced to live, like him, as misers. He was ruthless with booksellers, demanding lengthy credit and books on approval, and then refusing payment or the return of goods until compelled by law. His treatment drove several into bankruptcy, but he could always find others to accept his huge orders.

At the age of thirty he had to flee abroad to avoid creditors. The move only made matters worse because at that time, in the turmoil after the Napoleonic Wars, many great European libraries were being dispersed. Ignoring his debts, Phillipps bought manuscripts wherever he could, enriching his collection with items which would now be almost priceless. Meanwhile he had hired a printer, Adolphus Brightley, who arrived at Middle Hill to find that he was expected to lodge and work in Broadway Tower, a monument on a lonely hilltop. This was impossible since the Tower was dilapidated, its windows had no glass in them and the only water available was that which poured through the roof and down the walls. In any case its rooms were all occupied by some local indigents. Phillipps's agent, who had become adept at running the estate without spending money, took charge of the young printer, found him temporary lodgings and joined him in a plea for help to their absent employer. But not even a small sum could be spared for the printer's expenses. Like all Phillipps's dependants he had to learn to fend for himself. He and the agent somehow evicted the people from the Tower and patched it up sufficiently for the printing press to be installed. There Brightley worked for over three years, unable to leave because all his capital was invested in the materials of his trade. In that time he gave loyal service, learning Latin and Anglo-Saxon to assist his work of printing transcriptions of old manuscripts. Finally his employer's meanness and bad temper became too much for even his tolerance, his wages fell hopelessly into arrears and he gave notice. The string of printers who succeeded him suffered as badly, or worse, and left more promptly. Each in turn was set to work on Phillipps's catalogue of his manuscripts, and each used a different size, colour and type of paper for the work. The finished catalogue, which Phillipps distributed to certain libraries and the few scholars he respected, has a unique reputation as the book which was produced by the greatest number of printers.

Lady Phillipps's father, General Molyneux, saved the day by taking over management of the Middle Hill estate and arranging a settlement of its proprietor's debts. Phillipps was thus able to return home. Immediately he began a spate of book-buying which belittled even his earlier efforts. As crates and cartloads of paper poured into it, the interior of the mansion at Middle Hill rapidly shrank. Most of the rooms were unusable for normal purposes, being filled with books, as were all the corridors in which there was barely enough room for two people to pass. When the dining room became clogged with manuscripts Phillipps locked it up, and the family had to make do with one sitting room on the ground floor and three bedrooms upstairs, poorly furnished, with peeling wallpaper and broken panes. In order that the books might easily be removed in case of fire, they were stored in long, coffin-like boxes, piled one on top of another, the fronts of which opened downwards on horizontal hinges. The walls of the Phillipps' bedroom were so thickly lined with these boxes that only a few square feet of floor remained for Lady Phillipps's dressing-table.

The strain of keeping house under these circumstances, constantly persecuted by bailiffs and writ-servers and with no sympathy from her bibliomaniac husband, became too much for Lady Phillipps. She lost her spirits, took to drugs and died at the age of thirty-seven. Immediately after the funeral Phillipps began a search for her replacement. What he needed in a wife was money, nothing else. All his affections were given to books. 'I am for sale at £50,000,' he wrote to a friend. But it was not easy to find a docile bride with that size of dowry. It was ten years before Phillipps married again, and in that period he was continually active in negotiations with fathers of unmarried ladies. Munby reckons that he made seventeen serious bids before he finally closed a deal. His approaches were crude and pecuniary. One prospective father-in-law accused him, justly, of behaving like a Smithfield cattle dealer. Finally, after much haggling, he struck a bargain for a clergyman's daughter with £3,000 a year. She was stout and amiable, and the marriage went happily until in his last years Phillipps's eccentricities became intolerable.

He also offered his daughters on the marriage market, beginning when the eldest was twelve by proposing her to his old friend, Charles Madden, who had charge of manuscripts at the British Museum. But Henrietta Phillipps had ideas of her own. One of her father's agreeable habits was of hospitality to scholars. He enjoyed the company of the many visitors to Middle Hill who came to consult his manuscripts – although he was often unable to locate a particular document among the boxes and unopened crates of his collection. The fateful visitor was James Orchard Halliwell, a brilliant young scholar from Cambridge and one of the most enigmatic figures of nineteenth-century literature. He was a dandified youth of obscure birth whose manuscript studies had procured him the highest academic honours and election as Fellow of the Royal Society before his nineteenth birthday. Later he became the leading collector of Shakespearean documents and rarities and author of the acknowledged best Life of Shakespeare. He had the greatest influence in forming the modern Shakespeare cult at Stratford-on-Avon. He was also one of the few people ever to get the better of Sir Thomas Phillipps.

Phillipps had corresponded with Halliwell about manuscripts before inviting him to Middle Hill. The young man was ingratiating and presented himself as Phillipps's eager disciple. Once in the house he began courting Henrietta and promptly asked for her hand in marriage. Her father in his usual way turned the subject to money. Halliwell had little to show in the way of income or prospects, which were what Phillipps most required of a son-in-law. And there was another objection: some nasty rumours were going around about Halliwell's character and reputation. It was even said that he was that most dreaded enemy of the bibliomaniac — a sly book thief. Phillipps withheld his consent to the marriage and, when the couple married without it, was relentless throughout the rest of his life in persecuting them.

His first opportunity for revenge on his son-in-law came soon after the wedding. Halliwell was accused of stealing manuscripts from Trinity College, Cambridge, and then selling them. The evidence was black against him, but he defended himself vigorously, speaking at public meetings and issuing an explanatory pamphlet. Somehow the matter never came to court. Phillipps, who had been urging on the prosecution, was dismayed, and he became even more so when he realized that his estates, which were entailed upon his heir, would eventually pass to the Halliwells. Lawyers advised him that there was no way of preventing James Halliwell, through his wife, from inheriting Middle Hill. That being the case, Phillipps decided on a scorched-earth policy. Halliwell would succeed to a wilderness. Ignoring all protests from his heirs and trustees, he cut down the fine avenues and copses on the estate, ruining its appearance and value. With the money raised by the timber he bought an enormous mansion in Cheltenham, Thirlestaine House, and in 1863 began moving his library there from Middle Hill. This vast operation took more than eight months to complete. A fleet of over a hundred wagons, drawn by 230 carthorses, groaned and sometimes collapsed under the weight of the Phillipps Library on its journey over the Cotswolds. Thirlestaine House, with its central block and two wings, was so large that Phillipps moved about it on horseback while supervising the disposal there of his books and pictures. Middle Hill was left empty and derelict and allowed, even encouraged by Phillipps, to fall into ruin. Cattle roamed its gardens and ground-floor rooms, and nothing was done to prevent the local vandals from smashing its windows and remaining fittings – most of which Phillipps had himself removed so as to make the house useless to his heirs.

The last years at Thirlestaine House saw the culmination of Sir Thomas Phillipps's mania. Without ceasing to acquire more manuscripts he began a new collection of printed books. Thousands of volumes, both cheap and rare, were poured into his library. He bought indiscriminately, gripped by a terrible new ambition. 'I wish to have one copy of every book in the world!!!!!' he wrote to a friend. What with ordering books, unpacking, arranging and cataloguing them and corresponding with or receiving visits from scholars, he had no time for ordinary domestic life. He ate and slept among his books. His only diversions were printing learned texts and conducting his propaganda war against Roman Catholics. Catholic scholars were barred from his library.

The second Lady Phillipps detested Thirlestaine House. The parts not stuffed with books, she complained, were infested with rats, and the kitchen was in a separate wing on the other side of a road from the house, so dinners always arrived cold. She had a breakdown and was sent off to a cheap boarding-house in Torquay, where her husband kept her in embarrassing debt and sent angry letters in response to her pleas for money.

Phillipps's campaign of spite against his heirs was ultimately unsuccessful. When the old bibliomaniac died, aged eighty, Halliwell was energetic in repairing the roof of Middle Hill, finding a buyer for it and breaking the entail on the estate. For the rest of his life he was a rich man. His wife, Henrietta, died a few years after her father, and Mr. J. O. Halliwell-Phillipps (as he now called himself) went on to make his name as the first authority on the life and times of Shakespeare. Despite their quarrel he had always admired his father-in-law, and he imitated him in printing small editions of manuscript texts of literary, topographical or folklore interest. His particular form of bibliomania was love of rarities, so he would often buy back his own productions in order to destroy them, leaving just one or two copies in existence and thus defeating the main purpose of publishing in the first place. All his life he had collected and dealt in literary and other relics of Shakespeare, beginning with those he stole (including a *Hamlet* quarto of 1603 which he abstracted from Phillipps's library and mutilated to conceal its provenance). Early disgraces were in time forgotten and he became a revered figure of scholarship. His remarkable Shakespeare collection was housed in a strange bungalow complex, to which he kept adding new buildings, at Hollingbury Copse near Brighton. He referred to it as 'that quaint wigwam on the Sussex Downs which had the honour of sheltering more record and artistic evidences connected with the personal history of the great dramatist than are to be found in any other of the world's libraries'.

The most generous obituary on the death of Sir Thomas Phillipps was written by Halliwell, who praised him for his great learning. Madden of the British Museum crossly disagreed. He was an old rival of Phillipps, who had consistently topped his bids on behalf of the national collection at sales of precious manuscripts. He referred to him as the Monopolizing Bugbear. In reply to Halliwell he declared that Sir Thomas had no degree of learning or scholarship and that his publications were worthless because they contained so many errors. Phillipps had at some time picked a quarrel with almost every one of his friends, but many of them wrote kindly about him, remembering the more benevolent aspects of his bibliomania, his kindness to young scholars and his willingness to open his library to those capable of appreciating it. The monstrous form of his madness was so apparent that people made allowances for it, and he somehow retained the affections even of those he had most wronged or persecuted, such as his own family.

Disposing of the Phillipps Library was far beyond the powers of his heirs for several generations. Sales of its now incredibly valuable contents have been going on from the nineteenth century to the present. In sifting through the manuscripts, writes Munby, great treasures have come to light, items of unique worth which for a hundred years had lain buried within the Phillipps hoard. 'We may hope,' he adds, 'that *Bibliotheca Phillippica* has not yielded up all its secrets yet.'

JEWS, BRITONS AND
THE LOST TRIBES OF ISRAEL

D
eeply rooted in the culture of the British people is the mystical
notion that they are the true Israelites, the spiritual heirs or
even the blood descendants of the ten tribes made captive by
the Assyrians and dispersed from the Holy Land in the eighth century
BC. It is a belief which has taken many forms and given rise to many
strange obsessions, movements and turns of history. Those who have
fallen under its spell include not only cranks and eccentrics, so called,
but most respectable figures among English statesmen, nobles and
royalty. Representatives of the two extremes, described here, are Mr
Edward Hine (1825-91), who discovered the lost tribes of Israel in the
British Isles, and the seventh Earl of Shaftesbury (1801-85), who strove
to bring about the Second Coming by converting the Jews to the Church
of England.

It is difficult to make sense of ideas such as these without taking into
account the time-honoured tradition from which they derived, that of a
special relationship between Britain and the Holy Land. The origins of
that tradition have been traced into prehistoric times, most eloquently by
the historian of Atlantis, Lewis Spence, who thus begins his *Mysteries of
Britain:*

'To the peoples of antiquity the isle of Britain was the very home and
environment of mystery, a sacred territory, to enter which was to
encroach upon a region of enchantment, the dwelling of the gods, the
shrine and habitation of a cult of peculiar sanctity and mystical power.
Britain was, indeed, the *insula sacra* of the West, an island veiled and
esoteric, the Egypt of the Occident.'

Support for that image comes from Caesar's statement that the Druid
religion began in Britain and was best preserved there, and it comes also
from native legends, of the Holy Grail, King Arthur and his reputed

ancestor Joseph of Arimathaea, of which the modern christianized forms probably derive from prehistoric prototypes. The story that St Joseph and his twelve fellow-missionaries came to England from the Holy Land soon after the Crucifixion may reflect an even earlier legend; but the site of the world's first Christian church, supposed to have been planted at Glastonbury (the English Jerusalem) by St Joseph, still survives, together with its original sacred dimensions, and both the legend and the site have been of great service to English mystical nationalism. Also useful has been the phrase which Gildas, the first native historian in the sixth century, applied to the British in their battles with the Saxons. He called them God's Israelites.

Like modern English clergymen, who refer to their congregations as the people of Israel, Gildas may have intended a metaphor. But the identification of the British as the true Israelites has not always been taken metaphorically. The extreme Puritans of Cromwell's time, who rejected classical and pagan culture, studied Hebrew and named their children out of the Bible, sincerely believed that they were the chosen people of the Old Testament, reincarnated. In recognition of this, Praisegod Barebone and the other members of the Little Parliament of 1653 abolished the English constitution and replaced it with the old Jewish laws of Moses. They were spurred on by Oliver Cromwell, who read them the 68th Psalm ending, 'The God of Israel is he that giveth strength and power unto his people', and told his Parliament that they were the Israel to whom God's message was addressed and that they had been divinely chosen to preside over the establishment of his rule on earth.

The most radical of the Puritans, who were exiled for unruly or fanatical conduct, made their headquarters in Amsterdam; and the English Israelites there met the other branch of their nation, the Jews of Iberia fleeing the Inquisition. This happy reunion between Israel and Judah was obviously no chance coincidence, and the Puritans took it as a sign from God that the Millennium was at hand. Their interpretation of Scripture was that the English were destined to convert the Jews to Christ and then lead them back to the Holy Land, where they would produce the new Messiah, setting in train the prophesied events preceding the universal reign of God on earth.

In 1649 a pair of English Puritans in Amsterdam, Joanna and Ebenezer Cartwright, wrote home to their government, asking it to bring this about by, first, inviting the Jews back to England (from which they had been expelled after much persecution in the reign of Edward I) and then shipping them to the Holy Land, after their conversion of course. A similar proposal had been made some years earlier, under James I, in a book called *The World's Great Restauration* by a lawyer, Sir Henry Finch. He prophesied that the Jews, converted and restored to Palestine, would establish a mighty empire to which all temporal sovereigns should be prepared to yield up their powers – world government by christianized Jews in effect. This was taken by the authorities as meaning that King James should give up his throne to a Jew. Finch was arrested and had to use all his legal skill in explaining, successfully, that he had not quite meant it that way.

The Cartwrights' plea was more timely because they wrote in the year when Puritanism officially prevailed, King Charles lost his head and the Commonwealth was set up – a regime naturally receptive to millennial schemes based on biblical prophecy. Partly for religious reasons and partly as a stimulus to trade, Cromwell favoured readmitting the Jews, and the cause became popular. It was aided by news from Amsterdam about the ten tribes of Israel which, according to the Old Testament, were carried off into captivity in Assyria and never returned home. The news was that the lost tribes had just been rediscovered – in South America.

The story was told in a delightful book by a Rabbi, Manasseh ben Israel. It was called *The Hope of Israel* and it summarized travellers' tales of colonies of Jews found all over the world, along with theories of learned men about how the dispersed tribes had reached those distant parts. Several such colonies had been reported from America, still practising circumcision and rending their garments in times of grief, and one of the theories quoted by Rabbi Manasseh supposed that the tribes of Israel had grown so tired of persecutions that they decided to move as far away from the rest of mankind as possible. Thus they settled in Greenland and from there moved to Labrador and then on south. The original and exciting part of the book was an account by a friend of the author, a traveller called Aaron Levi, alias Antonius Montezinus, who had just returned from the West Indies and South America. There in the course of many adventures he had come across a remote community of bearded, light-skinned, though rather sunburnt practising Jews, who retained among themselves the Hebrew language and customs. They had travelled to America by the eastern route, passing through Asia and across the Bering Straits.

The Hope of Israel sold very well in England, appealing to the sort of readers who form the market for today's 'amazing facts' and UFO literature. It seemed an innocent publication, but it had a message. The intention of Manasseh, and of his Puritan allies who had had the book translated into English, was to draw attention to statements in the Old Testament (e.g. Deuteronomy 28.64) that the chosen people must be scattered to all the ends of the earth before they are restored to their homeland. Now that Israel had been found as far away as America, the only remaining 'end of the earth', according to Manasseh who probably did not mean the term unkindly, the only place where the Jews were still excluded, was England. The book was made a compelling argument for lifting the anti-Jewish immigration and other laws, and it partly succeeded. The laws were not revoked until after Cromwell's time, but they became neglected. Sephardic Jews began settling in England, and the scripture-reading natives looked on with approval, knowing from Isaiah (11.11) that one of the places where the Israelites would gather, in preparation for their return home and the consequent opening of God's kingdom, was the obviously British 'islands of the sea'.

The great eighteenth-century antiquary and speculative theologian, William Stukeley (who identified the doctrines of the old British Druids with those of the Church of England), carried the identification of Britain and Israel one step further. He transferred the Holy Land to Britain and invited the Jews to share in it. The true religion, he said, has flourished in Britain ever since the Flood, and the Jews are more at home here than in any other country. Here they are most likely to be converted to Christianity, following which 'we might hope for what many learned men have thought; that here was to be open'd the glory of Christ's kingdom on earth'.

The idea of the New Jerusalem in Britain, immortalized by William Blake, was an offshoot from the main branch of millenarian theory which had the Jews baptized in Britain and then settled in Palestine. Its ultimate fruit was the Balfour Declaration of 1917 which committed successive British governments, despite their many attempts to wriggle out of it, to the principle of a Jewish homeland, and thus produced the modern state of Israel. That issue was, of course, never intended and would never have been approved of by the mystical Zionists of Britain.

According to their traditional interpretation of scripture, the modern Israelis lack one essential quality: they have not been converted to the English Church. They have stubbornly refused to take the one step which since Puritan times has been considered necessary for the salvation of the world.

If the British have failed in their assumed mission to co-operate with the Jews in manifesting a Christian Messiah, it is not for want of trying. In 1808 was founded that remarkable crusade, the London Society for Promoting Christianity among the Jews. After a slow start it acquired all at once a rich, devoted backer and a valuable legend, and the Society quickly rose to become one of the most influential groups in Victorian England. The backer was Mr Lewis Way, a barrister, and the incident which turned him towards the Jews' Society (familiarly so called) occurred when he was riding near Exmouth in Devon. He happened to remark on a fine stand of oak trees, and was told that their name was the 'Oaks of à la Ronde' and that their late owner, Jane Parminter, had left a will forbidding anyone to cut them down until the Jews had been brought back into Palestine. Mr Way was so struck by the idea that he began reading his Bible, learnt from it of the British mission to convert the Jews and became a full-time benefactor of the Society founded for that purpose.

Many years later, when the Jews' Society was at the high peak of prosperity, its chief accountant happened to be near Exmouth and thought he would have a change from inspecting its books by checking up on its most famous legend. What he found, or rather did not find, shocked him, and he hurried back to London with the grave news that there was no reference in Jane Parminter's will to oak trees in connection with the Jews' restoration. The Society was thus forced into suppressing much of its literature, in which the Parminter story had been an important feature because of its proven ability to attract supporters to the cause of converting the Jews.

Throughout the nineteenth century the Society for Promoting Christianity among the Jews flourished mightily, with large and valuable premises in London, numerous missions abroad and a list of patrons including royal persons, the Archbishops of Canterbury and York, most of the English bishops and a host of other dignitaries. Its greatest period was in the thirty-seven years from 1848, when its President was Anthony Ashley Cooper, Earl of Shaftesbury.

Lord Shaftesbury and his Anglican Jews

Lord Shaftesbury was appropriately commemorated in the 1970s by the most eccentric of British postage stamps, bearing an image of an arm holding a domestic brush between two piles of crumbling brickwork. The reference may have been to Shaftesbury's agitation on behalf of young chimney-sweeps, resulting in the Climbing Boys Act and a great improvement in their conditions.

He was the prince of do-gooders, corresponding in his time to Lord Longford in ours, though on a grander scale. Tall, pale and cold-looking, he had a heart which bled for those of lesser fortune than himself, which included practically everyone, but particularly for the most lowly and oppressed of his fellow creatures. He went where no English gentleman had been before him, to the worst slums and foulest factories, down mines and into prisons and lunatic asylums, noting every class of misery, cruelty and injustice, ascertaining their causes, and then proceeding with cool determination to have them remedied. As Lord Ashley, before the death of his father, he entered the House of Commons in 1826 and started his life's work of reforming and humanizing the nation. His enormous influence behind the scenes and close friendship with the Prime Minister, Lord Palmerston, who was his stepfather-in-law, contributed to his spectacular successes in cleaning up early industrial Britain. He promoted most of the reformist legislation of his time, including the acts which regulated conditions in factories, mines and collieries, the treatment of lunatics and criminals and the standards of working people's dwellings. Children were his special concern. Having delivered them from industrial slavery he set about educating them, founding schools for the poor, institutions for their training, young men's Christian associations and the like.

From the abolition of slavery to the prevention of cruelty to animals most of the good causes he adopted had some success, and he became widely loved and trusted. On one occasion he was invited to a meeting by forty of London's leading thieves, who wanted advice about their future careers. Lord Shaftesbury addressed them, together with over four hundred of their lesser colleagues, and persuaded them that their best course was to take advantage of an emigration scheme he had arranged for them.

If anyone could have persuaded the Jews of their duty to fulfil prophecy by becoming Protestants and returning to the Holy Land, that person would have been Lord Shaftesbury. Of all his good causes it was the one dearest to his heart. Like the Puritans of an earlier age he conducted his life entirely in accordance with the word of God as given in the Bible. It told him to love his fellow men, feed the hungry, visit prisons and so on; and all these things he did. It also told him that the Jews must be brought to Christ and returned to Palestine, and he undertook that duty as willingly as he accepted any of God's other instructions.

Through his influence on Palmerston, Lord Shaftesbury procured the appointment of a British consul in Jerusalem, specially charged with protecting all Jewish settlers in the Holy Land whatever their nationalities. His motives were entirely religious, but he was cunning enough in his dealings with worldly ministers to mention some of the material benefits which might fall to the British government if it encouraged Jewish immigration to Palestine. That policy, he urged, would be effective in bringing stability to a strategically important area on the trade routes between Europe and Asia, while adding to the British Empire a new province which Jewish skills and industry would soon make prosperous. With such rational-sounding justifications as these, but prompted on a deeper level by the enduring belief among the English of their special relationship with the Jews and Israel, British governments from Shaftesbury's time constantly aided or permitted the restoration of the Jews to their homeland.

The success of this policy, as far as the British were concerned, depended on the success of the Society for Promoting Christianity among the Jews. It was not for their own sake that the Jews were to be replanted in the Holy Land, but for the fulfilment of prophecy. That meant they had to be converted. Lord Shaftesbury had no particular interest in Jewish religion and culture, which he saw as archaic survivals, useful no doubt in the long years of exile, but destined according to the Bible to be replaced by the higher code of Christianity. It never occurred to him that the Jews might have their own view of things, that they might prefer to remain Jews rather than become Anglicans. In the great tradition of philanthropists, he knew what was good for them and he was determined they should have it.

It is the Jews themselves who have been the stumbling-block to all English schemes for universal regeneration through their agency. The Society for converting them to Christianity was a splendid affair. Its subscribers were noble and generous, and its well-endowed missions were spread across the world, wherever there were Jews to convert. The only trouble was its lack of product. The Jews were given every chance. Schools were opened for their benefit, Bible classes and tea parties were held for them and copies of the New Testament were presented to any who cared to receive them. Yet in proportion to the effort and money put into the campaign, the number of converts was pitiful.

The Society's favourite missionaries were Anglican clergymen from Jewish families and former rabbis converted to Christianity. One of these was the Rev. Dr Michael Solomon Alexander, a professor of Hebrew and Arabic, whom Shaftesbury caused to be appointed as the first Anglican Bishop of Jerusalem in 1842. Another was Rabbi Ginsburg, a refugee from Poland, who as the Rev. J.B. Crighton-Ginsburg was posted to the mission in Constantine, Algeria. Accounts of the various missions are given in a book, *Sites and Scenes,* by the Rev. W.T. Gidney, historian to the Society for Promoting Christianity among the Jews. Many of them appear to have been quite successful, socially. Jews came to tea, accepted gifts of tracts and New Testaments and enjoyed their learned discussions with the Anglican ex-rabbis. They were also grateful for the good English education which the mission schools offered their children. But whenever the subject of their conversion was raised, the missionaries reported that their Jewish guests tended to become evasive. The few successes were made much of. In 1862 Crighton-Ginsburg celebrated his best year in which no less than three Jews were brought to Christ. But in neighbouring Tunis pickings were slimmer. Gidney records one convert in 1862, another in 1864 and yet another in 1885. At the mission in Persia, he says, 'Another baptism was chronicled in the spring of 1853.' The missionary in Morocco could not claim as much, but wrote consolingly in his report that 'the New Testament is rarely burnt or torn as it was some years ago'.

Strange as it may seem, the Society's greatest success was in converting rabbis. The reason was that it could offer them good posts in its various missions. For most Jews, however, converting to Christianity meant cutting themselves off from their own communities and losing their means of living. In its early days the Society's policy was to pay them a sum of money in compensation. The Jews naturally interpreted this as bribery, Lord Shaftesbury was against it for the same reason, and the practice was forbidden. But the missionaries urged that unless they could offer some material inducement to converts their task was hopeless, and semi-officially they were allowed to continue.

It is extraordinary how long the delusion lasted that the Jews could and should be converted to Anglicanism. Its consequences were not those intended, but they were certainly important. The historian Barbara Tuchman in *Bible and Sword* makes a firm link between the British obsession with the Jews, as the destined fulfillers of scriptural prophecy, and the eventual success of Zionism in Israel. The obsession, of course, has been all one way. The Jews have no particular reason to be obsessed with the British. They have naturally accepted British help in establishing themselves again in the Holy Land, but rarely seem to have understood why it was offered. Indeed, they were so puzzled by the marks of special favour which they received from the Puritans of Cromwell's time that the theory arose among them that the Lord Protector of England must himself be a secret Jew. It is said that they sent a mission from Holland to Cromwell's birthplace in order to investigate his pedigree and see if he was qualified to be the Messiah.

The cause of converting the Jews was one of Lord Shaftesbury's few failures and the one he most deeply regretted. Not everyone, of course, shared his enthusiasm for it. His own father, who was not so addicted to good works, prompted his chaplain, the Rev. H.H. Norris, to write a long book violently denouncing the folly of the Jews' Society. Many people recognized that the Society's aims were hopeless; others assumed its members must be crazy. During one of his spells of duty on the Lunacy Commission, Lord Shaftesbury was told that a woman before them must be mad because she subscribed to a society for converting the Jews. Shaftesbury had to remind the embarrassed advocate that he himself was President of that society. He always wore a ring with 'Jerusalem' engraved on it, and to the end of his life was convinced that one day the Jews would reoccupy that city under its Anglican bishop and do their duty by giving the world a new Christian Saviour.

Edward Hine and the British Israelites

The tendency in the British to identify themselves with the chosen people of Israel takes its most extreme form in the British Israelite movement. The Puritans believed that they were reincarnated Israelites,

171

but the B.I. historians have added a scientific dimension by showing that the present inhabitants of Britain are actual blood descendants of the lost ten tribes. Relying on the Bible, they have proved that the future of the British people is to migrate, or rather return, to Palestine and themselves undertake the responsibility of engendering a Messiah.

The honour of first making this discovery was claimed by Edward Hine of London, but in fact he merely improved on a theory put forward in 1840 by John Wilson in his book, *Our Israelitish Origin*. Some years previously the learned Wilson had been led by his studies to realize that the modern nations of Europe, particularly the Anglo-Saxons, were descended from those tribes of Scythia, an area north of the Black Sea and towards the Caspian, who were themselves descended from the ten tribes of Israel. By right of inheritance, therefore, it was 'the glorious privilege' of the British 'to preach the gospel for a witness unto all nations until the end come'. Several other scholars agreed with him, notably Sharon Turner, author of lengthy works on the history of the Anglo-Saxons, and Dr George Moore who had written a book called *The Lost Tribes or Saxons of the East and West*. These three were joined by another independent thinker, Professor Piazzi Smyth, the Astronomer Royal for Scotland and leading authority on the Great Pyramid. He had reached similar conclusions to Wilson from his reading of the prophetic scripts which he had found geometrically expressed in the dimensions of the Pyramid's inner passages. To interpret these it was necessary to use the 'pyramid inch' unit, differing by only one part in a thousand from the modern English inch and equal to a 500,000,000th part of the earth's polar axis. In scientific journals Piazzi Smyth urged the French to abandon their atheistic metre in favour of the Pyramid inch, whose preservation had been the sacred commission of the British. His prolix writings on the Great Pyramid as evidence of Britain's direct inheritance from Israel, though few people understood them, have been prominently displayed ever since in British Israelite literature.

All this came to the ears of Edward Hine when at the age of fifteen he attended one of Wilson's lectures. He knew at once that Wilson was right, and the knowledge made him a prophet. To the end of his life he preached the gospel of British Israel. But in one important matter he differed from Wilson who had included the Germans and other Europeans among the lost tribes. Hine believed that the true Israelites were to be found only in Britain and its colonies. The Germans, he decided, were Assyrians. Professor Piazzi Smyth thought much the same. When the King of Prussia in 1872 obliged all Germans to use the ungodly metric system, Piazzi Smyth wrote to Hine that he considered the Germans to have 'forfeited the claim to be true Israelites', and must thenceforward 'consider them as subjects of the beast's kingdom'.

Edward Hine was the thirteenth child in a family living at 6 York Place, City Road, London. The parents were religious but poor, and the children, after a short schooling, had to find work at a young age. Edward was good at business and rose from humble jobs in shops and warehouses to become a stockbroker and then manager of a penny bank. An incident in his schooldays gave him an important prejudice. A party of Egyptian boys had been sent over for a term, with one of whom he had become friends. After they had returned home he was horrified to be told that those of the boys who had failed an examination had been beheaded, his little friend among them. This inclined him ever after to the side of the Israelites in their quarrels with the Egyptians.

In 1869 he retired from business and began his real career as preacher, lecturer, writer and editor on behalf of British Israel, or Identity as he called it. The pattern of events which he foresaw and did his best to bring about will not be unfamiliar to readers of the earlier part of this chapter. The British would come to realize that they were Lost Israel; they would send representatives from every part of Britain and the colonies to populate the Holy Land; there they would be united with the tribes of Judah and Levi, the present-day Jews; from this must follow the Second Coming. Even the first stage, the acknowledging of Identity, would bring material benefits to the people of Britain: the abolition of war, crime and poverty and the appearance of a godly government willing to reform the tax system.

In his view of the part to be played by the Jews within the grand scheme Hine was more realistic than Lord Shaftesbury and the grandees of his missionary Society. As the tribes of Judah, the Jews must necessarily return, together with the British Israelites, to the Holy Land. But there was no need to convert them first. Their role was to rebuild the Temple of Jerusalem according to the divine pattern, revive and broadcast the Law of the Old Testament and sing the Song of Moses. In harmony with that music the ten tribes from Britain would sing the New Testament Song of the Lamb. Hine's picture is in happy contrast to the reality achieved by his rival idealists of the Shaftesbury school. A visitor to Bishop Alexander's Anglican church at Jerusalem in 1844 found the congregation consisting of eight converted Jews and one or two tourists. Hine's dream of an Anglo-Jewish choral society might have worked better.

One of Hine's early works was *Seventeen Identifications*. This was later expanded into *Twenty-Seven Identifications*, and in 1874 it achieved completion as *Forty-Seven Identifications of the British Nation with the Lost Ten Tribes of Israel*. These identifications were the characteristic marks of the Israelites, as given in the Bible, which Hine recognized in the British of his day. In the scriptures he found that latter-day Israel must be a nation occupying islands north-west of Palestine, possessed of many colonies all round the earth and consisting of people unlike the Jews in speech and physiognomy. This chosen nation, so the Bible told him, must be the leading world power, and the natives of its colonies must be in the process of dying out. The identification relied on a passage from Jeremiah 30, where God said that He would 'make a full end of all nations whither I have scattered thee', and Hine took this as meaning that the Aborigines of Australia, the Maoris, the Cape Kaffirs and the American Indians were fated to follow the native Tasmanians into extinction.

The Irish too were said to be dwindling in number, and this was in accordance with prophecy, because (apart from the Ulstermen, who were the tribe of Dan) they were not Israelites at all but Canaanites. The fact was well demonstrated by the Book of Numbers, which says of the Canaanites that they would be 'pricks in your eyes, thorns in your sides, and shall vex you in the land wherein ye dwell'. This identification brings to mind a proposal made by James Harrington in the seventeenth century. In his *Oceana* he suggested that Ireland should be sold to the Jews for their habitation, thus solving two problems at one stroke.

By his talents as a speaker and energetic pamphleteering, Edward Hine acquired a considerable following. His magazine, *Life from the Dead*, provided a monthly forum for articles and lively discussions on the various proofs of Identity. One of the chief of these was the Coronation Stone, otherwise known as the Stone of Destiny and Jacob's Pillar. In Hine's mythology it had been brought to Ireland by the tribe of Dan, and its migration by way of Scotland to the Coronation Chair in Westminster Abbey was a fulfilment of prophecy, because wherever Israel was that stone was certain to be with them. There were also discussions on how best to implement the return of the British people to the Land of Israel. One suggestion was that the urban poor should first be sent there together with the Jews – paid for by Rothschild.

Hine claimed that Queen Victoria knew about his plans and thought favourably of them. Apparently she had learnt of them through one of his followers, the artist Edward Corbould, who often talked with her on the subject. She once said with a smile that when Mr Hine's ideas prevailed she was quite ready to transfer her government to Palestine.

In 1884 Edward Hine decided on a bold step, to make a missionary tour of the United States of America and persuade the people there that they were really the tribe of Manasseh. To finance the trip he sold his entire stock of writing and pamphlets to a disciple, Mr Loveland. For a time all went well. Beginning in Brooklyn, he found audiences for lectures and was invited to preach in churches. An early convert to the idea of America as Manasseh was General Winfield Scott Hancock, the hero of Gettysburg, who in 1880 had narrowly failed to become President. Americans, like the Ephesians, have always been receptive to new theories and new speakers; in letters to Mr Loveland, Hine wrote enthusiastically about the attention he was receiving.

From the East Coast he travelled to Cleveland, Ohio, and from there too his letters were optimistic. He had met a remarkable man, Charles Latimer, who had the gift of dowsing. He also knew the best way to make use of it. Wrote Hine: 'He is the most successful man in discovering oil-wells in America. He goes about with a divining rod in his hand, which discloses to his pulse where a spring lies.' What was more, he was a natural Israelite, for he had used the money from his first oil-well to start a magazine, *International Standard,* in which he vigorously opposed the metric system for reasons of religion and the Great Pyramid. Hine proposed to him that the next time he found an oil-well he should start a British Israel magazine with Hine as editor. But either Mr Latimer found no more oil-wells or he kept the profits to himself, for the subject was never again mentioned.

From Cleveland Hine's mission moved up to Canada, survived some cold weather and poor audiences and was then established in Buffalo. Some of his letters took an odd turn. It was the Jubilee year of 1887, and Hine was anxious to know if the Coronation Stone had spoken or made any movement when the Queen was in Westminster Abbey. He thought that an International Conference would shortly be held, where the question of transporting the British Israelites and the Jews to the Holy Land would be discussed. Also he had heard that the ancient mound of Tara in Ireland was to be excavated. In it, he believed, would be found the evidence needed to convince the Conference to do its duty. This evidence consisted of 'the ark, Urim and Thummim, the title deeds in the earthen vessel and credentials of Identity'. He urged his followers to acquire these things before they were removed by the archaeologists. Some years later the earthworks of Tara were seriously damaged by an excavating party of British Israelites in search of the Ark of the Covenant.

During his three years in America the missionary had had his ups and downs; more than once Mr Loveland and others back home had to help him with sums of money. In Buffalo he hit rock bottom. 'I am in great distress,' he wrote, 'and know not my future. My failure is in Buffalo. I have been here so long because I have no money to move away. I have been evicted and lost all my clothes and goods, am destitute, a stranger in a strange land, friendless, helpless and hopeless; have not had a full meal for a month, am dirty, ragged and in tatters; precisely in the condition that Joshua might be expected to be in, and do not know at all what is to become of me – all seems dark. I am aged, have grown infirm, and badly ruptured with always a swimming in my head. Walk about the streets ready to fall, inclined to think my mission in life has ended, and that this is my last letter. . . . People at home have been secretly working against me. I am too honest to steal, too proud to beg, too old to work, and have no trade at my hands. . . .' He had become a vagrant.

The trouble was that he had fallen among a population of Germans and Poles, who were not particularly interested in whether the British were or were not the true Israelites. Also, popular sympathy at that time was for Irish Home Rule, and there were no audiences for lectures on English mystical nationalism. But Hine's classic hard-luck letter had its deserved effect. A return ticket was sent from England; he travelled home, stricken in health and even poorer than when he had left, and died three years later in the house of a kind disciple who looked after him.

The British Israelite movement has continued to flourish up to the present, with many overseas branches in the Dominions and former colonies. In 1919 it developed into the British Israel World Federation under the royal patronage of Princess Alice. It has since attracted many other grand patrons, and its present offices are appropriately sited at 16 Buckingham Gate, in the shadow of the Palace. Its manifold publications denounce moral laxity, progressive clergymen, the Common Market, metrication, Communist intellectuals and similar menaces. On the positive side it encourages the reading of scriptures, particularly those which tell of the Anglo-Saxon-Norman-Celtic race's destiny as the Chosen People.

In recent times, of course, the British Israelites have had to change their tune somewhat. The identifications which seemed so convincing in Hine's era, to do with Israel ruling throughout the earth and pushing the natives of the colonies into outer darkness, no longer appear so applicable to Great Britain. And there is consternation at Buckingham Gate over the Anglo-Israelite descent on Jerusalem having been pre-empted by the Jews, who have got there first. In the British Israel World Federation today one detects a certain jealousy of the Jews, natural perhaps. Yet their most treasured document is a letter from a former Chief Rabbi which offers hope for a reconciliation to come. It was written in 1919 to one of their officers, Captain Merton Smith of Sunningdale, who must almost have fainted when he opened it, for it certainly concedes important points in the British Israelite case. The Chief Rabbi ruled as follows:

'1. The people known at present as Jews are descendants of the tribes of Judah and Benjamin with a certain number of descendants of the tribe of Levi.

'2. As far as is known, there is not any further admixture of other tribes.

'3. The ten tribes have been absorbed among the nations of the world. (See II Kings Chap. 17, more especially vv. 22 and 23.)

'4. We look forward to the gathering of all the tribes at some future day. (See Isaiah 27, 11-12; and Ezekiel 37, 15-28.)

'With the Chief Rabbi's cordial greetings.'

The only uncertainty is how Judah, Benjamin and the Levites will recognize their brother tribes when the British Israelites gather at Jerusalem to claim their share of the Holy Land.

DOUBTS ON SHAKESPEARE,
AND A BACONIAN MARTYR

T
he notion that some person or persons wrote the Works of Shakespeare is a perfectly sensible one, but sense and certainty fall away when it comes to identifying the author or, as some think, group of authors. The problem of who wrote Shakespeare is like a problem of theology which, not being susceptible to first-hand proof, must be decided by faith alone. Such topics, where no one's opinion can be proved better than anyone else's, naturally provoke the liveliest controversies. Theories about the authorship of Shakespeare abound. They fill literally thousands of volumes. The Stratfordians, who attribute the works to William Shakspere, the Stratford-on-Avon actor and businessman, are convinced that they alone have the right answer, but so are their oldest rivals, the Baconians, and so are dozens of other schools, the Oxfordians, the Marlovians, the champions of Pembroke, Derby, Rutland, Raleigh and so on. The list of claimants is enormous. Queen Elizabeth is on it, and so are Robert Burton, Daniel Defoe and obscure characters whose names are virtually unknown to anyone but their promoters. A Frenchman, Jacques Pierre, has been suggested, and an Arab, Sheikh Zubair, the Great Sheikh. Evidently there is some doubt about the question of Shakespeare authorship, but that doubt is rarely admitted. Most writers on the subject are dogmatists, first selecting their candidate and then trimming the evidence to fit him, or her. The most reliable are the agnostics, notably the late Sir George Greenwood, M.P., who proved in a number of tediously long books that the author of the plays was an unidentified person who, for reasons best known to himself, wrote under the name of 'Shake-speare'.

All the advantages in the debate, of course, lie with the Stratfordians. They dominate the institutions of English literature and derive prestige, as well as a large income, from the display of dubious shrines and relics in Shakspere's native town. On reading their literature, however, particularly where they deign to mention the question of authorship, the layman finds clear indication that all is not well in their camp. Instead of arguing their own case and reasonably refuting those of their opponents, the Stratfordians tend to lose their tempers. They wax furious and abusive towards all who challenge Stratfordian orthodoxy; and when scholars resort to calling their rivals charlatans and lunatics it means that they are unsure of their ground. The source of the Stratfordians' unease is soon identified: it lies in the unsatisfactory life and character of their candidate for authorship, William Shakspere.

The only recorded facts about Shakspere's early life are: that his father was an illiterate local tradesman; that he was christened in Stratford-on-Avon parish church on 26 April 1564; that at the age of eighteen he married at an unknown church a pregnant woman seven or eight years older than himself, registered as Anne Hathwey. Within six months she had a daughter and later bore twins, a boy and a girl. At some time in his twenties Shakspere evidently went to London, for the next document in his life, dated 1595, lists him as one of a group of actors who had played before Queen Elizabeth. Similar records occur in 1598 and 1608, and he is also known to have acquired a small share in the Globe Playhouse. In his early forties he retired to Stratford, to a large house he had bought, where his only recorded activities were money-lending, suing debtors for minor debts and accumulating property. The source of his wealth is unknown, and so are important details of his life, such as where, if at all, he was educated and to what extent he was literate. No manuscripts or examples of his handwriting are known, apart from six alleged signatures, wretchedly scrawled as if by someone unaccustomed to holding a pen. Three of the signatures are on the famous will of 1616, in which Shakspere left most of his property to his daughter, and to his wife merely his 'second-best bed'. Bequests of small items such as rings and a silver bowl are specified, but the will contains no mention of books or literary properties. Shakspere's funeral was on 25 April 1616. His riches earned him a monument in Stratford church alongside that of his fellow usurer, John Combe. It featured his effigy in bust with one hand resting on a wool sack, a symbol of trade. Much later this hand was dignified by the addition of a quill pen.

Apart from rumours and legends gathered many years after his death, nothing else of any significance is known about the life of Shakspere.

The facts shed no light on his supposed career as a playwright, nor do they seems to provide adequate material for a biography. Yet hundreds have been published, including lengthy studies of Shakspere's Boyhood, Shakspere's Schooldays and other periods in his life of which there is not a single record. The humour of this appealed to Mark Twain, a firm anti-Stratfordian and a wavering Baconian. In one of his books, *Is Shakespeare Dead?*, he compared the writing of a Life of Shakespeare to an attempt which he made as a boy, together with his Sunday-school teacher, at writing a Life of Satan. Only five facts, he found, are given about Satan in the Bible, so:

'We set down the five known facts by themselves, on a piece of paper, and numbered it "page 1"; then on fifteen hundred other pieces of paper we set down the "conjectures," and "suppositions," and "maybes," and "perhapses," and "doubtlesses," and "rumors," and "guesses," and "probabilities," and "likelihoods," and "we are permitted to thinks," and "we are warranted in believings," and "might have beens," and "could have beens," and "unquestionablies," and "without a shadow of doubts" – and behold!

'*Materials?* Why, we had enough to build a biography of Shakespeare!'

Among the 'rumours' and 'perhapses' about Shakspere's life are that he stole venison and was whipped and imprisoned for it; that he helped his father as a butcher; that he was a merry wag and good company in a tavern, and that he began his theatrical career by holding horses for play-goers. Not many of these anecdotes suit the Stratfordians' case, but they can point to Ben Jonson's verses, prefixed to the First Folio edition of Shakespeare's works in 1623, addressing the author as 'Sweet Swan of Avon'. However, the partisans of the Earl, or alternatively the Countess, of Pembroke believe that the river referred to was the Wiltshire Avon which flows past the Pembroke seat at Wilton. The Baconians say that, since Jonson was Francis Bacon's private secretary, he could have been party to a conspiracy to hide the real authorship of the plays by attributing them to a nonentity from Stratford. They note Jonson's comment, strangely emphasized, that Shakespeare never 'blotted a line' and take it to imply that no one ever saw the man writing and that he produced fair copies of other people's works. There is more than one contemporary hint that Shakspere was a copier or plagiarist. Jonson himself is thought to have had Shakspere in mind in his poem, 'Our Poet Ape', about a contemporary writer 'that would be thought our chief', who steals work from other authors. Robert Greene the dramatist called Shakspere 'an upstart crow, beautified with our feathers ... in his own conceit the only Shake-scene in the country' – in other words an arrogant plagiarist.

For those who care to take sides in the authorship debate there is a profusion of arguments all round. The purpose here in summarizing a few of the main issues is to provide a background to the activities of the extraordinary characters who have thrown themselves whole-heartedly into the subject. The earliest, and the great majority, are Baconians. An important part of their case is that the author of Shakespeare could not have been a simple rustic, because his works show him to have been a refined philosopher and courtier, a soldier, sailor, traveller, scientist, diplomat and much else besides. He was evidently proficient in Latin, Greek, French and Italian, and had access to rare, esoteric works, some of them unpublished. His vocabulary is said to be larger than that of any other writer. Above all, they say, the person who wrote Shakespeare was a lawyer. A whole string of lawyer-authors have testified to his unerring use of legal jargon and his detailed knowledge of lawyers' talk and customs. This suits the Baconians because Francis Bacon was a notable lawyer, rising to become Lord Chancellor. He also possessed many of the above qualities attributed to the author of Shakespeare. This is a strong feature of the Baconian case, only slightly marred by the insistence of most other parties to the dispute that their candidates possessed similar qualities. The worst performers in this talent contest are the Stratfordians, for at an age when William Shakspere should have been studying law he is said to have been engaged outside the theatre, holding horses for the audience.

The death of William Shakspere in 1616 was marked by no obituaries or public tributes, and it was several generations before interest in his biography developed. At the end of the eighteenth century the Rev. James Wilmot, Rector of Barton-on-the-Heath, set about gathering materials for a life of his fellow Warwickshireman. He first made enquiries of old families in the neighbourhood of Stratford-on-Avon, but none of them had memories or notes of the man. The sage of Stratford must have had books, Wilmot reckoned, but though he combed private libraries within fifty miles of the town he was unable to locate a single Shakspere book or manuscript. This made him suspicious, and when he went on to compare Shakspere's life with the character of the author of Shakespeare, Wilmot realized that there had been a mistake. The learned man of philosophy, law and science who wrote the plays could not possibly have been the 'country clown' from Stratford whose lack of schooling would have barred him from the company of the scholars and great men of his time. Following other clues, Wilmot decided that the true author of Shakespeare was Francis Bacon. He put aside his proposed biography and never published his conclusions.

Before his death Wilmot had all his papers burnt, and no one would have known of his researches had it not been for a visit he received in 1805 from an Ipswich Quaker, James Cowell, who had also been prowling round Stratford in search of Shakspere traditions. In Wilmot's house he said he was perplexed by the total silence of local people on the subject, and late one night, after dinner, Wilmot initiated him into his Baconian theory. Cowell became a convert and, on his return to Ipswich, declared his new convictions in two papers which he read to outraged members of the local philosophical society. These papers were not rediscovered till 1923, by which time the Shakespeare-Bacon controversy was in full spate.

It was begun in earnest in the middle of the nineteenth century by an American lady, Miss Delia Salter Bacon, distinguished as the first in a long line of American writers who have devoted themselves to the demolition of the Stratford myth. Nor is that her only claim to distinction. She made a brilliant name for herself as a lecturer and pioneer of popular education and, had she not become obsessed with the Shakespeare authorship question, she would probably have achieved her ambition for fame in literature.

Her family were New England Puritans, but Delia Bacon was born in a log cabin in Ohio, built by her father, David Bacon, a Congregational clergyman and missionary. In 1800 he had been sent out West by the Connecticut Missionary Society to convert the Indians to the Calvinist doctrine; but the tribes were not impressed and he made little headway against his Catholic and other more enticing competitors. Determined to persist, he walked back home the next year to fetch his wife, who accompanied him into the wilderness.

It was said in New England at the time that one could scarcely meet a man who did not have the ground-plan of an ideal city in his waistcoat pocket. David Bacon's plan was for a model religious community in the wilds, far from the vices of civilization. To accomplish it, he trekked back once again to Connecticut, where he obtained rights to some twenty square miles of land south of Lake Erie in the Western Territories. In 1807 he began surveying the new settlement and building his cabin, which also served as the Congregational church. Delia was born on 2 February 1811, the fifth of the Bacons' seven children, and the community was further populated by a few families inspired by Bacon's idea of reviving the spirit of Puritan religion in the wilderness. Thus was born the town of Tallmadge, now a suburb of Akron, Ohio. It bankrupted its founder. The trickle of settlers was not enough to fund Bacon's investment. In failure and ruin he was forced to retreat with his family to Hartford, Connecticut, where in 1817 he died in poverty.

From her father Delia Bacon inherited strong will and ambition. She always found it easy to impress people and find friends and backers. As a little girl she was adopted by a rich lady of Hartford, and between there and her mother's poor home in New York State she spent her childhood. She had to work for her keep and there was little time for education, but she was determined to rise in the world and took every opportunity for reading and study. When she was fourteen her benefactor gave her a year at a local school run by the Beecher sisters, early champions of women's education. The Beechers, Catherine and Mary, were not all that much older than Delia, and the youngest of them, Harriet, was her junior. Harriet helped with teaching while also attending classes, and later acquired fame as Harriet Beecher Stowe, author of *Uncle Tom's Cabin*.

When her year's schooling was over Delia found a job as a teacher while planning to start a school of her own. An elder sister agreed to become her partner, and after two attempts had failed for lack of funds the Bacon girls found backers for a school at Jamaica, Long Island. Their mother was invited to take over the housekeeping and care of boarders. Delia was always susceptible to illness and nervous attacks, and at Jamaica she caught malarial fever and suffered bouts of insanity. For this and other reasons the school collapsed. Delia, aged nineteen, took refuge with the family of her eldest brother, Leonard, who had become Pastor of the First Congregational Church at New Haven, alongside Yale College. In the intervals between teaching and illness she had been writing stories, and in 1831 she found a publisher for her first book, *Tales of the Puritans*. It did not, as she had confidently expected, bring her instant fame and fortune, but she was now an experienced educator and kept herself by giving well-attended classes at New Haven. That same year she won a prize of $100 in a short-story competition, defeating no less a rival than Edgar Allan Poe. Against the wishes of her strict brother she went to New York, was introduced to the world of the theatre and tried her hand at play-writing. At the same time she gave public lecture courses in history which were considered both learned and entertaining, but when her second book, the dramatic *Bridge of Fort Edward*, came out in 1839 and failed to cause any notable sensation, Miss Bacon called off her campaign to take New York by storm and returned to her class in New Haven.

Her ambitions had left little time for love, but at the age of thirty-four she fell, almost fatally. She took up with a man ten years younger than herself, Alexander MacWhorter, a theological graduate of Yale. For a time their friendship was idyllic. They travelled together and shared intimate secrets. MacWhorter was the first to be told of Delia's amazing new idea that the author of Shakespeare was not the 'booby' from Stratford, as she called him, but possibly Raleigh or Bacon. In return, she had to listen to his theory, also considered startling by those who understood it, that the names given to God in the Hebrew Old Testament prove an unbroken line of revelation from antiquity to Christian times.

Leonard Bacon disapproved of his sister's romance and Delia herself began to grow uneasy. The young man was a long time in proposing. Delia thought that he had given hints of an engagement but they were never followed up. He was fascinated by her but hung back from committing himself. It may have been the odd fervour with which she discussed Shakespeare that put him off. At any rate the affair became a public scandal. Catherine Beecher, interfering on behalf of women's rights, put it about that Delia was being misused. Leonard Bacon accused his sister's suitor of deceit, treachery, unchristian conduct and so on, while MacWhorter's friends rallied to him. Throughout the Congregational Church and the divinity department at Yale people took sides. Delia found herself famous, though not at all in the way she had intended. MacWhorter was given an ecclesiastical trial with Delia as a witness, in which everyone's allegations of what had passed between the lovers were publicly aired and analysed. The judges, not surprisingly, were confused and could not decide who was to blame, but Delia's reputation suffered. Nor was she helped by Catherine Beecher's loyalty in publishing a book, *Truth Stranger than Fiction*, setting out at length Delia's side, as she saw it, in the quarrel with MacWhorter. Reviewers accused Miss Beecher of scandal-mongering. Delia felt that she had been used to further her friend's own ambitions.

The whole business had hurt her personally, but she was determined that it should not hurt her career. She gave lecture courses throughout the eastern towns of America with a brilliant season in Boston during the winter of 1850-51. An excellent publicist, she knew how to attract the support of influential people. On the platform her subject was history. She emphasized its importance as a key to understanding the present, describing the rises and falls of ancient cultures and the contributions they had made to modern thought. The Bostonians found themselves enlightened by her thesis and charmed by her appearance and style. Brought up among evangelical preachers, Delia knew how to excite an audience. Reviews tell of her flashing eyes, slim figure and graceful manner. It was not only young people, eager for education, who flocked to her lectures; she pioneered adult education by holding classes for mature ladies, and even gentlemen condescended to be instructed by her. She was no feminist in the sense of wearing bloomers or demanding the vote – she had no interest in politics; but her independent achievements made her a model of the emancipated 'new woman'.

In Boston Delia Bacon further developed her ideas on the authorship of Shakespeare and began to talk about them to friends. She gained a number of important converts among literary people, including for a time Ralph Waldo Emerson who agreed to act for her in finding a publisher for her proposed book on the subject. In her mind was growing the obsession which shaped the rest of her life and finally took it over altogether. The evidence of Bacon as Shakespeare could only be found in England, in some family tomb perhaps. To England therefore Delia had to go. She began looking for sponsors for the expedition and collecting letters of introduction to the leading English scholars. To raise funds she decided to give a season of lectures in New York.

For her second attempt on New York Delia had the advantage of a growing reputation, but she had stiff competition. Among lecturers advertised for the winter of 1852-53 was William Makepeace Thackeray, and there were courses by other notables such as Frederick Law Olmsted, the brilliant landscape designer whose works were to include

New York's Central Park. The rival lecturers would occasionally meet at evening parties where alliances were formed and hints exchanged on the art of attracting audiences. In society as well as on the lecture platform Delia Bacon made a great impression. Her subject that season was eastern literature, history and cultures over a period of 6,000 years. Long emancipated from the narrow Puritan perspectives of her youth, she quoted from the sacred books of ancient oriental religions as well as from the latest works of archaeology and science, paying tribute to the guiding hand of Providence which made a unity of all human experience. Her attention to both esoteric doctrines and modern scientific thought provoked suspicion among strict church-people that Delia Bacon was becoming a heretic. With her usual flair for publicity she denounced such rumours, challenging her critics to produce a 'committee of divines' to judge her orthodoxy. The promised confrontation excited the press, but the judicial divines never appeared. Delia's heresy was to flourish in a more sensational cause.

The crowning success of her New York season was finding a backer for the trip to England. He was Charles Butler, a banker and admirer of Francis Bacon. After a visit from Miss Bacon he became her admirer too. Assured of his support she set sail for England in the spring of 1853.

One of her first acts on reaching London was to send Emerson's letter of introduction to Thomas Carlyle. He replied with an invitation to his house in Chelsea. At Emerson's request James Spedding, the great Bacon scholar, was also invited. The evening was a great success. When Delia revealed her Bacon-Shakespeare theory Spedding was struck dumb with amazement. Carlyle's response was a huge laugh and an expression of disbelief; but he had taken an immediate fancy to Delia and the two became firm friends. For most of Delia's time in England Carlyle did all he could to help her, even offering a room in his house as her lodging. Delia, however, felt that Jane Carlyle was not quite so keen on her as her husband, so she tactfully refused. She later explained that she had had to break off with the Carlyles – 'for there are *two* of them'.

Like many of the anti-Stratfordians who followed her, Delia Bacon believed that documents to solve the Shakespeare authorship question might be found in one of the old writers' tombs, Spenser's perhaps or Bacon's. Her first attempt at literary grave-robbing was at St Albans. Escorted there by one of her American admirers, Mr Ogden, Charles

Butler's brother-in-law, she tried to persuade the beadle at the church to open up the Bacon sepulchre, but neither he nor Lord Verulam, Bacon's descendant, to whom she later applied, would give consent. The atmosphere of St Albans appealed to her and she stayed there in lodgings for almost a year, working on her book and negotiating with publishers, before returning to London.

For the next year and a half she occupied rooms above a greengrocer's at 12 Spring Street, Paddington. There she became reclusive, her monomania grew dangerously and she suffered bouts of severe illness. Another problem was money. Charles Butler withdrew his support and she had to depend on small loans from friends, family and American officials in England. During her first stay in London, Butler had visited her and offered to introduce her into high society, but Delia had no time for grand parties. Together they had visited Carlyle, who struck up a warm friendship with the American banker and was greatly benefited by Butler's offer to manage his trans-Atlantic investments. But Delia's sponsor had not reckoned on her stopping so long in England. In June 1854 he sent her a final sum of £50 which was intended for her fare back to America. Delia felt that so far she had accomplished nothing and refused to return home empty-handed. When the money was spent, she was saved by her Paddington landlord, Mr Walker. He had once been a butler in domestic service, and after he had been kind enough to demand no rent off her for a period of six months, Delia wrote that he was a far more gentlemanly Butler than her former patron.

After several disappointments Emerson finally persuaded an American publisher to offer $200 advance on Delia's book, and another offer was received from *Putnam's Magazine* for a series of four articles on the authorship of Shakespeare. This Delia preferred, and the first of the articles was published by *Putnam's* in January 1856. They paid $55 for it, the only money Delia was to receive for her Shakespeare writings, for *Putnam's* then refused to print the rest of the articles. They considered her evidence too philosophical and allusive and not sensational enough for their readers. They had also been frightened by the vehemently hostile reaction of a Shakespeare scholar whom they had consulted on the articles. While pioneering Baconianism Delia Bacon was also creating an active Stratfordian reaction. Meanwhile, in England, Carlyle recommended a number of possible London publishers, but these, when approached, were not interested in taking on Delia's book. One of them,

Chapman and Hall, sent her a stately rejection note, declining to have any part in 'an attack on one of the most sacred beliefs of the nation and indeed of all nations'.

In failing health and desperately short of money, Delia appealed to Nathaniel Hawthorne who was serving as American consul in Liverpool. His official duties had proved onerous, inhibiting his literary work, and the necessity of being polite to an endless stream of American visitors in need of help had caused him to swear that he would never willingly be polite to anyone ever again. He had never met Delia, but he knew about her from mutual friends, was intrigued by her story and responded generously to her letter. In the summer of 1856 he called on her in London and fell immediately under her spell. Though sceptical of her theories he adopted her as a worthy cause and devoted much time and money to supporting her and advancing her work. Whatever the cost, her book should be published, he resolved, and he engaged to find a London publisher for it.

Later that summer Delia moved to Stratford-on-Avon for her final, desperate assault on the Shakespeare mystery. In the 'Old Player's' tomb, she believed, would be found the documentary evidence to confirm her thesis, but she had deliberately refrained from seeking it until her book came out. Now she could delay no longer. Her brother in America had always disliked her ideas on Shakespeare and opposed her journey to England, and he would send money only on condition that Delia used it for a boat ticket home. The rest of her family took a similar line and Delia knew that it was now or never. In Stratford with her usual luck she immediately found a sympathetic landlady and cheap, comfortable rooms, where she settled down to planning her attempt on the tomb.

It took place on an evening in September. On the promise that she would create no disturbance, Delia had persuaded the clerk of Stratford church to unlock the door and leave her inside for a few hours. In a letter to Hawthorne she described what happened. With candle and lantern she entered the church, followed by her terrified landlady who handed her a shovel and then fled. The moment of truth was at hand; but as she contemplated the bust of the Old Player and went over in her mind the clues in Bacon's writings which had led her to the tomb, she was suddenly seized by doubt. Even were she strong enough to open the stone tomb by herself, it might prove to be empty. The convictions which had sustained her for so long now deserted her. When the clerk returned late at night as arranged to escort her from the church, Delia meekly followed him. Later she met the Vicar and so charmed him that he actually agreed to the opening up of the tomb, but Delia's heart was no longer in the enterprise and she never took it further.

A letter from Hawthorne brought news that he had succeeded in finding a publisher for her book on condition that he himself contributed a preface to it. This, when produced, did not at all satisfy Delia. Hawthorne had praised her constancy, heroism, lofty intellect and other worthy attributes, but he could not disguise his fundamental disbelief in her anti-Stratfordian thesis. Delia required warmer support than Hawthorne could honestly supply. She rejected the preface and started a quarrel. Hearing of this the publishers withdrew their offer, but Hawthorne, without telling Delia what he had done, took upon himself the costs of publishing, appointed an editor to put in order the long rambling work and arranged for half the edition of a thousand copies to be sold by his own publisher in America.

In 1857 *The Philosophy of the Plays of Shakspere Unfolded* by Delia Bacon, with Nathaniel Hawthorne's revised preface, finally appeared in the bookshops. Unaware of who was paying for it, the author had added greatly to Hawthorne's costs by making extensive changes to the printed proofs and writing further long chapters. His kindness proved expensive, and he also jeopardized his reputation by his association with a book he knew would strike many critics as outrageous and insane. Yet even when reproached by Delia for faithlessness he made no complaint. He even undertook her personal affairs, writing to dissuade her brother from persecuting her with orders to return home. In return, the Rev. Leonard Bacon bracketed Hawthorne with those he accused of encouraging his sister's delusions and leading her on into madness.

Her mind broke not long after her book came out. Through years of frustration, neglect, loneliness and poverty she had lived for the day when her revelations about the authorship of Shakespeare would burst upon an astonished world. When the moment came there was a long silence before reviews appeared, mostly expressing disdain or incomprehension.

The Philosophy of the Plays of Shakspere Unfolded is exceedingly hard to read. The question of who really wrote the works of Shakespeare is never clearly answered, but an accumulation of hints gives the impression that the mastermind behind them was Francis Bacon, with Sir Walter Raleigh, Edmund Spenser, Sir Philip Sidney, the Earl of Oxford and other enlightened scholars conspiring to bring about a philosophical reformation through the medium of the plays, political censorship making it impossible for them to publish their ideas openly. Solving the authorship question is but incidental to the author's main purpose, which is to enlighten her own generation by revealing the noble philosophy to be found within the Shakespearean plays. The true writers of these works, the Elizabethan Men of Letters or 'the Few' as Delia Bacon refers to them, were learned scholars in the classical tradition, and they were also keenly interested in the explorations, discoveries and scientific developments of their own times. They realized that the constricted, medieval view of the world was no longer appropriate, and they conspired to liberate humanity from ignorance, superstition and tyranny. Queen Elizabeth was sympathetic to their aims, but her political sense warned her that the humanistic philosophy of the Men of Letters might have an unsettling effect on the institutions of her government. She would not therefore permit the radical reform in education which Raleigh and his group desired, but she encouraged them to exert their influence gradually through the medium of art and literature. The energies of the Men of Letters were thus diverted harmlessly away from politics, and their genius produced the high culture of the Elizabethan Age which Delia Bacon believed to be the finest ever to have flourished on earth.

Throughout all her sufferings she had been sustained by the conviction that *The Philosophy of the Plays of Shakspere Unfolded* would complete the task of elevating human consciousness which the Elizabethan Men of Letters, because they were prevented from speaking out plainly, had been unable to accomplish. The awesome responsibility weighed heavily on her brain and had an unfortunate effect on her style of writing. Her unfolding of the philosophy in Shakespeare was done in a series of long, rambling, complicated allusive sentences, which have baffled even her devoted readers. No wonder the literary critics were puzzled.

To Delia, of course, their reaction to her book was a crushing disappointment. The idea grew in her mind that she was being systematically persecuted, and other delusions followed. She began to claim, though in her right mind she knew it to be untrue, that she was a descendant of Francis Bacon. One day the new landlord of rooms she had moved to in Stratford asked for his rent, which she could not pay. She had a fit and screamed out of the window for a lawyer. The landlord called a policeman and doctors followed. One of them was the Mayor of Stratford, who took her under his care, settled her affairs, hired a nurse and communicated with her family and Hawthorne. Even in madness Delia never lost her ability to attract loving helpers. The landlord whom she had abused remained loyal, and she stayed on with him until her worsening condition made necessary her removal to a private local asylum.

Fortunately one of Delia's nephews, Leonard's son, was on his way back to America from naval service in the Far East and thought to call on his aunt at Stratford. On seeing her state he spent his pay on a ticket to America and took her home. Back in Hartford, in a 'retreat', Delia spent her last year, sometimes calm and lucid, sometimes beset with painful delusions. On 2 September 1859 she died.

Though she never managed to open Shakspere's tomb, Delia Bacon succeeded in igniting a controversy which for more than a century has blazed away merrily. Nathaniel Hawthorne in his *Recollections of a Gifted Woman* suggested that only one person had actually read her remarkable book. The reader referred to was a radical Boston journalist, William D. O'Connor. Miss Bacon's tragic story made a strong impression on him, and so did her thesis. He wrote several books in her defence and became the most articulate champion of the other anti-Stratfordian writers of his time. These rapidly increased in numbers and influence. Doubts on the authorship of Shakespeare were expressed by John Greenleaf Whittier the 'Quaker poet', Walt Whitman, Oliver Wendell Holmes and Delia's faithful agent Emerson. Henry James, whose uncle was a friend of Delia's, declared: 'I am "a sort of" haunted by the conviction that the divine William is the biggest and most successful fraud ever practised on a patient world.' But he added, 'I find it *almost* as impossible to conceive that Bacon wrote the plays as to conceive that the man from Stratford, as we know the man from Stratford, did.'

In Britain an important convert was made of the Prime Minister, Lord Palmerston. His Baconian views were formed under the influence of a pamphlet written by a reclusive landowner in Sussex, William Henry Smith. It appeared just before Delia Bacon's book came out, and she persuaded Hawthorne to write to Smith accusing him of plagiarism,

191

which he denied. It seems that Baconianism was in the air at the time. Smith's thesis was not like Miss Bacon's, being derived from the comparison of similar phrases in the works of Bacon and Shakespeare. He avoided public controversy, partly because he did not want 'literary mud cast at him' and partly because the subject excited him too much and was bad for his health. Like most of the early Baconians he was confident that the movement would rapidly prevail through its own merits. His old age was enlivened by the promise of a new book which, he had heard, would complete the rout of the Stratfordians and establish the claims of Bacon once and for all. It was called *The Great Cryptogram: Francis Bacon's Cipher in the So-Called Shakespeare Plays* and its author was Mr Ignatius Donnelly, known to the press as the Sage of Ninenger, the Apostle of Protest and the Prince of Cranks, who is the hero of the following chapter.

In this frame from her film, *Heartbeat in the Brain*, Amanda Feilding is cutting her hair in preparation for boring her skull with an electric drill. The photograph below, taken twelve years later, shows her with Joey Mellen and their son, Rock, outside their Chelsea gallery. (33, 34)

James Orchard Halliwell (right) had an
early reputation as a book thief. His
marriage to a young heiress was
vigorously opposed by her father, Sir
Thomas Phillipps (below), who was the
most fanatical collector ever known of
books and rare manuscripts. Halliwell
survived the persecutions of his father-
in-law and finally inherited his estate.
He became chief promoter of the
Shakespeare cult at Stratford.
(35, 36)

Edward Hine (right) laboured throughout his life to convince the British people that they were the Ten Lost Tribes of Israel. He prophesied their imminent return to the Holy Land, followed by the Second Coming of Christ. Some of his notions were shared by the philanthropist and reformer, Lord Shaftesbury (below), whose ambition was to expedite the Millennium by converting the Jews to Christianity. (37, 38)

Sir Edwin Durning-Lawrence was one of the many distinguished lawyers who have attributed the works of Shakespeare to Francis Bacon. The evidence in his book, *Bacon is Shake-speare*, featured anagrams and ciphers, and he pointed out that the engraving of Shakespeare's bust at Stratford, published in Dugdale's *Warwickshire* in 1656 (below, left), bears little resemblance to the figure seen today (below). The quill pen in the Bard's hand was, he claimed, a later addition. (39, 40, 41)

The mechanism on the right was designed by Dr Orville W. Owen of Detroit as an aid to deciphering the works of Shakespeare and other contemporary playwrights, which he believed to have been written by Francis Bacon. His researches informed him that Bacon's manuscripts were concealed beneath the River Wye. The elaborate excavations he conducted there in 1911 were reported with the illustration, below, in a contemporary magazine. (42, 43)

Delia Bacon of Connecticut was the first active Baconian. Her trip to England in 1853-58, and attempts to open the tombs of Bacon and Shakespeare, cost her her sanity. Below is the statue of Francis Bacon at Trinity College, Cambridge. *Sic sedebat* – 'Thus he would sit' – says the legend beneath. This led the Baconian researcher, Orville Owen, to see cryptic significance in the line from *King John*, 'My dear Sir, thus leaning on my elbow I begin...'. (44, 45)

Ignatius Donnelly, the radical Minnesota politician, founder of heresies and the first to attempt deciphering Shakespeare's works to show they were written by Bacon. Below is a page from his copy of *King Henry the Fourth* after he had used it for purposes of working out Bacon's hidden message. (46, 47)

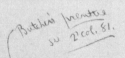
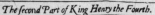

The photograph of 'flying saucers around a mother ship' was taken by George Adamski (above), the 1950s UFO prophet. On the left is the Earl of Clancarty (Brinsley le Poer Trench), pioneering UFO writer. (48, 49, 50)

CONGRESSMAN DONNELLY,
THE GREAT HERETIC

The greatest uncelebrated man in American history must surely be Ignatius Donnelly. His public career was spectacular, but he was not the sort of person who has statues raised and streets named in his honour, the reason being that he was a heretic. In fact he was an heresiarch, a founder of heresies, and a relentless opponent of orthodoxy in any field. His most famous book, *Atlantis: the Antediluvian World,* marked the beginning of 'Atlantology' and popular belief in a lost continent as the source of world civilizations. With his next book, *Ragnarök,* Donnelly introduced the theory, later popularized by Immanuel Velikovsky, that the earth was once almost destroyed by a giant comet. He was also the first person to decipher Shakespeare.

He became a figure of dread, not only to the upholders of orthodox scholarship, but also in the world of politics. His rabble-rousing oratory, his raking up of scandals and his vehemence in denouncing all kinds of conspiracies and rackets made him at times the most hated man in American public life. At other times he was said to be the most popular. Everything he did attracted publicity, and when it became known that the formidable Donnelly had deciphered the coded messages which Francis Bacon had woven throughout the works of Shakespeare, Baconians everywhere felt that their day of triumph was at hand.

The decoding of Shakespeare was seen by Donnelly as the crowning achievement of a life which had already been so full of incident and rare adventure that no one but he would have thought any further crowning necessary. It began on 3 November 1831 in Philadelphia, where his parents had settled after migrating from Ireland. His father, Dr Philip Carroll Donnelly, was in medical practice there. The Donnellys were a lively, cultured family and there were constant parties or musical and literary evenings at their house on Pine Street. One of Ignatius's sisters,

Eleanor C. Donnelly, became a prolific author and poet, admired and even imitated by such notable contemporaries as Longfellow and Tennyson. Ignatius himself at the age of nineteen published a book of sentimental poems by which he was soon so ashamed and embarrassed that he became one of those authors who strive throughout their lives to buy up and destroy their earlier productions.

After schools in Philadelphia and a spell in a lawyer's office Ignatius Donnelly was admitted to the Bar of Pennsylvania and in 1855, aged twenty-four, he was nominated for the State Legislature. But his ambitions were more free-ranging. The following year, soon after his marriage, he and his wife set off to seek a fortune in the West. After a long rambling journey by steamboat up the Mississippi, through Iowa and by way of Chicago they arrived at St Paul, Minnesota, where Donnelly was horrified to see how the local farmers and settlers were being exploited by usurers. Money was being lent at up to 60 per cent. From then on his life was dedicated to combat with what he called 'the shameless plutocracy'. His first move was to buy a square mile of land (640 acres) south of St Paul and build a house. Like many Americans of his century, including Delia Bacon's father and others mentioned in this book, Donnelly dreamed of a model city where the ideals of the New World republic would be realized. He divided up his acres into lots, creating the new town of Ninenger, and advertised for citizens. There was a great response, and as he walked about the porch of his house, watching Ninenger grow around him, its young proprietor worried that he was going to make so much money that he would have trouble spending it.

That problem never arose, because the year after its foundation Ninenger began rapidly dissolving. A financial panic discouraged settlement in Minnesota and ruined Donnelly, forcing him into bankruptcy. He remained stranded in Ninenger while his colonists with teams of horses dismantled their houses and took them off elsewhere. But he made the best of a bad job by turning the deserted lots of his city over to wheat and became a farmer.

Oratory was one of the greatest of Ignatius Donnelly's many talents. His bellowing voice easily attracted crowds, and he soon became famous as the best rhetorical entertainer in the West. The Minnesotan farmers were amazed and delighted by his witty phrases and epigrams and the wide vocabulary with which he expounded his original, violently radical ideas. In 1857, the year of Donnelly's ruin, Minnesota became a State in the Union and from the very start it was a hotbed of bribery and corruption. Its politics were dominated by the big Eastern corporations, its politicians were mostly bought men, and its people had very little say in the management of their own affairs. Their only champion, and a very effective one, was Ignatius Donnelly. They sent him to the State Legislature and in 1859 he became Lieutenant-Governor of Minnesota. Throughout the rest of the century he conducted populist campaigns on behalf of the various movements he founded, such as the People's Party and the Anti-Monopolists, sometimes winning, sometimes defeated by the abusive propaganda directed at him by his powerful opponents.

In 1862 Donnelly entered national politics as a Republican Congressman, and in Washington he was also effective. He successfully urged the purchase of Alaska in 1868, and through all his eight years in Congress he never ceased from exposing conspiracies in big business and politics, naming the guilty parties and making many powerful enemies. They in turn characterized him as an irresponsible demagogue and managed to prevent his election for a third term in Congress. He returned to Ninenger and to the localized battlefield of Minnesota politics.

The positive side of Donnelly's campaign was for popular education. Ignorance, he said, is even worse than slavery. His house at Ninenger, like the Donnelly household in Philadelphia, was a centre of local life and culture. Some of the writers who gathered around him contributed to a magazine he started, *The Anti-Monopolist,* which with Donnelly's satirical and outspoken editorials achieved for a time a large circulation. Like all his other enterprises, however, it eventually failed, and so did a farm which he had bought and was then forced to abandon. For four years up to 1878 he served a spell in the Minnesota Legislature, but by the end of 1880 his fortunes were at a low ebb. Broken and driven from politics by his rich opponents, besieged in his house by creditors and bailiffs, Donnelly turned to literature.

He was a well-read man, and during his time in Washington he had taken advantage of the Library of Congress to pursue further studies. The tragic history of Delia Bacon had made a strong impression on him. He was convinced that she was right about Shakespeare, and he was also convinced that she had been suppressed by the same sort of despotic authorities in literature as were trying to suppress him in politics. 'She was persecuted into the mad-house and the grave', he wrote, 'by men who called themselves scholars and gentlemen. Their asinine hooves beat upon the great sensitive brain of the shrinking woman, and every blow was answered by a shriek. And when, at last, they had, by their onslaughts, destroyed her intellect, the braying crew wagged their prodigious ears, and in stentorian chorus clamored that her insanity was indubitable proof of the falsehood of her theory.'

Delia Bacon became one of the great causes which Donnelly took up and to which he devoted the latter part of his life. In about 1870 he had begun the stupendous labours of which the climax was the publication eighteen years later of his book on the Shakespeare cipher. In it was a convincing refutation of the Stratfordians' claim that Delia's insanity was associated with the insanity of her theory. Triumphantly Donnelly pointed out that the Stratfordian author of the first book written against Delia and the Baconians, one George H. Townsend of London, had also gone mad before committing suicide.

Through the winter of 1881–82 Donnelly was hard at work in his study in Ninenger. Papers on the Shakespeare question were laid aside to make room for others on subjects which had long occupied his mind. In *Atlantis: the Antediluvian World* he attempted to put right what he saw as the total corruption of history. He explained at one stroke the myths and sacred histories of all peoples and discovered the origin of all cultures. Plato located the drowned island of Atlantis in the ocean beyond the Straits of Gibraltar, and where Plato left off Donnelly's imagination took over. He identified Atlantis as the original Garden of Eden, Garden of the Hesperides, Elysian Fields, Mount Olympus, Asgard of the Eddas and Earthly Paradise where human affairs were once conducted in peace and happiness. Atlantean colonists initiated the cultures of Egypt, America, the Aryan and Semitic races and the Bronze Age in Europe. After the deluge which destroyed their continent, surviving Atlanteans dispersed to different parts of the world, and their tales of the disaster were perpetuated in myths of the Great Flood and other forms of cataclysm which occur universally. Donnelly had compiled an impressive catalogue of similarities between the myths, folklore, anthropology and artefacts, as well as the forms of animal and plant life, of the continents bordering on the Atlantic Ocean. His proof of the reality of Atlantis rested on the cumulative effect of all this evidence rather than any single piece of it. All that was needed for the perfection of the thesis was some object or record of undoubted

Atlantean provenance, and Donnelly proposed that the nations of the earth should deploy their 'idle navies' for that purpose. 'A single engraved tablet dredged up from Plato's island,' he wrote, 'would be worth more to science, and would more strike the imagination of mankind, than all the gold of Peru, all the monuments of Egypt, and all the terra cotta fragments gathered from the great libraries of Chaldea.'

The idea struck an important target. After reading *Atlantis,* the British Prime Minister, Gladstone, proposed to his Cabinet that a task force of the Royal Navy should be sent into the Atlantic to probe for the lost continent. The scheme was vetoed by the Treasury on the ignoble grounds that it would cost too much.

Quotations from the Bible and other ancient texts were again used by Donnelly in his next book, *Ragnarök: the Age of Fire and Gravel,* to support his theory that the earth was once struck by a giant comet. Reviewing it, the London *Daily News* called its author 'a stupendous speculator in cosmogony'. The *Pall Mall Gazette* commented: 'America, the land of big things, has, in Mr Donnelly, a son worthy of her immensity.' Donnelly's books were not merely compilations of facts and observations; his enthusiasm and the visionary tone of his writing were the qualities which chiefly made them successful. *Atlantis: the Antediluvian World* remains popular to this day, turning the heads of imaginative readers and providing the cornerstone for all the numerous studies in Atlantology that have come after it.

Having cleared the decks for what was to be the great work of his career, Donnelly beamed the full glare of his intellect onto the Shakespeare problem. He had long been convinced that Bacon was the true author of the plays attributed to Shakespeare, but the question which puzzled him was why Bacon should have allowed the credit for them to be taken by the humble actor. One day he was looking through a book belonging to one of his little sons, *Every Boy's Book,* and came across a reference to Francis Bacon having been interested in ciphers. In a flash came to him the thought, 'Could Lord Bacon have put a cipher in the plays?' No sooner had he conceived the idea than he was convinced by it. If Bacon had encoded messages in the texts of the Shakespeare plays he must have intended that somebody at some future time would understand them, and Donnelly made up his mind that he would be that person. During the winter of 1878–79 he re-read the whole of Shakespeare, looking for key words which would give away the secret of the cipher, expecting to find a clear statement such as, 'I, Francis Bacon, of St Albans, son of Nicholas Bacon, Lord Keeper of the great Seal of England, wrote these plays, which go by the name of William Shakespeare.' Nothing so unequivocal presented itself, but the more he read the more Donnelly noticed certain words, phrases and peculiarities of punctuation which seemed superfluous to the meaning of the texts. It also seemed to him that their occurrence was determined by some numerical rule, but try as he might he could not discover it. The procedure, as he described it, was laborious and frustrating.

'I tried all the words on page 53, on page 54, on page 55. I took every fifth word, every tenth word, every twentieth word, every fiftieth word, every hundredth word. But still the result was incoherent nonsense. I counted from the top of the pages down, from the bottom up, from the beginning of acts and scenes and from the ends of acts and scenes, across the pages, and hop, skip, and jump in every direction; still, it produced nothing but dire nonsense.'

In trying to crack the cipher which Bacon had written into the Shakespeare plays Donnelly claimed that he had used up two tons of paper. He never let himself doubt that it was there, and his continued failures over the years to discover it merely spurred him on to fresh efforts. It occurred to him that the key must be in the original printing, so he obtained a facsimile copy of the First Folio edition of the plays as published in 1623. Even with this aid the secret of the cipher long remained elusive. Donnelly wrote that he envied the interpreters of the Egyptian hieroglyphics on the Rosetta Stone their comparatively simple task. Gradually, however, daylight began to creep in. Certain words in the plays, if taken in a certain order, made the kind of sense he was looking for. He seemed to discern a numerical formula behind their selection, but it was very complicated and its principles were unclear. Finally he decided that the cipher words were situated in order, counting up or down the page columns, as multiples of the page numbers on which they occurred. By a mysterious process which he would not reveal (in order, he said, to protect his copyright) Donnelly arrived at certain numbers which, in combination with certain other numbers or 'modifiers' and varied by some elaborate but vague calculations, indicated the special words which comprised Bacon's cipher messages. This cipher only worked for passages in the two parts of the play *Henry IV*. The other plays contained different ciphers which

Donnelly had not worked out, but the small part of Shakespeare which he had been able to decode yielded a strange harvest.

Every word of all the sentences in the following chapter grows out of the number 327:

	Word.	Page and Column.	
516—167=349—22 *b* & *h*=327. 498—327=171+1=			
172+10 *b* & *h*=182.	182	76:1	Seas ⎤
516—167=349—22 *b* & *h*=327. 447—327=120+1=	121	75:1	ill ⎦
516—167=349—22 *b* & *h*=327—30=297—50 (76:1)=	247	76:2	said

Observe, here, how precisely the same number brings out *seas* and *ill;* compare the numbers in groups; — 516—516; — 167—167; — 349—349; — 22 *b* & *h*—22 *b* & *h*; — 327—327; — and going up the first column of page 76 with 327, we find *seas;* while going up the first column of page 75 with 327 brings us to *ill.*

	Word.	Page and Column.	
516—167=349—22 *b* & *h*=327—284=43. 447—43			
=404+1=405+3 *b*=408.	408	75:1	that
516—167=349—22 *b* & *h*=327—254=73—15 *b* & *h*=			
58. 448—58=390+1=391.	391	76:1	More ⎤
516—167=349—22 *b* & *h*=327—50=277—50 (74:2)			
=227—1 *h*=226.	226	74:1	low ⎦
516—167=349—22 *b* & *h*=327—254=73—50 (76:1)			
=23—1 *h*=22.	22	76:1	or
516—167=349—22 *b* & *h*=327—30=297—254=43			
—15 *b* & *h*=28.	28	75:2	Shak'st ⎤
516—167=349—22 *b* & *h*=327—248=79. 193—79			
=114+1=115+ *b* & *h*=(121).	(121)	75:1	spur ⎦
516—167=349—22 *b* & *h*=327—254=73—15 *b* & *h*=			
58. 498—58=440+1=441.	441	76:1	never
516—167=349—22 *b* & *h*=327—50=227—7 *b* & *h*=	220	76:2	writ
516—167=349—22 *b* & *h*=327.	327	76:1	a
516—167=349—22 *b* & *h*=327—145 (76:2)=182.			
498—182=316+1=317.	317	76:1	word
516—167=349—22 *b* & *h*=327—193=134. 248—			
134=114+1=115.	115	74:2	of
516—167=349—22 *b* & *h*=327—254=73—15 *b* & *h*			
=58—5 *b*=53.	53	74:1	them.

I will ask the skeptical reader to examine the foregoing three remarkable combinations of words : *seas-ill* (Cecil), *more-low* (Marlowe), and *shak'st-spur* (Shakspere). Remember they are *all derived from the same root-number, and the same modification of the same root-number:* 516—167=349—22 & *h* (167)=327; — and that they are *all found in four columns !* Are there four other columns, on three other consecutive pages, in the world, where six such significant words can be discovered?

Above is an example of Donnelly's decoding. By use of his arcane number formulas he extracts from three pages of *Henry IV, Part 2*, Bacon's hidden statement, 'Seas ill [Cecil] said that More low [Marlowe] or Shak'st spur [Shakspere] never writ a word of them.' Other extracts depict the Stratford man in disgusting detail as coarse and poor-spirited, prematurely aged and suffering from several diseases and disfigurements including consumption, pox and goitres. He was fat, greedy and debauched, and his ill-bred character is illustrated in the cipher by several discreditable anecdotes. Donnelly had conceived a violent dislike for Shakspere, reflected in his decodings; and if his readings were correct the peasant from Stratford must indeed have been a vile creature. But it is sadly apparent that Donnelly's monumental labours were in the service of pure self-delusion. He was interested in spiritualism, and the weird babble of voices which come through in his cipher messages are more typical of the products of spirit seances than of Bacon's or any other sane person's style of speech. Donnelly's readers were asked to believe that Bacon went to the trouble of encoding in his Shakespeare writings nothing more than a series of pointless anecdotes and stupid comments. As to the plays themselves, Donnelly regarded them as merely 'marvelously complicated padding around a wonderful internal narrative'.

The Great Cryptogram, almost a thousand pages long, was published in two large volumes. The second volume was about the cryptogram while the first contained all the other evidence that Donnelly could muster against Shakspere and for Bacon as the author of the Works. As a kind of reflection of Donnelly's many-sided character, the two volumes are so different from each other that they might have been written by two different people.

In the first Donnelly uses the same technique as in *Atlantis*, of compiling and comparing facts. He sets down what is known of the respective characters of Shakspere, Bacon and the author of the plays as revealed in his writings. Also listed are similar phrases and passages in the works of Bacon and Shakespeare. For some of these parallels Donnelly was indebted to his correspondent Mrs Henry Pott, a learned English authority on Bacon and an enthusiastic Baconian. He paid tribute to her industry and gave as an example of it: that in order to prove Bacon the first person to have used the phrases, 'Good morrow' and 'Good day', she had read through no less than six thousand works dating from the time of Bacon or earlier. The first volume of *The Great Cryptogram* is clear and scholarly and makes lively reading. The case for Bacon as Shakespeare has never been better exhibited, and Donnelly makes no bones about his hatred and scorn for the Stratford pretender. He derides his very name, illustrating its despicable character with an anecdote of a person called Shakspere who was so ashamed of his low name that he changed it to Saunders.

It has often been said that if Donnelly had published only the first volume of *The Great Cryptogram* with a different title, it would have been widely respected. Yet it contained no conclusive evidence that Bacon wrote Shakespeare. Donnelly's proofs, like those in *Atlantis,* were cumulative, and he felt the need for a more dramatic confirmation of his thesis, something like the 'single engraved tablet' which he wanted dredged up from the sunken continent. The direct words of Lord Bacon, speaking through his cipher, were intended by Donnelly to have the same effect as would that engraved tablet. Bacon's contribution, however, filling the second volume of *The Great Cryptogram,* ruined the sale of the book. Hostile reviewers fastened on that volume and made easy sport of it. Parodists, using the same numbers and methods as Donnelly, extracted from the same pages of *Henry IV* alternative messages such as, 'Don nill he, the author, politician and mountebank, will worke out the secret of this play', and 'Master Will I am Shak'st spurre writ the play'. Donnelly became something of a laughing-stock, but he also made converts and found defenders. Among these was William O'Connor, the old champion of Delia Bacon. The year after *The Great Cryptogram* was published O'Connor brought out a book called *Mr Donnelly's Reviewers,* in which he vigorously assailed the critics who had spoken ill of *The Great Cryptogram* and accused them of taking part in a publishers' conspiracy to suppress the book.

If there was such a conspiracy it was ill conceived, for neither in politics nor literature was Donnelly ever long suppressed. He bought the plates of his book from the dissatisfied publisher and planned a little house to contain them in his garden in Ninenger. 'That building will be my monument of colossal failure,' he wrote in his diary. But in the end the book did not fail. It recovered from its bad reviews and, through its author's energetic promotion, sold out and was several times reprinted.

Eleven years later he followed it up with a smaller book, *The Cipher in the Plays and on the Tombstone,* where he hinted that 'malign and secret influences behind the curtain' were conspiring against the cause of Bacon. One can dispute the authorship of the sacred Gospels with impunity, he observed, but to doubt the authorship of Shakespeare is to stir up opposition so intense and virulent that it can not easily be accounted for. Donnelly suspected that the Rosicrucians were behind it. They obviously knew that Francis Bacon, who was one of them, wrote the Shakespeare plays, but perhaps they believed that the times were not yet ripe for that knowledge to be revealed. Donnelly disagreed. The world, he believed, was at a crisis. The power of big business was threatening to enslave humanity, and the only possible opposition to it was a government which enacted the philosophy of Francis Bacon. The first step towards bringing that about was to convince the world that Bacon wrote Shakespeare.

The year that *The Great Cryptogram* was published, Donnelly travelled to England, was entertained at the House of Lords and lectured at both Oxford and Cambridge Universities about, or rather against, Shakespeare. He led a debate at the Cambridge Union on 'Did Francis Bacon write the Shakespeare plays?' and was only narrowly defeated, most members abstaining from the vote. His interest in spiritualism led him in search of Bacon's shade at St Albans, following in Delia Bacon's footsteps. In the church there he experimented with a magnetic compass, and found that wherever he stood its needle always pointed to Bacon's monument.

The campaign of writing, travelling, debating and lecturing on behalf of Bacon would have occupied most other people's entire energies, but throughout it Donnelly kept up his political and other activities. In 1887 he re-entered the State Legislature as leader of the Farmers' Alliance and then began another project, to impress his views on the world through a series of novels. The most successful of them, *Caesar's Column*, was published in 1890 and described what was to happen a hundred years later, when everything that Donnelly most feared had come to pass. The businessmen had won. They dwelt in great cities, powered by the earth's magnetic currents, and dined in wonderful restaurants where every imaginable dish was available at the press of a button and news from any part of the world was shown on individual television screens. Their society was maintained by slave labour, but finally the under-dogs revolted, destroyed the state armies by aerial bombardment and massacred the ruling classes. The victims were cemented into a huge pillar to commemorate the revolution. As soon as it was completed, the mob turned on their leaders and lynched them also. Authority was entirely thrown over, civilization collapsed and most of the people died from violence or starvation. The narrator of these events was in New York, from which he escaped in an airship. He and his party flew to Europe, where similar revolts had taken place, and then on to Africa. They settled in a quiet part of Uganda and dedicated themselves to building the ideal civilization of the future.

Donnelly's anxiety about the power of capitalism was expressed in the propaganda of his People's Party, most of which he wrote himself. At the age of sixty-seven he disgusted his children by marrying a second wife, a girl of twenty-one. Two years later he was nominated by the People's Party as their candidate for Vice-President. The populist movement swept the Mid-West, but the election of 1900 was won by the Republicans. Their President, McKinley, was assassinated the following autumn, and 1901 was also the year of Donnelly's death. There were times in his career when it seemed as if he might achieve power in the United States, and had he became president the history of our times could have been very different. But there was never any real chance of that happening. Ignatius Donnelly could never bear to be orthodox. In every battle of his life he consistently supported the opposition against the authorities. His avoidance of being on the winning side in any issue seemed almost deliberate. If ever he had looked likely to become President of the United States, he would doubtless have found some new outrageous heresy to sabotage his campaign.

Shakespeare waiting to receive Bacon's play?
A suggestive illustration from a cipher manual of 1624.

SHAKESPEAREAN DECODERS
AND THE
BACONIAN TREASURE HUNT

The list of judges and distinguished lawyers who have pleaded the case for Francis Bacon as author of Shakespeare includes such names as Judge Holmes of the Missouri Supreme Court, Judge Stotsenburg of Indiana, the English judge Lord Penzance, Sir Edwin Durning-Lawrence and others of equal weight. If these people's pronouncements were as powerful in literature as in their courts, Bacon would long have been established in his claim. But the trouble with the Baconian case is that the evidence supporting it is all circumstantial. That sort of evidence may convince lawyers, but it has not impressed the literary judges. In their view the Shakespeare authorship belongs to William Shakspere by right of tradition and the Baconians' claim must be supported by positive proofs if their appeal is to be heard. What is demanded of the Baconians is documentary evidence that Francis Bacon himself ever claimed to have written Shakespeare.

In none of his known writings did Bacon ever make such a claim, but since Donnelly's time many people have believed that he made it secretly by means of a cipher. Bacon was certainly interested in cryptology, the art of encoding and decoding hidden messages, and he may have practised it as an agent of the Tudor government. His expert knowledge of the subject is revealed in a passage in his *De augmentis scientiarum* which begins:

'Let us proceed then to Ciphers. Of these there are many kinds: simple ciphers; ciphers mixed with non-significant characters; ciphers containing two different letters in one character; wheel ciphers; key-ciphers; word ciphers; and the like. But the virtues required in them are ... that they be easy and not laborious to write ... and lastly that they be if possible such as not to raise suspicion.'

This was published in the same year as the First Folio edition of the Shakespeare plays, in 1623, and Baconian cryptologists have found significance in the coincidence of dates, suggesting that Bacon's intention in *De augmentis* was to provide the key to a cipher which he had written into the works attributed to Shakespeare. Hundreds of people have devoted many years, even lifetimes, to cracking the supposed Bacon cipher, and almost all of them have claimed success, or partial success, through codes, anagrams, acrostics and other cryptic devices. Their efforts range from the interpretation of a few words or phrases in the Shakespeare canon to full-blown decipherings of entire works, not only Shakespeare's but those of other contemporary writers whose productions, or those generally accepted as such, might also have been written by Bacon.

An example of the anagrammatic approach to Shakespeare studies is that of the lawyer, Durning-Lawrence, who referred to the Stratford player as 'a drunken, illiterate Clown, who could not write so much as one letter of his own name, and was totally unable to read a single line of print'. In the most uproarious of Baconian works, *Bacon is Shake-speare* (an assertion he repeats in capitals throughout the book) he gives as one of his main proofs an anagram of the famous 'long word' HONORIFICA-BILITUDINITATIBUS, which occurs in *Love's Labour's Lost*. Rearranging its letters, Durning-Lawrence produced the Latin sentence, HI LUDI F. BACONIS NATI TUITI ORBI, meaning 'These plays, F. Bacon's offspring, are preserved for the world.' This was by no means the first Baconian anagram which the 'long word' had been made to yield: it is a favourite toy of heretical decoders. But Durning-Lawrence claimed his interpretation was uniquely correct, because in the First Folio edition of *Love's Labour's Lost* the word is the 151st (not counting italicized words) on page 136 and occurs in the 27th line, while the sum of the numerical values of the first and last letters in each of his Latin words (if a $=1$, b$=2$ etc.) is 136, the rest of the letters add up to 151 and there are 27 letters in HONORIFICABILITUDINITATIBUS. It 'surpasses the wit of man', declared Durning-Lawrence, to construct any other anagram with the same qualities from the long word. He offered a hundred guineas if anyone could do it. The challenge was soon taken up. A Mr Beevor of St Albans offered an alternative anagram of the long word, ABI INIVIT F. BACON HISTRIO LUDIT, which he translated 'Be off, F. Bacon, the actor has entered and is playing.' This phrase lacks the numerical qualities of

Durning-Lawrence's, but it evidently amused the good lawyer for he generously sent Mr Beevor his cheque for a hundred guineas.

Dr Owen's cipher wheel

This type of Shakespearean cryptography, involving anagrams and acrostics, has obvious appeal to lovers of literary puzzles and crosswords, and thus it has attracted many practitioners. They are the small fry of Baconian decipherers, the elite among them consisting of those, like Donnelly, who have produced long narrative passages from their decoding of Shakespeare plays. In that grand tradition the leading figure is Dr Orville W. Owen of Detroit. He was a physician with a good practice and a great love for the writings of Shakespeare which he would read on journeys between patients. One day there came into his mind some words spoken by the Bastard in King John:

'My dear Sir, thus leaning on my elbow I begin . . .'

These words struck him as superfluous and odd and made him suspect the presence of a cipher. This happened when he was about thirty years old, and for the next eight years, up to the early 1890s, he searched through the works of Shakespeare, Bacon, Greene, Peele, Marlowe, Spenser and Burton, all or most of which he attributed to Francis Bacon, in pursuit of further clues. Finally, by methods he never quite made clear, Owen managed to squeeze out from these works a very long, rambling message from Sir Francis Bacon, written in blank verse and containing elaborate instructions on how his writings were to be decoded.

There is an obvious strangeness about this procedure which has always mystified Owen's commentators. Having found and applied the key to unlocking Bacon's cipher, only then did he receive from Bacon the key by which his cipher was to be unlocked. It seems as if he went about things in the wrong order. Nevertheless, once he had obtained Bacon's instructions to his decipherer, Owen was scrupulous in following them out to the letter. This was no mean task. The instructions, besides being dreadfully wordy and vague, demanded immense labours from whoever cared to carry them out. The cipher ran through all Bacon's hidden works – Shakespeare, Marlowe, Spenser etc. – and all these had to be searched through for certain key words which the instructions did not precisely name. These were clues to other words or phrases of which the secret narrative was made up. The instructions were insistent that only someone with intuition could properly follow them, and Owen, who was a spiritualist and went very much by his intuition, felt himself uniquely qualified or even 'chosen' to be Bacon's interpreter.

One of the instructions told him to:

> Take your knife and cut all our books asunder,
> And set the leaves on a great firm wheel
> Which rolls and rolls, and turning the
> Fickle rolling wheel, throw your eyes
> Upon FORTUNE, that goddess blind, that stands upon
> A spherical stone, that turning and incessant rolls
> In restless variation.
> Mark her the prime mover:
> She is our first guide.

Owen constructed such a wheel. It consisted of two great revolving drums on which was rolled a canvas strip 2 feet wide and 1,000 feet long. As ordered, he cut up all his books of Bacon, Shakespeare and the other named authors and stuck them page by page onto the canvas. By cranking the drums in either direction he could pass the entire hidden Bacon canon under his eyes at whatever speed required. As the writings revolved he marked all sentences containing the 'guide' words, Fortune, Nature, Honour, Reputation and Pan, which led him to 'key' words such as Love and King or their synonyms, Devotion, Adore, Majesty, Highness and so on. These did not themselves constitute the message but indicated the occurrence of cipher text in the same or neighbouring sentences. Owen dictated the marked sentences to secretaries he had hired for the project, and they typed them out and filed them under the appropriate guide or key word. From the thousands of bits of paper thus obtained, Owen selected and put together the component parts of Bacon's cryptic outpourings.

The product was enough to fill six volumes, five of which Owen published between 1893 and 1895 as *Sir Francis Bacon's Cipher Story*. In the story was revealed for the first time the inside information on Queen Elizabeth's life and reign. It turned out that she had been married secretly to the Earl of Leicester and that Bacon was their son. He had been brought up in ignorance of this, but when he discovered who his real mother was and realized that he had been done out of his rights as heir to the throne, he made a scene. The Queen learnt that he had written *Hamlet,* took it as a personal attack on her and caused him to be banished to France. Elizabeth, according to the cipher, was eventually strangled by Robert Cecil to stop her from acknowledging Bacon her rightful heir.

This idea that Francis Bacon was the son of Queen Elizabeth has taken a strong hold on the minds of Baconians and occurs again and again in their literature. Many decipherers since Owen have claimed to have found confirmation of it. There is in fact a curious piece of evidence which might be taken to support it. On a wall of Canonbury Tower in north London, where Bacon once lived, is an old inscription recording the names of all English monarchs from William the Conqueror to Charles II. In the space between Elizabeth I and her successor, James I, are traces of a name. It has been deliberately chiselled away, apart from the initial letter which is F. The name could therefore have been Francis Bacon and the inscriber could have been asserting his royal rights. The fact that Nicholas Bacon left all his money to his other sons and nothing to Francis might also be taken as a hint of doubt about Francis's paternity.

After four volumes of Francis Bacon's cipher story had been worked out and published, Owen's assistants were so well trained that they were able to compile a fifth volume on their own. Some of those who visited the works believed, or were persuaded by Owen to believe, that they also could manipulate the cipher. One of them, a writer for the Detroit *Tribune,* published a long article about Owen's method and how, by following it, he personally had been able to elicit messages from Bacon. On the other hand, the expert cryptologists, William and Elizabeth Friedman, in their critical but good-humoured book on the anti-Stratfordian decipherers, *The Shakespearean Ciphers Examined,* say that Owen's system was so loose and subjective that it cannot really be called a system at all. It may be that his wheel, which produced narratives through a mixture of chance and intuition, was really an instrument of divination, a sort of crystal ball. Looking into it, Owen was not so much deciphering as recording messages from his own unconscious mind, or from the spirit world, according as one prefers to believe. But whatever the source of his material, Owen was sincere in his belief that it had been written into Elizabethan texts by Sir Francis Bacon in order to lay claim to the authorship which he could not acknowledge in his lifetime and to the right of birth which he had been denied. When people accused Owen of having made up the cipher stories out of his own head, he published a testimonial from a friend stating that he had 'never shown the slightest sign of possessing unusual or extraordinary literary skill, or genius'. Such extraordinary skill, it was implied, would have been necessary for compiling Bacon's secret reminiscences. But Owen may have had an excellent helper, for he claimed that his work was often intruded upon by Bacon's ghost.

The search for Bacon's boxes

The Baconian obsession, it appears, has three different forms which develop one from the other. The first involves arguments about the respective lives and literary styles of Bacon and Shakespeare. When those prove inconclusive, the next stage is the search for ciphers or anagrams in Shakespeare's works; and when these are disputed or ignored and fail to convince, all that is left is treasure-hunting, the search for Shakespeare's or someone else's manuscripts to decide the authorship question once and for all. Shakespearean treasure-hunts begin with Delia Bacon's abortive attempt on the Stratford tomb in 1856 and they are not confined to Baconians. In 1956 Mr Calvin Hoffman, the American Marlovian, author of *The Man Who Was Shakespeare*, managed to open the Walsingham tomb at Chislehurst in an unsuccessful search for documents which, he hoped, would prove Marlowe to have been that man. But of all such delvers for buried papers Dr Owen was the most ambitious and adventurous.

Owen's promotion from decipherer to treasure-hunter came at a critical time in his life. His Baconian labours had distracted him from medical practice and absorbed most of his money, and only a faithful few had been convinced by his cipher. Even the editors of Baconian journals held aloof from it. He needed a breakthrough, and one came with his discovery of a new form of cipher. This one worked by letters rather than words and sentences. Owen started at one of his key words and spelt out messages letter by letter, moving up, down, diagonally or sideways like a king in chess. That provided its name, the King's Move Cipher. Applying it to Sidney's *Arcadia*, which he also attributed to Bacon, Owen obtained the information which set him on his new tack. The gist of it was that Bacon had concealed manuscripts and other

217

treasures in a number of boxes which he had buried somewhere near a castle and the confluence of the rivers Severn and Wye. Abandoning his wheel, Owen set off for England with his wife and young children.

Also in the expedition was its principal backer, Dr Prescott of Boston, whose wife, Kate, wrote a gossipy account of their adventures in a book called *Reminiscences of a Baconian.* They were veterans in the Bacon cause. Some years earlier they had been to Stratford-on-Avon in company with Mrs Elizabeth Wells Gallup, a former assistant of Owen who had made her name as an independent decipherer of Shakespeare. Using a different key from Owen's, the Bi-lateral Cipher described by Bacon in *De augmentis,* she obtained similar information about Queen Elizabeth and how she was really Bacon's mother. In America, Mrs Gallup found a patron, Colonel George Fabyan, a flamboyant character who spent much of the fortune he had made in textiles on supporting and publicizing the work of Baconian decipherers. She was installed in Fabyan's research institution on his estate at Geneva, Illinois, where she spent the best part of her life working out Bacon's hidden messages in the works of Shakespeare and other authors. Many of the scholars whom Fabyan induced to visit Geneva were impressed by her results, which were obtained through microscopic analysis of the different kinds of type-face found in early editions of Shakespeare, but the Friedmans assert that these results could be repeated by no one else, not even her own students. Fabyan also helped to fund Owen's expedition.

The Prescotts were its advance guard. They booked rooms for the party at a hotel in Chepstow, the nearest town to the spot indicated by Owen's cipher, and prepared the ground by identifying some of the landmarks it mentioned. Sure enough, there was a ruined castle at Chepstow, and when Owen arrived other landmarks were located, just where the cipher had said they would be. Thus encouraged the expedition set to work.

The great Bacon treasure hunt lasted intermittently for fifteen years, from 1909, the date of Owen's original excursion, to the last efforts in 1920 and 1924 which were directed by his followers. It provided moments of high hope and excitement and a high level of employment for Chepstow labourers. To open the campaign Owen hired a boatman to row the party up and down the Wye in search of a cave where, according to the cipher, Bacon's boxes were hidden. The most likely place was thought to be some holes in a cliff near the castle. They were inaccessible, so ladders and scaffolding had to be erected before workmen could enter and excavate them. Some interesting features of old Chepstow were uncovered by the diggings, but nothing of Bacon's, and work was suspended for a year, the Prescotts returning to America while Dr Owen stayed in Britain to mull over his cipher.

The failure of the first season's work was soon explained. From a reworking of the cipher Owen discovered that Bacon had later removed his boxes from the cave where they were first hidden, and reburied them in a chamber he had constructed below the river Wye. This was confirmed to him by the arrival of an anonymous letter. Its writer quoted Ben Jonson's lines to the Droeshout portrait of Shakespeare in the Folio, beginning:

> This figure that thou here seest put
> It was for gentle Shakespeare cut,

and informed Owen that the second line could be anagrammed to read:

> Seek, sir, a true angle at Chepstow – F.

In the tradition of mystical treasure-hunters Owen was receptive to clues of that sort, and he took it for granted that Bacon had inserted the anagram in a line of someone else's verse as a guide to the whereabouts of his boxes. It does not seem to have occurred to him that such a line can be anagrammed in dozens of different ways to produce any nonsense required. If Bacon, Ben Jonson or whoever wrote the line had concealed an anagram in it, their message could equally well have been 'Seek a sure triangle at Chepstow' or 'Seek for a castle; swag put in there' or 'Stalk treasure, Owen – cheap gifts' or even 'Forget it! Shakespeare cult wanes.' Dr Owen wasted no time with such unhelpful alternatives. He accepted the version sent by the unknown correspondent and began digging pits in the bed of the river Wye.

The faithful Prescotts rejoined him for this new enterprise, and another patron was the Duke of Beaufort, the owner of Chepstow Castle, who allowed Owen to rummage round it and appointed an engineer, Fred Hammond, to assist him. He also provided Mr Harry Pirie Gordon, a young man from Oxford, to supervise the proceedings. Both these agents fell under Owen's spell, and with the Duchess of Beaufort they joined enthusiastically in his quest. In return for his support the Duke stipulated that Bacon's cache, when found, should be presented to the Nation.

Owen was never quite sure how to work out the 'true angle at Chepstow' or how to reconcile the conflicting clues to the location of Bacon's treasure provided by the cipher. This meant that many different sites had to be probed. At each of the likely spots, workmen had to sink piles and shafts into the river bed, pump out water, shovel mud and excavate with pickaxes. Often they would continue far into the night, working by the light of flares and always alert to the erratic movements of the Wye and the danger from floods. The winter of 1910-11 was cold and rainy, but Owen was constantly by the river, directing the diggings and infecting both workers and spectators with excitement. Every time a pick struck solid rock he was sure that the quest was at an end and that Bacon's storeroom had at last been found. On one occasion some large stones were unearthed and the doctor cried out, 'We're onto it boys I guess!' But it was not to be. The only significant find was a stone cistern, empty, with marks on the lid which Owen fancied were cryptic signatures of Bacon.

After months of hard, unprofitable labour, the excavation programme was brought to an abrupt end by Colonel Fabyan withdrawing his support. The treasure-hunters, who had thought themselves on the brink of triumph, were disappointed but not disheartened. Owen had a way of instilling faith in his followers. Their only complaint was about his unwillingness to initiate them fully into the mysteries of the cipher, thus denying them the opportunity to work out the secret of Bacon's hiding-place for themselves. However, when the outbreak of war in 1914 made further explorations impossible, and Dr Owen went back to Detroit, he allowed the Prescotts access to his latest cipher work. With the benefit of fresh clues, they embarked on another season's treasure-hunting at Chepstow. Their diggings in the cellar of the old castle nearly brought down its walls, but all they found was an iron handle. This, they believed, belonged to the box where Bacon had stored his treasures. The box itself never turned up.

In 1924 yet another expedition from America appeared at Chepstow. It was led by Mr Harold S. Howard, an old associate and backer of Owen, who had also financed the Prescott party. His approach was to hire a boatman to search along the banks of the Wye for a hidden flight of steps which he thought was referred to in the cipher. The Duke of Beaufort's man, Mr Hammond, still active in the hunt, kept to the old idea that Chepstow Castle was the right place to look, and numerous

Baconians and mystics, who assembled from all over the country to assist the enterprise, each had ideas of their own. Howard finally settled on a grotto in nearby Piercefield Park as the most likely repository for the treasure, but its owner was alienated by his eccentric behaviour and denied him access.

That same year, Dr Owen died in Detroit after a long illness. He never lost faith in his cipher, but at the end he advised others to avoid the Bacon obsession which had cost him his health, fortune and reputation and gained him nothing. It had also prevented him from developing other interests in which his brilliant imagination might have been better employed. He was said to have invented an anti-gravity machine which was rejected by the US Government, to whom he offered it, with the excuse that it reminded them of the perpetual motion devices beloved by cranks. The Friedmans, who knew Colonel Fabyan, heard from him that Owen had also discovered the secret of how Christ walked on the water. The technique came from Francis Bacon, who had confirmed it by experiment and written it into one of his ciphered works decoded by Owen. It had to do with sound and the use of high-frequency vibrations. Fabyan hired a scientist to repeat the experiments and claimed that, while not exactly successful, they did produce some notable advances in the field of acoustics.

Dr Owen's warning against involvement with the Bacon-Shakespeare controversy seems to have been little heeded, for many since his day have tried their hands at unravelling Bacon's cipher, and the sport is still going on. But after the retirement of its two giants, Owen and the still more formidable Mrs Gallup, its standards declined. Many Baconians had pinned their hopes on the Owen and Gallup ciphers, and when even these, the products of such ingenuity and patience, could make no real impression on Shakespearean orthodoxy, they were naturally somewhat disheartened. Since its golden age at the turn of last century the Baconian movement has never been quite the same. All that can be said in favour of Bacon's authorship of Shakespeare has already been said and can only be repeated, and few converts have ever been made by any of the proposed ciphers. It seems that the only way out of this dead end is through another Baconian treasure hunt, as ambitious as Dr Owen's but more successful in its outcome.

Sigmund Freud and the case of Mr Looney

If Baconism has somewhat declined this century, other schools have grown up and flourished. In 1920 an English schoolmaster, J.T. Looney, published *'Shakespeare' Identified,* putting forward the claims of Edward de Vere, seventeenth Earl of Oxford, poet, playwright and courtier, whose volatile character and career were similar to those of Shakespeare's Hamlet. Looney had written his book some years earlier; its delayed appearance was due to the cowardice of his first intended publisher, who was frightened of being laughed at and insisted that Looney adopt a nom de plume. Very properly Looney refused to be ashamed of his name, and his book was eventually brought out by Cecil Collins who went on to publish many other 'Oxfordian' books. Soon they were flowing thick and fast. De Vere is an attractive candidate, and his case gained influential support, notably from Dr Sigmund Freud. The Father of Psychoanalysis recognized the author of Shakespeare as an early adept of his own profession, and ridiculed the notion that his great predecessor could have been the boor from Stratford. On the other hand, Edward de Vere, whom Freud called 'the nobly-born and highly cultivated, passionately wayward, to some extent *déclassé* aristocrat', had all the qualities, psychologically speaking, which Freud attributed to the true Shakespeare. When Freud adopted a belief he expected his followers to adopt it also, and those among them who obstinately retained the Stratfordian faith were a source of irritation to him. His English colleagues warned him how dangerous it was to question the National Hero – particularly in the name of Looney – but Freud insisted on publicizing his Oxfordian faith. Only once did he yield, when James Strachey, the translator of his *Autobiographical Study*, shamefully objected to being associated with the name Looney and deleted a passage where it appeared. Freud accused him of nationalistic narcissism and insisted on including the name in the American edition.

A common criticism of the Stratfordians is that they are excessively fond of mocking their opponents; and cruel chance has fed their wit, not only with Looney, but with such names as George Battey, who thought Shakespeare had been written by Daniel Defoe, and S.E. Silliman, a Marlovian author.

Christoper Marlowe, though a late entry to the race, is a well-backed outsider in the Shakespeare stakes. His main handicap is that he was killed in a pub brawl in 1593, long before most of Shakespeare was written – or so it is recorded. But Mr Calvin Hoffman, a former Broadway critic, suggests in his book, *The Man Who Was 'Shakespeare'*, that Marlowe's murder was a put-up job. Marlowe at the time was facing arrest for blasphemy, atheism and other atrocities, and it is possible that his homosexual protector, Thomas Walsingham, faked his death and smuggled him away to the security of his estate, Scadby Park near Chislehurst. If that was the case, Marlowe would have had the best of reasons for not publishing under his own name.

The young school of Marlovians have shown a precocious tendency towards treasure-hunting. After the failure of Hoffman's rifling of the Walsingham tomb their interest became fixed on Canterbury, where Marlowe was born. Several of their writers have hinted at a conspiracy against him in his native city. One of them, observing that his birthplace had recently been torn down for shop development, enquired at the city's information office why he was not more celebrated there, and was told that Marlowe was still disliked in Canterbury because every time he paid a visit home he was drunk.

Another Marlovian author, David Rhys Williams, wrote that on a visit to Canterbury he met Dr William Urry, the city archivist, who showed him 'a carton containing (we understood him to say) over 500 newly discovered documents concerning Marlowe, either directly or indirectly, many of which identified him as Shakespeare'. Dr Urry was working on a report to be published about them. That was before 1966 when Mr Williams's book came out. A letter recently addressed to Dr Urry (January 1983) was kindly replied to by the present archivist, Miss Anne Oakley, with the sad news that Dr Urry had died two years ago, his book uncompleted. As to the documents, she said, 'they mostly concern the misdemeanours of the Marlowe family which were very extensive'.

The Marlowe and Oxford schools have both produced cryptographers, not nearly so ambitious as the Baconians, but still good in their minor way. Oxford himself was inclined to make play on his name, Vere or Ver, and his followers have done likewise. Their favourite among the Shakespeare Sonnets is the 76th, which is also quoted by the other schools as hinting at their candidates. It starts:

> Why write I still all one, ever the same,
> And keep invention in a noted weed,
> That every word doth almost sel my name,
> Showing their birth and where they did proceed?

'Weed' means disguise and 'sel' means either sell, tell or spell, according to whichever literary expert one follows. The phrase 'every word' preceding it can be anagrammed as Eyword Ver or Eword Very, which does indeed almost sell, tell or spell the name Edward Vere.

Another near-anagram, perhaps a rather better one, is here presented as an original offering to the Oxfordians. The well-known dedication to the Sonnets reads: TO. THE. ONLIE. BEGETTER. OF. THESE. ENSVING. SONNETS. Mr.W.H. ALL. HAPPINESSE. AND. THAT. ETERNITIE. PROM-ISED. BY. OVR. EVER. LIVING. POET. WISHETH. THE. WELL-WISHING. ADVENTVRER. IN. SETTING. FORTH. T.T. The Oxfordians have been attracted to the phrase OVR EVER LIVING because Ever is an anagram of Vere. But one can do better than that with an anagram of the entire phrase – VERO NIL VERIVS, – perfect except for the last letter (s taking the place of G), and possibly significant because VERO NIL VERIUS, meaning 'There is nothing more true than the truth', was the motto on the coat of arms of Edward de Vere!

The most audacious anagram of the Marlovians is the subject of William Honey's *The Shakespeare Epitaph Deciphered*, where it is said that Christopher Marlowe looked like William Shakspere and took advantage of that by arranging to have Shakspere murdered and then assuming his personality. It was therefore Marlowe who was buried at Stratford-on-Avon. Honey's main proof of this comes from anagram-ming the malediction carved on the Stratford gravestone. The inscription was renewed in the eighteenth century, and its original form is known only from records of that time.

With slight adjustments to the normal rules of the game, explained in his book, Honey produced the following anagram of the malediction showing what the writer really meant to say.

> Good ffrend who wishes for Shakespeare
> To digge the dust: entombed heae:
> Playes by the man, verses hys sonnets
> And Christopher Marlowe's bones.

With so many excellent proofs and so many worthy candidates to choose among, it is no easy matter to decide who one thinks Shakespeare really was. It is all very well for the Stratfordians, Baconians etc., but not everyone can aspire to their certitudes. Perhaps the 'groupists' are right and the author was a combination of Oxford, Marlowe, Bacon, Derby, Rutland, Raleigh, Buckhurst, Dyer, Greene, Peele, Kyd, Jonson, Burton, Defoe, Florio, Sherley, Spenser, More, Paget, Dekker, Webster, the Earl and Countess of Pembroke, Queen Elizabeth, King James and all the other claimants – or some permutation among them – assisted maybe by an obscure rustic from Stratford-on-Avon. It would be nice to know the answer, and perhaps some day we will. But if ever the authorship of Shakespeare is established beyond doubt by the discovery of some indisputable item of proof, it will be a sad day for followers of this most classic controversy, which has produced so many colourful characters and inspired such heroic feats of imagination and fanaticism.

EMINENT UFOLOGISTS

On 24 June 1947 an American pilot, Kenneth Arnold, observed a chain of nine brilliant objects flying in formation over the Cascade Mountians in the State of Washington. They were moving at a faster rate than any known aircraft could manage, and Arnold compared them to saucers skimming and bouncing off the surface of water. In newspaper reports they were referred to as 'flying saucers'.

Flying saucers proliferated. Within a few years thousands of similar sightings had been reported, and the rumour spread that earth was being visited by extra-terrestrial spacecraft. This was apparently confirmed in 1952 when an American mystic, George Adamski, was observed by six witnesses in conversation with a handsome, young, fair-haired Venusian who had just stepped out of a flying saucer in the California desert. His account of the meeting, supported by the witnesses' affidavits, was appended to a book, *Flying Saucers Have Landed*, written by an Irish landowner of an old and eccentric family, Desmond Leslie.

The effect of the book was sensational. It was published in many languages, and droves of people responded with descriptions of flying saucer sightings, meetings with their occupants and other weird experiences. One of Leslie's correspondents was the Honourable Brinsley le Poer Trench, advertising manager to a chain of London journals. He had never himself seen a flying saucer but the subject appealed to him. If it were true that beings from other planets were beginning to appear on earth, people and governments should be alerted to what was happening and preparations should be made to receive the visitors. A meeting was called at le Poer Trench's London flat, attended by Desmond Leslie and a few other interested people. They each put up £10 to start a magazine, *Flying Saucer Review*. Its first editor was Derek Dempster, aviation correspondent of the *Daily Express*, who was succeeded the following year by le Poer Trench. Flying saucers later became known more professionally as unidentified flying objects or UFOs, but the *Flying Saucer Review* kept its name and earned fame as the oldest and most reliable of UFO journals.

George Adamski came to Europe in 1959 and stepped immediately into the headlines by gaining an audience with Queen Juliana of the Netherlands. Neither party published an account of whatever passed between them, but the Dutch press was scandalized. Adamski was found to be the leader of a California cult, the Royal Order of Tibet, and lecturer on esoteric lore at a monastery he had founded at Laguna Beach. Panic spread through Holland at the idea of the Court being infested by a new Rasputin. The UFO missionary withdrew to Switzerland, where a series of lectures had been arranged for him by an admirer in Basle, Miss Lou Zinsstag.

Since the encounter in the California desert Adamski's UFO experiences had multiplied. Like many other 'contactees' he claimed to be in constant telepathic communication with the space beings. They had allowed him to film their flying saucers, entrusted him with their messages to mankind and taken him on trips to the moon and several planets. Lou Zinsstag, who recently published a book on Adamski in collaboration with long-serving UFO-investigator Timothy Good, says that she was inclined to believe most of Adamski's claims, partly because she considered him an honest character and partly because of some extraordinary experiences she had in his company. He had a mediumistic type of charisma. Poltergeist disturbances seemed to follow him around, and his associates were often impressed by his gift for telepathy. In Basle he received regular visits from mysterious young men who, he hinted, were natives of other worlds. Lou Zinsstag herself had some encounters with these people. They looked much like ordinary folk, but could be identified by their habit of responding automatically to orders directed at them by thought. Adamski said that many people from outer space were walking about the world disguised as humans. One whom he met in Copenhagen in 1963 handed him a package to be delivered personally to the Pope. Attended by his Swiss admirer, he set off for Rome where, he said, a Papal audience had been arranged for him. He was seen to enter a small door in the side of the Vatican, emerging an hour later with the news that the dying Pope John XXIII had received the package from him with the words, 'This is what I have been waiting for.' Another momentous visit he claimed was to the White House with a message for President Kennedy, urging him to fly to an Air Force base where a friendly space craft had landed. Kennedy rushed off to the base, apparently, and had a long talk with the crew, but was not invited for a flying saucer ride. Thus was confirmed the most enduring suspicion among UFO students, that the authorities know a great deal more about flying saucers than they pretend.

A cousin of Lou Zinsstag was the great C.G. Jung. He took seriously and deplored the official suppression of news about flying saucers, which he had learnt about from the writings of a former US Air Force major, Donald Keyhoe. The major had also informed him that flying saucers are sometimes apparent on radar screens. This persuaded Jung that they could not be of a purely psychological nature. Without ruling out the extra-terrestrial or any other possible explanation, he suggested that the aerial apparitions were 'symptoms of psychic changes' to be expected at the beginning of the Age of Aquarius. In his book, *Flying Saucers, a Modern Myth of Things Seen in the Skies*, Jung went deeply into the subject – to the embarrassment of his disciples, who did their best to play down the master's enthusiasm for ufology. His cousin kept him informed on the latest developments in the field, and astonished him with her collection of UFO photographs, including those taken by Adamski. She tried to arrange a meeting between the two men, but Jung was wary and would not join the list of Adamski's famous acquaintances.

Apart from a modest income from his books, Adamski made no money out of his exploits, and his early followers were impressed by his sincerity. They were also thrilled by the items of wisdom he passed down from the Space Brothers – which happen to have included many of the ecological doctrines that became popular a decade later. Then suddenly he seemed to deteriorate. His claims grew wilder and contradictory and the space messages trailed off into trivial moralizings. Disciples were shocked by the discovery that the details he had given of his alleged space travels were largely repeated from a science-fiction story he had written some years earlier. Even his closest adherents began to waver in their faith, and the cause of the Space Brothers lost the best part of its following. The name of Adamski was banned for a time from the pages of *Flying Saucer Review*.

After he died in 1965 his reputation started to mend. Desmond Leslie had always stood by his co-author and, with Lou Zinsstag and other loyalists, found ways of accounting for Adamski's lapses. He had once said that the original Brothers who had guided his mission were due to be replaced by another shift. These newcomers may not have been as wise and benevolent as the first bunch; they may even have misled Adamski deliberately, perhaps in order to discredit him for having revealed forbidden knowledge. There was also the possibility of mischief by the CIA or some other secret agency with an interest in suppressing the space message by confusing its oracle. A feature of UFO literature is the repeated claim by flying saucer witnesses, investigators and writers to have received visits from sinister men dressed in black or in black Cadillacs, frightening them off the subject. George Adamski moved always in the midst of such phenomena. Eventually they may have overwhelmed him.

So say his apologists, and maybe they are not far off the track. As many of its students have become aware, the subject of flying saucers is rather like practical occultism, tending to manifest its phenomena to those who invoke them. Since Adamski's time – and long before it – there have been cases which parallel his, even though they provide no real explanation of it; cases of prophets inspired by other-worldly beings, flourishing in wisdom and attracting a following, only to be misled and made fools of by the powers they relied on. John Keel, the best of all UFO writers, gives some striking examples in his book, *Operation Trojan Horse,* the most dramatic being that of the Brazilian UFO prophet, contactee and author, Aladino Felix.

Under the name Dino Kraspedon, Felix in 1959 published *My Contact with Flying Saucers,* describing his first encounter some years earlier with planetary beings and the interesting things they told him about their method of space travel and the true nature of the universe. Like Adamski, he began to have regular visits from the Venusians, and often came across them in public places. He became an inspired preacher and made a name for himself as a prophet. He accurately foretold a number of local disasters and, to a television audience, the assassinations of Martin Luther King and Robert Kennedy. Then he predicted an outburst of terrorism in São Paulo. This duly took place. Banks, police stations and the American consulate were among important buildings blown up by a mysterious gang. When finally they were rounded up by the police, their leader turned out to be the famous Aladino Felix. On being arrested he declared himself an agent of the Venusians, whose coming rule on earth he was expediting.

John Keel is one of several writers who have described the strange incidents and phenomena that came to haunt their personal lives when they began specializing in the subject of UFOs. 'Within a year after I had launched my full-time UFO investigation effort in 1966,' Keel wrote, 'the phenomenon had zeroed in on me. My telephone ran amok first, with mysterious strangers calling day and night to deliver bizarre messages "from the space people". Then I was catapulted into the dreamlike fantasy world of demonology. I kept rendezvous with black Cadillacs on Long Island, and when I tried to pursue them, they would disappear impossibly on dead-end roads. . . . Luminous aerial objects seemed to follow me around like faithful dogs. The objects seemed to know where I was going and where I had been. I would check into a motel chosen at random only to find that someone had made a reservation in my name and had even left a string of nonsensical telephone messages for me. I was plagued by impossible coincidences, and some of my closest friends in New York, none of whom was conversant with the phenomenon, began to report strange experiences of their own – poltergeists erupted in their apartments, ugly smells of hydrogen sulfide haunted them. . . . More than once I woke up in the middle of the night to find myself unable to move, with a huge dark apparition standing over me.'

A distinguished victim of his own interest in the UFO problem was the psychologist Dr Wilhelm Reich. From observations of unidentified luminous objects over his laboratories at Rangeley, Maine, Reich concluded that they were animated by the 'orgone energy' which he believed to be the universal force of life. He began experimenting on passing UFOs, using an instrument of his own design to liquidate them by drawing off their energy. Succeeding in this, he became convinced that the objects were inter-galactic spacecraft, navigating the universal orgone stream, and that their means of propulsion could be discovered and reproduced. Reich's obsession with the subject led to a change in his character and a series of disasters, ending with his arrest and death in prison.

Meanwhile, at the offices of the *Flying Saucer Review* normality continued to reign. UFO happenings were soberly reported and discussed, and no one sought or suffered personal contact with them. Brinsley le Poer Trench completed his spell as editor and went on to write seven books about UFOs, concentrating on their reported activities in ancient and Biblical times and originating many of the ideas later popularized by the best-selling Erich von Däniken. In his latest, *Secret of the Ages,* he reveals that most UFOs come, not from space, but from bases inside the earth, which is hollow and inhabited. There are entrances at each pole, and contact with the interior is also possible by way of a secret tunnel system beneath the earth's surface, built in ancient times by colonists from space. These people are still present, within the hollow earth and in caverns deep beneath our feet. They are constantly kidnapping people, twisting their minds and returning them to the surface as their programmed agents, in preparation for their forthcoming invasion of the upper earth. As proof of the hollow earth, Brinsley le Poer Trench displays a satellite photograph which does indeed show a large black spot, possibly a cavity, at the North Pole. The American agency responsible for the photograph has, of course, a quite different explanation of it.

With his advanced views, seniority, dignified appearance and kindly, approachable manner, Brinsley le Poer Trench is perfectly qualified for the position he has achieved as leader of the international UFO movement. His recipe for the harmony of nations is to stimulate their common interest in the mysteries of space. In 1967 he founded Contact International as a means of linking UFO study groups in different countries, in many of which he has attended meetings. One of his missions was to Japan, where his books are popular, to officiate at the launching of a new UFO religion and the unveiling of a monument to the Space Brothers. His reputation in Japan was noted by Mr Honda the famous motor-manufacturer, who came to London in 1983 and invited le Poer Trench to a reception. He was anxious to know the methods by which UFOs are propelled. A letter containing all the known or surmised details was sent off to him, but the magnate has not yet responded. If the instructions he received were correct, it is possible that earth's answer to the space-ships of other planets will be a Japanese model now under construction at the Honda factory.

It seemed appropriate to ufologists the world over when in 1975 Brinsley le Poer Trench inherited the title Earl of Clancarty and a seat in the House of Lords. His performance there lived up to all their expectations. Upon taking his seat in Parliament's Upper Chamber, Lord Clancarty began pressing the Government to open their files on flying saucers. Like many other ufologists he is convinced that the world's leaders have secret information on the nature of the phenomenon which they dare not release for fear of causing panic. Throughout his career he has argued strongly against that supposed policy. The public, he believes, should be prepared for the shock of extra-terrestrial contact. In January 1979 he succeeded in persuading the House of Lords to debate the subject.

It was the first time that UFOs had been the subject of debate in a national legislative assembly, even though several heads of government have seen the objects and professed interest in them. Idi Amin once enjoyed a UFO sighting on the shores of Lake Victoria and wisely explained that it meant 'good luck to Uganda'. Sir Eric Gairy, who ruled the Caribbean island of Grenada for several years before losing office in a coup, was a most active ufologist. Following a sighting of his own in 1975, he persuaded the United Nations to hold a UFO debate and urged them to declare 1978 the Year of the UFO. The debate took place, and Gairy astounded a conference of his fellow Commonwealth prime ministers by addressing them at length on the UFO problem; but the Year of the UFO was opposed by both the Americans and Russians and nothing came of it.

Some years before his rise to fame, Jimmy Carter spotted a UFO, and in his presidential campaign in 1976 promised to disclose all that was officially known about them. After his election, however, the pledge was either forgotten or found to be impracticable.

The historic House of Lords UFO debate attracted a number of members who had never before shown interest in the proceedings there. Lord Clancarty opened it by summarizing the UFO phenomenon and calling on the British Government to take the initiative in setting up an international agency to study it. He was warmly supported by Lord Kimberley, Liberal Party spokesman on aerospace, who deplored government secrecy on the matter of UFOs and told of a hidden pact between the United States and the Soviet Union to exchange UFO information but to withhold it from other nations. The speakers who followed mostly declared themselves against UFO censorship. Lord Gainford described a personal sighting, and the Bishop of Norwich raised an interesting theological point, relating to the old question as to whether inhabitants of other planets have immortal souls. His merciful conclusion was that redemption through Christ obtains throughout the galaxies.

The success of the debate encouraged Clancarty to form the House of Lords All Party UFO Study Group, bringing to light some previously unsuspected UFO enthusiasts, such as Lady Falkender, the former aide of Mr Harold Wilson. Several of its members are elderly politicians who once served in government, but unfortunately none of them knows or can remember anything important about state UFO secrets. Admiral of the Fleet Lord Hill-Norton, a recently converted ufologist, now laments the opportunities he missed, in the days when he was First Sea Lord, of studying the Navy's UFO intelligence.

There seems in fact to be little justification for all the talk about official cover-ups. UFO researchers over four decades have achieved almost nothing towards explaining the phenomenon, and there is no good reason to suppose that governments or their secret agencies are better informed than anyone else. The problem has more sides to it than can be covered by the simple theory of inter-planetary spacecraft. In the early days of Adamski, when UFO fever was raging, there were many who expected that ambassadors from space would shortly be landing on the White House lawn or somewhere else purposeful. When that failed to happen, ufologists became introspective and turned to examining aspects of their subject which were not necessarily connected with visitors from other galaxies. John Keel pointed out that most items of UFO lore were precisely those of traditional folklore in space-age dress. The modern reports of people being abducted by space beings and taken to other worlds continue the age-old theme of capture and levitation by fairies or spirits. In many of these cases, both the ancient and modern versions, the victim is returned in a state of trance or shock, and the experience may have a lasting effect on his character. In traditional societies a person who is taken away by spirits is marked out as a future witch-doctor or shaman, and many UFO-contactees develop mediumistic powers which, for lack of proper function, may actually drive them insane. Adamski's may be a case in point. Thus a growing belief among ufologists is that their subject has less to do with extra-terrestrial contacts than with the perpetual mysteries of life on earth. There is no telling, of course. This earth may well have received visitors from other galaxies, who could reappear at any moment. It is therefore reassuring that, in the event of an incursion by space invaders, Lord Clancarty and the lords and ladies of his All Party Group are there to deal with them.

BIBLIOGRAPHY

A dreadfully persistent lover

Arthur M. Sullivan. *New Ireland*, vol. 1, pp. 382-410. London, 1897.

Ada Jane Arbuthnot. 'The Arbuthnot Abduction', in *Memories of the Arbuthnots of Kincairdshire and Aberdeenshire*. London, 1920.

Carden Miscellany, no. 3. Singapore, 1975.

The strange adventure of a Somerset genealogist

Sir Ian Stuart-Knill, Bart. *The Pedigree of Arthur*. Sidmouth, 1971.

Kingdom Voice magazine. January and February 1972.

Loyalists of the flat earth

'Parallax' (S.B. Rowbotham). *Zetetic Astronomy*. Birmingham, 1849; second edition London, 1873.

—. *Experimental Proofs*. London, 1870.

R.A. Proctor, *Myths and Marvels of Astronomy*. London, 1878.

John Hampden, *Is Water Level?*. Chippenham, 1870.

William Carpenter. *'Common Sense' on Astronomy*. London, 1863-66.

—. *Water, Not Convex*. London, 1871.

—. *Wallace's Wonderful Water*. London, 1875.

—. *One Hundred Proofs that the Earth is Not a Globe*. Baltimore, 1885.

Alfred Russel Wallace. *My Life*. London, 1905. Account of the Old Bedford Level experiment, II, 365-76.

The Field. London, 26 March 1870, p. 285. On the Old Bedford Level experiment.

William Edgell, *Does the Earth Rotate?*. Radstock, 1914.

E.A.M. Blount. *Adrian Galilio*. Malvern, 1898.

—. *Flat or Spherical?*. Kingston Hill, 1905.

—. (ed.), *The Earth* journal. Wimbledon, 1900.

Albert Smith (ed.). *Earth Not a Globe Review*. Leicester, 1893-97.

English Mechanic and World of Science. London, LXXX, 1904. Correspondence on Old Bedford Level experiment.

Irving Wallace. *The Square Pegs*. London, 1958. Chapter 1.

Martin Gardner. *Fads and Fallacies in the Name of Science*. New York, 1957. Chapter 2.

Charles K. Johnson (ed.). *Flat Earth News*. Lancaster, California, 93539-2533.

The community that dwelt within the earth

Dr. Cyrus Teed ('Koresh') and U.G. Morrow. *The Cellular Cosmogony, or, The Earth a Concave Sphere*. Chicago, 1898.

Elliott J. Mackle. 'The Koreshan Unity in Florida 1894-1910'. Unpublished thesis, University of Miami, Florida, 1971.

—. 'Cyrus Teed and the Lee County Elections of 1906' in *The Florida Historical Quarterly*, July 1978.

The diehard priest who opposed capitalism

Jeremiah O'Callaghan. *Usury or Lending at Interest ... Proved to be Repugnant to the Divine and Ecclesiastical Law and Destructive to Civil Society*. London, 1828.

William Cobbett. *History of the Protestant Reformation*. London, 1829.

'O'Callaghan, Jeremiah', in *New Catholic Encyclopedia*.

A most conservative M.P. and the royal boycott of Lincoln

Arthur R. Maddison. *An Account of the Sibthorp Family*. Lincoln, 1896.
Christopher Sykes. *Two Studies in Virtue*. London, 1953.
—. 'Colonel Sibthorp: the Festival Centenary', in *History Today*, May, 1951, pp. 14-20.

The first lady of conspiratology

Nesta Webster. *The French Revolution*. London, 1919.
—. *Secret Societies and Subversive Movements*. London, 1924.
—. *Spacious Days: an Autobiography*. London, 1950.
—. *World Revolution: the Plot against Civilization*. London, 1921.
Richard Gilman. *Behind World Revolution*. Ann Arbor, 1982.
Robert Eringer. *The Conspiracy Peddlers*. Mason, Michigan, 1981.
Gary Allen. *None Dare Call it Conspiracy*. Seal Beach, California, 1972.

The man who got letters from statues

Baron Ludwig de Gueldenstubbé. *Pneumatologie positive*. Paris, 1857.
Frank Podmore. *Mediums of the Nineteenth Century*. New York, 1963.

Two unusual landowners

Henry Wilson and James Caulfield. *The Book of Wonderful Characters*. London, 1869, pp. 93-106. On Lord Rokeby.
Sir S. Egerton Brydges. *Public Characters*. 1817, I. On Lord Rokeby.
Gentleman's Magazine. London 1800, pp. 1219-20. On Lord Rokeby. 1804, p. 785. On H.L. Warner.
Edward Hasted. *The History of Kent*. Canterbury, 1801, vol. viii, p. 57. On Lord Rokeby.
S.J. Pratt. *Gleanings in England*. London 1801. On H.L. Warner.

The consolation of a jilted Latvian

Edward Leedskalnin. *A Book in Every Home* Homestead, Florida, 1936.

—. *Magnetic Current*. Homestead, 1945.
Pamphlets and postcards illustrating the works of Edward Leedskalnin are sold at Coral Castle, US 1 at SW 286th Street, Miami, Florida.

The judge who visited wild men

James Burnett, Lord Monboddo. *The Origin and Progress of Language*. 1733-92.
—. *Ancient Metaphysics*. 1779-99.
William Robertson (ed.). *Account of a Savage Girl Caught Wild in the Woods of Champagne*. Edinburgh, 1768.
William Knight. *Lord Monboddo and Some of his Contemporaries*. London, 1900.
E.L. Cloyd. *James Burnett, Lord Monboddo*. Oxford, 1972.

A crusader for thoroughbred people

Karl Pearson. *The Life, Letters and Labours of Francis Galton*. Cambridge, 1924.
D.W. Forrest. *Francis Galton: the Life and Works of a Victorian Genius*. London, 1974.
Hesketh Pearson. 'Uncle Frank', chapter in *Extraordinary People*. New York, 1965.
Francis Galton. *Inquiries into Human Faculty*. London, 1883.
—. *Memories of my Life*. London, 1908.
—, and others. *The Prayer-Gauge Debate*, ed. John O. Means. Boston. 1875.
Stephen Jay Gould. *The Mismeasure of Man*. New York, 1981.

The inventor of frozen battleships

David Lampe. *Pyke, the Unknown Genius*. London, 1959.

The last of the old Welsh Druids

Roy Denning. 'Druidism in Pontypridd', in *Glamorgan Historian*, vol. 1, pp. 136-145.
Keith Woolnough. 'The Golden Chain', unpublished manuscript.
Elijah Waring. *Recollections and Anecdotes of Edward Williams*. London, 1850.
Gentleman's Magazine, 1789, pp. 976-77.
Prys Morgan. *Iolo Morganwg*. Cardiff, 1975.
Owen Morgan ('Morien'). *The Winged Son of Stonehenge and Avebury*. Pontypridd, 1900.
Islwyn ap Nicholas. *A Welsh Heretic: Dr William Price of Llantrisant*. Swansea, 1973.

Jerusalem in Britain and other findings of a revisionist geographer

William Comyns Beaumont. *The Mysterious Comet.* London, 1932.
—. *Rebel in Fleet Street.* London, 1944.
—. *The Riddle of Prehistoric Britain.* London, 1946.
—. *The Private Life of the Virgin Queen.* London, 1947.
—. *Britain the Key to World History.* London, 1949.
—. 'After Atlantis: The Greatest Story Never Told', manuscript to be published with critical and biographical notes by Robert Stephanos.
—. ('Appian Way'.) *The Riddle of the Earth.* London, 1925.

The people with holes in their heads

Joseph Mellen. *Bore Hole.* London, 1975.
—, and Bart Huges. *The Scroll.* London, n.d.
Amanda Feilding. *Blood and Consciousness.* London, 1978.
—. Film: *Heartbeat in the Brain.*

Bibliomaniacs

Seymour de Ricci. *English Collectors of Books and Manuscripts.* Cambridge, 1930.
A.N.L. Munby. *Essays and Papers.* London, 1977.
—. *Portrait of an Obsession* (adapted by Nicholas Barker from the five volumes of Munby's *Phillipps Studies*). London, 1967.
W. Roberts. *The Book-Hunter in London.* London, 1825.
Holbrook Jackson. *The Anatomy of Bibliomania.* London, 1950.
T.F. Dibdin. *Bibliomania.* London, 1809.

Jews, Britons and the lost tribes of Israel

Barbara Tuchman. *Bible and Sword.* London, 1957.
J. Wilson. *Our Israelitish Origin.* London, 1840.
Rev. W.T. Gidney. *The History of the London Society for Promoting Christianity Amongst the Jews from 1809 to 1908.* London, 1908.
—. *Sites and Scenes: a Description of the Oriental Missions of the LSPCJ.* London, 1897.
'Ben-Israel'. *Memoir of Edward Hine.* London, 1909.
Edward Hine (ed). *Life from the Dead.* London, 1873.
—. *Forty-Seven Identifications of the British Nation with the Ten Lost Tribes of Israel.* London, 1874.

Manasseh ben Israel. *The Hope of Israel.* London, 1650.

Doubts on Shakespeare, and a Baconian martyr

S. Schoenbaum. *Shakespeare's Lives.* Oxford, 1970.
F.E. Halliday. *The Cult of Shakespeare.* London, 1957.
Gilbert Slater. *Seven Shakespeares.* London, 1931.
Vivian C. Hopkins. *Prodigal Puritan.* Harvard, 1959.
Delia Bacon. *The Philosophy of the Plays of Shakspere Unfolded,* with preface by Nathaniel Hawthorne. London, 1857.
Theodore Bacon. *Delia Bacon, a Biographical Sketch.* Boston, 1888.
Martin Pares. *A Pioneer. In Memory of Delia Bacon.* London, 1958.
Irving Wallace. 'The Lady who Moved Shakespeare's Bones', in *The Square Pegs.* New York, 1957.

Congressman Donnelly, the great heretic

Ignatius Donnelly. *Atlantis, the Antediluvian World.* New York, 1882.
—. *Ragnarök: the Age of Fire and Gravel.* New York, 1883.
—. *Caesar's Column.* Chicago, 1890. New edition with biographical introduction by Walter Rideout, Harvard, 1960.
—. *The Great Cryptogram: Francis Bacon's Cipher in the So-called Shakespeare Plays.* Chicago, 1888.
—. *The Cipher in the Plays and on the Tombstone.* London, 1899.
Henry Wellington Wack. 'Ignatius Donnelly', in *American Baconiana,* I, February 1923.
Martin Ridge. *Ignatius Donnelly. The Portrait of a Politician.* Chicago, 1962.

Shakespearean decoders and the Baconian treasure hunt

Sir Edwin Durning-Lawrence. *Bacon is Shakespeare.* London, 1910.
W.F. and E.S. Friedman. *The Shakespearean Ciphers Examined.* Cambridge, 1957.
Orville W. Owen. *Sir Francis Bacon's Cipher Story.* Detroit, 1894.
Kate Prescott. *Reminiscences of a Baconian.* New Haven, 1949.

Calvin Hoffman. *The Man Who Was 'Shakespeare'.* London, 1955.

William Honey. *The Shakespeare Epitaph Deciphered.* London, 1969.

Eminent Ufologists

George Adamski. *Inside the Space Ships*, with foreword by Desmond Leslie and biographical notes by Charlotte Blodget. London, 1956.

—, and Desmond Leslie. *Flying Saucers Have Landed.* London, 1953.

Lou Zinsstag and Timothy Good. *George Adamski – The Untold Story*, with foreword by Lady Falkender. Beckenham, Kent, 1983.

John Keel. *Operation Trojan Horse.* London, 1971.

C.G. Jung. *Flying Saucers. A Modern Myth of Things Seen in the Skies.* London, 1959.

Brinsley le Poer Trench. *Secret of the Ages: UFOs from Inside the Earth.* London, 1974.

The House of Lords UFO Debate. Transcript from Hansard with foreword and afterword by Lord Clancarty and notes by John Michell. London, 1981.

SOURCES OF ILLUSTRATIONS

Adamski Foundation (50); Arbuthnot, A.J., *Memories of the Arbuthnots*, London, 1920 (1); Bacon, Theodore, *Delia Bacon: a Bibliographical Sketch*, Boston, 1888 (44); Beaumont, W.C., *A Rebel in Fleet Street*, London, 1944 (31), *Britain – The Key to World History*, London, 1948 (32); 'Ben-Israel', *Memoir of Edward Hine*, London, 1909, by courtesy of The British Israel World Federation, London (37); Blount, E.A.M., *Adrian Galilio*, Malvern, 1898 (3, 4); British Museum, London (35); Carpenter, W., *Water, Not Convex*, 1871 (6); Chipault, A., *Chirurgie opératoire du système nerveux*, Paris, 1894, I (page 152); Coral Castle Inc. (18, 19); Donnelly, Ignatius, *The Great Cryptogram*, Chicago, 1888, II (47; page 207); Dugdale, William, *Antiquities of Warwickshire*, 1656 (40); Edgell, William, *Does the Earth Rotate?*, Radstock, 1914 (7); Feilding, Amanda, and Joseph Mellen (33); Gordon, Alexander, *The Lawrences of Cornwall*, London, 1915 (39); Güldenstubbé, Ludwig de, *La Réalité des esprits*, Paris, Strasbourg, 1857 (17); Harries, Pauline (34); Honig, Evelyn (9); *Illustrated London News*, 2 March 1946, ill. by G.H. Lavis (25); 9 September 1893 (29); 11 March 1911, ill. by Cyrus Cuneo (43); Johnson, Mr and Mrs Charles K., *Flat Earth News*, Box 2533, Lancaster, California, U.S.A., 93539-2533 (5); *Kay's Caricatures*, 1784 (22); Koresh, *The Cellular Cosmogony*, Estero, 1922 (8, 10, 11); Lincolnshire Recreational Services, Usher Gallery, Lincoln (12); Mansell Collection (38); Owen, Orville W., *Sir Francis Bacon's Cipher Story*, Detroit, 1894 (42); Parallax, *Zetetic Astronomy*, 2nd edn, London, 1875 (page 32); Peacock, T.L., *Melincourt, or Sir Oran Haut-Ton*, London, 1896 edn, ill. by H. Townsend (20); Pearson, K., *Life, Letters and Labours of Francis Galton*, Cambridge, 1924 (23, 24); Pontypridd Public Library (30); Price, Dr William, *Gwylellis Yn Nayd*, 1871, Pontypridd Public Library (28); *Punch*, vol. 20, 1851 (13); Selenus, Gustavus, *Cryptomenices et cryptographicae libri IX*, Lüneburg, 1624 (page 211); Smith, Edwin (41, 45); Universal Pictorial Press & Agency Ltd (49); Wilson, Henry, and James Caulfield, *The Book of Wonderful Characters*, London, 1869 (21; page 81).

INDEX

239